Victimology

Victimology

Edited by
Israel Drapkin and
Emilio Viano

Lexington Books
D.C. Heath and Company
Lexington, Massachusetts
Toronto   London

Library of Congress Cataloging in Publication Data

Drapkin Senderey, Israel, 1905–   comp.
Victimology.

1. Victims of crime – Addresses, essays, lectures. I. Viano, Emilio,
joint comp. II. Title.
HV6030.D7   364   73-13044
ISBN 0-669-91033-3

Published simultaneously in Canada.

Printed in the United States of America.

International Standard Book Number: 0-669-91033-3

Library of Congress Catalog Card Number: 73-13044

FOR REBECCA AND SHERRY LEE

364
D766

Contents

Preface

Criminology, as a field of study, is a recently developed discipline, having been in existence for about a century, and is still a growing one. While scholars from the behavioral sciences group were developing theories about human behavior in general, criminologists focused on criminal behavior. Thus, for the early criminologists, the main subject of study was the criminal. However, in recent years the focus has shifted to the crime itself, not only as a legal entity but as a complex situation reflecting the interaction between different actors and the cultural norms and expectations of society; as the product of the intricate interplay of emotional, rational, incidental, and situational factors.

Consequently, attention and interest have developed about the *victim* as an integral part of the criminal situation. Scholars have begun to see the victim not necessarily just as a passive object, as the neuter or innocent point of impact of crime into society, but as eventually playing an active role or possibly contributing in different measure to his own victimization. During the last thirty years, there has been a spur of speculation, debate, and research on the victim, his role, the criminal-victim relationship, the concept of responsibility, the crime motive, and on behaviors that could be considered provocative. At the same time, certain types of criminal behavior have been identified as being victimless.

Thus the study of crime has acquired a more realistic and complete outlook. Criminologists have recognized the different elements that constitute a crime, and they study them within their dynamic context, attempting to understand their interrelationship and therefore detect explanatory patterns. Much of the preliminary study of crime from this comprehensive point of view has been of an inventory-taking nature. This is, of course, a basic prerequisite for the development of systematic typologies and theories.

Although the founders of criminology were themselves aware of the crucial importance of the criminal-victim relationship, it was not until the 1940s that a high level interest in the victim developed. Von Hentig's paper entitled "Remarks on the Interaction of Perpetrator and Victim" (1941) and his book, *The Criminal and His Victim* (1948); Mendelsohn's paper "New Bio-psycho-social Horizons: Victimology" (1947); and Ellenberger's study on the psychological relationship between the criminal and his victim (1954), all underlined the importance of studying the criminal-victim relationship in order to obtain a better understanding of crime and its origins and implications. Since then, numerous scholars have focused their efforts on this aspect of the criminal situation. As a result, a considerable body of literature on the victim has been developed.

Meanwhile, a movement for the recognition of the victim as deserving more effective remedy than the traditional action in tort was begun by the late English penal reformer Margery Fry (1955). Her call for reform was first heard in New Zealand in 1963. In that year, the New Zealand Parliament established the first crime compensation tribunal, with discretionary power to award public compensation to the victim or his dependents where he had been injured or killed through the commission of certain specified offenses. In the following year, the Tory government in England announced a similar, but nonstatutory program. In America, the first jurisdiction to adopt the compensation principle was California. Its program was enacted in 1965 and put in operation two years later. Since that time, similar or related programs have been established in New York (1966); Hawaii (1967); Massachusetts (1967); Maryland (1968); Nevada (1969); and most recently, New Jersey (1971). Today, many propose a different and further step to provide for the compensation of persons injured by certain criminal acts – an insurance system.

The interest of scholars and professionals on victims and their relationship with their criminals has now reached a significant momentum. International recognition that victimology is indeed a vital branch of the study of crime has been given at the First International Symposium on Victimology held in Jerusalem in September 1973.

This book represents an ambitious effort to review the growth and the major achievements of victimology during the past thirty years. This will be accomplished by offering reading selections chosen with essentially two major themes in mind. The first theme indicates the conceptual shape of the field to the reader by exposing him: (1) to several major efforts at delineating appropriate levels and units of analysis; (2) to attempts to specify key relationships between and among relevant factors, conditions, and variables; and (3) to important questions concerned with the practical implications of scholarly efforts to understand vicitimization in modern Western societies. The second theme is reflected in articles which in our judgment represent significant attempts at empirical research in this difficult and complex field. They have produced new facts, demonstrable relationships, and more clearly defined hypotheses, all of which are essential in order to establish guidelines for future understanding.

While the articles comprising this reader reflect the scope and diversity of interests in the field of victimology, they have been organized to underline five major points of reference.

Part I, "Origin and Scope of Victimology," consists of four articles designed to acquaint the reader with the development of victimology as a specialized concern within criminology.

Each of the six articles in Part II, "The Victim-Offender Relationship," discusses a crucial point: the relationship between the offender and the victim, and its implications.

Part III, "The Victim and His Society," calls attention to the fact that the concept of victimization should not be limited only to select types of interpersonal relationships. A broader definition of who the oppressors and who the victims are may be necessary.

The five articles in Part IV, "The Victim and the Administration of Justice," comment on several problems facing society and the parties involved in a case of victimization from the point of view of the justice system. The measure of victimization present among a given population, the controversial legal requirement of corroboration in instances of sexual assaults, the jury's reaction to the personality of the victim and of the offender, problems of moral and scientific responsibility stemming from the use of drugs for medical purposes, are the major issues discussed in this section.

Part V, "The Social Reaction to Victimization," consists of five readings dealing with the theme of victim compensation and treatment at the hands of the state.

Thus this reader is meant to provide scholars and students with an overview of past accomplishments in the field of victimology as the necessary background for further work and study. Like any collection of readings, this one is partial rather than exhaustive. While this volume attempts to offer its readers a truly international selection, most contributions are from the English-speaking world because they are more numerous. However, at the end of each of the five parts, a bibliography of selected works from the international scholarly community will provide helpful information to those who desire to further pursue their readings.

The quality of the works represented here is by necessity uneven, but the historical significance of some of them is unquestionable. With these caveats in mind, we feel that this book provides a sound introduction to the field of victimology in that it forces the reader to recognize not only the complexity of the issues and realities involved but also the wide range of scholarly efforts put forth during the last thirty years to meet the challenge. In fact, we conceived this reader as a testimonial and an overview of these efforts, and we truly endeavored to make it so. If we succeeded, we take pride in having contributed to the formal recognition and establishment of victimology as an essential branch of criminology.

We wish to express our thankfulness to the authors and publishers who gave us permission to publish for the first time, or reprint, and edit their works. We wish also to thank Miss Barbara Levey of Lexington Books for her able editorial assistance.

September 2, 1973
Israel Drapkin

Emilio Viano

Part I
The Origin and Scope of Victimology

Introduction

The concept of "victim" appears among the most ancient ones of humanity. Inextricably connected with the idea and the practice of sacrifice, the notion of victim belongs to all cultures. Most religions, for example, are fundamentally sacrificial. Early ritual literature from all regions of the world offers abundant clues to the study of sacrifice and of its victims — human, divine, animal, or inanimate. The epics and mythological sources provide sufficient evidence pointing to the existence of the different types of sacrifice and victims, and they contain a wealth of symbolic elements connected to those rituals and practices.

The Oxford English Dictionary (vol. XII, 1961) defines *victim* as:

1. "a living creature killed and offered as a sacrifice to some deity or supernatural power." This concept has, for example, been applied to Christ as an offering for mankind.

2. "a person who is put to death or subjected to torture by another; one who suffers severely in body or property through cruel or oppressive treatment; one who is reduced or destined to suffer under some oppressive or destructive agency; one who perishes or suffers in health, etc., from some enterprise or pursuit voluntarily undertaken. In weaker sense: one who suffers some injury, hardship, or loss, is badly treated or taken advantage of, etc."

There is a rather well-developed vocabularly in English connected with the notion of victim:

a. victimhood, "the state of being a victim;"
b. victimizable, "capable of being victimized;"
c. victimization, "the action of victimizing, or fact of being victimized, in various senses;"
d. victimize, "to make a victim of; to cause to suffer inconvenience, discomfort, annoyance, etc., either deliberately or by misdirected attentions; to cheat, swindle or defraud; to put to death as, or in the manner of, a sacrificial victim; to slaughter; to destroy or spoil (plants) completely;"
e. victimizer, "one who victimizes another or others;"
f. victimless, the absence of a clearly identifiable victim other than the doer, for example in a criminal situation.

1

Even before the development of scholarly studies on the subject, several writers focused their attention on the victim. The novels of Daniel Defoe *(Moll Flanders, Colonel Jack)*, the satirical work on murder by Thomas de Quincey *(On Murder Considered as one of the Fine Arts)*, a novel by Franz Werfel *(Nicht der Mörder, der Ermordete ist Schuldig)*, some passages in *The Prophet* by K. Gibran, all express important ideas and observations on the victim and his relationship with the offender.

During the nineteenth and twentieth centuries, a few scholars discussed the victim's role in a criminal situation. But it was not until after World War II that the study of the victim acquired a more rigorous scientific nature by employing the methodology of empirical research. The publication of Von Hentig's *The Criminal and His Victim* in 1948 marked the beginning of *victimology* — that branch of criminology which primarily studies the victim of crime and everything that is connected with such a victim.

The articles by Mendelsohn and Nagel reprinted here offer the reader interesting information on the initial stages of victimology, on the discussion and controversy which surrounded them, and on the spread of the idea of victimology in various countries. Schafer's "The Beginnings of 'Victimology'" reviews and summarizes the works of scholars who can be considered the pioneers of victimology. Daniel Glaser discusses the introduction of a new methodology — the victimization survey — and its theoretical and practical implications.

1

The Origin of the Doctrine of Victimology

Beniamin Mendelsohn

The idea of Victimology occurred to my mind in the following manner:

A) As the natural corollary of the conception set forth in my first study *Method to be used by counsel for the defence in the researches made into the personality of the criminal* (Revue de Droit Pénal et de Criminologie, Bruxelles, août-sept.-oct. 1937, page 877). Convinced that a 'well conducted defence cannot be based on untruth' (page 883), I once more took the trouble that I had previously taken at the outset of my profession as a barrister, of drawing up for my own use, a scientific method of study of a criminal case. In general this method consists of the following measures (which explains my gradual evolution towards the conception of Victimology). a) A questionnaire containing more than 300 questions, concerning the branches of criminology and associated sciences (pages 882-883) couched, as far as possible in simple language. b) The same questionnaire is given to the accused and to some of those around him, with the object of being able to complete and compare the material collected and to go through the proofs. c) To the sources of information indicated above is added, of course, the report of the trial in the lower court, and what the accused testifies (independently of the replies given in the questionnaire), the opinion of the expert witnesses, and the results of a social enquiry — when such is necessary and is possible in practice. (I have presented this method here only in rough outline for the purposes of demonstration.) Thus the defence comes to be the result of the best documented facts and the application of well established law. By this method I have in detail gone into: 'The personality of the accused from the bio-psycho-social point of view and, parallelly, into the 'data concerning the personality of the victims' and even of their social relations (page 883).' This method has been applied by me throughout my practice of the profession of a barrister specializing in criminology.

B) As one of the results of the application of the method indicated above (A), I have published my study on *Rape in criminology* (Giustizia Penale, Roma, 1940, Parte I-a — I presupposti del diritto penale, VI della 5-a serie, Fasc. I-II-III-IV), which appeared after the outbreak of the second world war. This time I have concentrated my researches *on the victim* from the bio-psycho-social point of

Reprinted from *Excerpta Criminologica* (Abstracts on Criminology and Penology), 1963, 3 (3): 239-244 by permission of *Exerpta Criminologica* and the author.

view, and his relationships with the delinquent, within the framework of rape and – to some degree – of other crimes against morality. Chapter II treats the subject of: 'The phases of the struggle for possession between the aggressor and the victim. The extent to which the woman is able to resist rape'. I pointed out the possibility of resistance on the part of the woman by the almost inexpugnable position she occupies on account of the topography of the sexual organs in the female body. . . . They have the following features: a) They are not situated at the extremities of the body, exposed to attack; b) They are sheltered in the most hidden place of the external portion of the human body; c) They do not constitute a prominence but a cavity – that is to say, they are sheltered within the body; d) They are protected by two lower limbs that possess a great mobility, a great radius of action of defensive and offensive nature and a great power of resistance and are served by the most powerful muscles in the human system, sustaining and transporting all the weight of the body. I would add: the various muscles have well deserved the title of: Castitatis custodes! The following exceptions are mentioned: (I) A very great disproportion between the physical strength of the aggressor (or aggressors) and that of the victim. (II) The state of unconsciousness of the victim (early age, anaesthesia, fainting, drunkenness, hypnotism, alterations of the mental state, stupefiants, etc.).(III) The element of surprise in an abnormal position favourable to the neutralization of the resistance of the victim and to the perpetration of sexual intercourse. (IV) Threats strong enough to break down the will to resist. Finally, I remarked that, from the psychological point of view, the resistance of the victim may be lessened also by the circumstances listed here: (1) The familial, authoritative or hierarchical relations existing between the accused and the victim. (2) The volcanic temperament of the victim, which may obscure the reasoning faculty. (3) The libertine social surroundings of the victim . . . . (4) The superiority of the social milieu of the accused in relation to that of the victim.

Chapter II – at the end – points out that it is absolutely necessary to take into consideration the degree of exhaustion of the victim, and also that the power of the aggressor should not be appraised by that of the individual in his normal condition but according to what it is when under the influence of his unleashed primitive instincts; that his physical strength is the resultant of the combination of two primitive instincts: the sexual and the aggressive; and that his strength may be exaggerated by the morbid sexuality of the delinquent, or by alcohol, etc.; or it may be diminished by a violent blow. To avoid a mistaken interpretation, the following remark was added: 'we are far from admitting that a woman must either fight for the defence of her virginity like an athlete in an arena or else be considered to be at fault – such is not the theme of our study. Moreover, no juridical law can demand that anyone should be a hero! The point that we wish to make is simply that the court – whose appreciation of the facts is of sovereign quality – should be careful to take account of all the real possibilities of the woman's defence, every time that it is not a question of rape but

of a consented act or a simulated resistance. In every case it must weight up all
the circumstances which may throw light on the happenings.'

Attention is also drawn to threats that may really intimidate the victim,
taking into consideration her personality, that may force her to yield from fear,
and that may be directed against some other member of the family (Garraud,
Garçon, etc.). Chapter IV treats the problem of 'the degree of specific credibility
of the woman with regard to her complaints about offences against her modesty'.
The victims are divided from the psychological and juridical point of view into
the following categories and the subject is developed in detail (here I only indicate the title of each category). I) Adult witnesses. II) Minor boys between the
ages of 16 and majority (article 79 of the French code of criminal procedure and
article 161 of the Roumanian code. Charles II) have the right to give evidence
under oath in the same way as other witnesses. III) Minors below 15 years of age
do not take the oath and are heard only as informers. (V) The statements of
young girls under the age of 15 when giving evidence should be received with
greater caution than those of minor boys of the same age. V) The depositions of
girls under 16 years should be taken with still more reserve in questions of
assaults against decency. VI) Depositions of the group of minor girls. VII) Minors
with pathological consitutions. Chapter II ends with the conclusion — from the
juridical point of view — that the sexual act is possible only under the following
circumstances: 1) With the consent of the woman, or in cases of simulated resistance — which does not constitute a crime; 2) without the consent of the victim,
and in spite of the latter's resistance — which is a crime; 3) with the consent of
the victim but with resistance reduced in proportion to the intimidation, the intellectual and social level, the physical disproportion, the degree of consciousness and the position in which the victim has been surprised. In these conditions
the sexual act is a crime.

I think that there is a way of treating this subject which fits perfectly into a
treatise on victimology. The title *Rape in victimology* would harmonize better
with the contents of my article.

C) As a result of the same manner of thinking and as a consequence of the
method set forth above (A), it is applied to several cases of 'crimes passionnels'
in which I have pleaded before the Court of Criminal Justice in Bucharest
between 1934 and 1951. It was while preparing for the trial of Stephan Codreanu
arraigned in 1945 for a crime passionnel that I began to elaborate the doctrine of
Victimology. It was a case of double murder: The accused had with premeditation killed his wife and her lover. He had for several years continued to live with
his wife after the divorce. He was always invited by her to stay on the first and
the fifteenth of the month, under the pretext of preparing the lessons with their
little daughter, whom he adored. He would eat with the family and she poured
out all her sweetness to keep him for the night, but the next day she would turn
him out of the house, having first of all taken all his money. The lover — a
young soldier — would ridicule him. He was sentenced to 12 years, but the sen-

tence was mitigated and he was released after 5 or 6 years. There can be no doubt that, had it had not been for the perversity of his former wife, he would never have been guilty of two crimes.

D) In 1946 the manuscript *New bio-psycho-social horizons: victimology* was circulated among the specialists of Bucharest (medico-legal experts, psychiatrists, psychoanalysts, barristers). This manuscript was intended for a work of considerable size, but I have only published the summaries of a few chapters in specialist reviews.

E) In March 1947, at the invitation of the Roumanian Society of Psychiatry, I made a communication on Victimology in the amphitheatre of the State Hospital 'Coltzea' in Bucharest.

F) In 1948, Prof. Dr. Hans von Hentig published in Yale a very interesting study entitled *The criminal and his victim,* and in 1954 Prof. Dr. Henry Ellenberger (Topeka, Kansas) made an important contribution to this subject in his study *Relations psychologiques entre le criminel et sa victime* (Revue internationale de criminologie et de police technique, No. 2/1954, Genève). I have quoted these two studies because – in contrast to various other works that only skim over the question – these attack the very essence of these problems. Between the studies of Prof. von Hentig and Prof. Ellenberger on the one hand, and ours on the other hand, there are statements and viewpoints that are identical, even though the terms employed are different. Thus, what we designate as the 'penal couple' – that is to say, the victim-criminal – appears in Prof. von Hentig's work under the name of 'doer-sufferer'; and what we have named 'Victimology' is called 'Victimogenesis' by Prof. Ellenberger. It is also interesting to note that the training of the two authors is completely different, one being a psychiatrist and the other a barrister specializing in criminology. What is especially noteworthy is that this new scientific conception took concrete form after the second world war, almost simultaneously at the two different sides of the globe, in two worlds completely separated from one another and without any intellectual contact between them, Roumania being at that time completely shut off behind the Iron Curtain. These facts confirm our opinion that Victimology is a scientific reality which impresses itself on the human consciousness by its scientific quality. Nevertheless, we must point out a fundamental difference between the points of view of Prof. von Hentig and Prof. Ellenberger on the one hand and of ourselves on the other hand. The former consider the study of the victim as a chapter of criminology, whereas we consider it as a separate science, which, because of its structure and its aim should be independent. The reasons which have led us to this conclusion can be found in my study *Victimology, present day science – La victimologie, science actuelle (*Revue de Droit Pénal et de Criminologie, Bruxelles, avril 1957, page 519).

G) The same text appeared under the title of *A new branch of bio-psycho-social science: Victimology (*Revue Internationale de Criminologie at de Police Technique, Genève No. 2/1956). *Victimologie* (Etudes Internationales de Psycho-sociologie Criminelle, Paris No. 1/1956) was a summary of a part of our incomplete and unpublished study: *Horizons nouveaux bio-psycho-sociaux: la victimologie.*

H) In 1954 at the International Congress on Social Defence at Antwerp, my work was mentioned for the first time in the general report by Judge Versele (Brussels).

The Spread of the Idea of Victimology in Various Countries

My *Victimology* appeared in English and French in several papers. In Japanese in the Japanese Journal of Legal Medicine and Criminology, Vol. 24, No. 6/1958, published in continuation of the report of Prof. Dr. Shufu Yoshimasu, professor of the Section of Psychological Medicine, and in the translation of Dr. Osamu Nakata, assistant professor in the Medical University of Tokyo.

In Paris the daily newspaper *Combat* in its issues of 6.6.1958, 27.8.1958, and 21.8.1958 published articles under the signature of Alexandre Wexliard (Paris, at the present time professor at the University of Ankara) and M. Mellot, the former adopting the idea of Victimology in its entirety — with powerful supporting arguments — and the latter only admitting it within the scope of criminology.

Geneva. On several occasions during the debates at the meeting of the European consultative group on the prevention of crime and the treatment of offenders (1958) the problems of Victimology were mentioned.

Belgium. At the suggestion of Prof. Paul Cornil, the Dutch-Belgian conferences dedicated their meetings of December 19 and 21, 1958, to the problem of Victomology. Four papers were read respectively by the professors: Paul Cornil (Brussels), Nagel (Leiden), Callewaert (Ghent), and Noach (Utrecht). Several meetings were held in 1958 on Victimology during the University Seminar on Criminology and the programme contained a study of Victimology on its agenda.

Prof. Paul Cornil opened the new academic year of the University seminar on criminology with a lecture on Victimology. A certain number of sessions were reserved for a study of this doctrine. A victimological *movement* began to take shape in Belgium and developed in the following years. The April number 1959 of Revue de Droit Pénal et de Criminologie was dedicated to Victimology (120 pages). This number contained the following articles: Prof. Paul Cornil, *The contribution of Victimology to criminological science.* Prof. Willy Callewaert, barrister (Ghent), *Victimology and fraud.* B. Mendelsohn (Jerusalem), *Victimology — a present day science.* Prof. Dr. Dellaert (Louvain), *First comparison of criminal psychology and Victimology.* Aimé Racine, barrister (Brussels), *The child as the victim of immoral acts committed on its person by an ascendant.* L. de Bray (Brussels), *Some observations on the victims of crimes.* This number also published some detailed accounts of the discussions, suggestions and resolutions adopted by the Dutch-Belgian conferences.

Gerda de Bock, director of the course of studies at the University of Ghent, presented a report *Justice et publicité* to the Belgian and Luxemburg Assembly on Penal Law. Published in the Rev. de Droit Pénal et de Criminologie (Brussels), No. 1/1960, p. 35-65. Beginning with page 57 the subject is treated from the point of view of Victimology. The results are related to a careful social enquiry in Ghent. Though no victimological question was introduced into the questionnaire, the subjects of the enquiry, of their own account, supplied data concerning problems of Victimology. They were of sufficient value to be recorded and shown in the results of the work.

Italy: (1958) Professor Dr. Domenico Macaggi of the Faculty of Law and director of the Medico-Legal Institute has included Victimology in the list of subjects for theses for the Doctorate. A thesis on Victimology has been prepared by Miss Maria Grazia Anduini-Plaisant.

The Netherlands: Prof. Dr. W.H. Nagel, *Victimologie,* Tijdschrift voor Strafrecht LXVIII (1959). Prof. Dr. W.M.E. Noach, *Het Slachtoffer en de rechtspraak,* Strafrechtspraak (An anthology 1959). p. 29-43.

France: Etudes internationales de psycho-sociologie criminelle No. 4/ 1959 includes an article critically analysing the matter under the title *La Victimologie* and bearing the signature of Me. Claude-Roland Souchet, barrister of the Paris courts. The same appeared in La Vie Judiciaire in its number of December 1959. I was invited to take part in the International Congress of social prophylaxis (Paris, September 26, 1959) under the presidence of Mr. M. Patin, president of the Supreme Court, Criminal Section, and to present a report from the victimological point of view on a selected subject, but was unable to participate.

Dr. N. Duc, *Considérations sur la criminologie et la victimologie des attentats aux moeurs à propos de 35 cas personnels* (Annales de Médecine Légale, Paris, Année XLI, No. 1/1961, pages 55-58). Abstracted in English in Excerpta Criminologica, No. 5/1961, page 455.

Dr. Louis Gayral, director of studies in the Faculty of Medicine of Toulouse. In his work on general psychiatry, in the chapter on forensic medicine, he introduces some considerations on Victimology.

Jean Geraud, Professor in the Faculty of Medicine of Toulouse, established Victimology as a subject for the degree of doctor.

Dr. R. Lafon, *Quelques propos sur la Victimologie (* Annales de Médecine

Légale, Paris, Année XLI, No. 1/1961, page 24) (Excerpta Criminologica No. 4/1961, page 349).

Dr. R. Lafon, Dr. J. Trivas, Dr. J.-L. Faure and Dr. R. Pouget, *Victimologie et criminologie des attentats sexuels sur les enfants et les adolescents* (Annales de Médecine Légale, Paris, Année XLI, 1961, p. 97-105) (Excerpta Criminologica No. 5, 1961, p. 454) Cl. R. Souchet, barrister-at-law, Paris: *La Victimologie*, in Etudes Internationales de Psycho-sociologie Criminelle, Paris, No. 4/1958, pages 13-14). Idem reprinted in La Vie Judiciaire, Paris, December 1958. Idem summary published in Excerpta Criminologica, No. 1/1960, page 24.

Argentina: Prof. Luis Jemenes de Assua gave in 1958 a series of lectures on Victimology at the institute of penal law and criminology of the University of Buenos Aires, for candidates for the degree of doctor. Prof. L.H. de Assua, together with Dr. Eduardo Aguira Abarrio, Dr. Maria H. Pen, Dr. Octavio Iturbe of the Board of Governors of the Institute and the students who had taken the course, collect these studies together in a book on Victimology.

Dr. O. Iturbe gave a lecture on Victimology at the Criminological Society. He also published a study on the same subject called *Victimologia, nuevo enfoque criminologica de la victima del delito*, in 'La Revista Penal y Penitenciaria' No. 87-90, Enero-Diciembre 1958. Tome XXI, pages 199-223. (Excerpta Criminologica, No. 1/1960, 23).

Japan: Dr. Shûfu Yoshimasu, professor of Medical Psychology of the Faculty of Medicine, and Prof. Dr. Tanemotu Furuhata, president of the Japanese Academy of Criminology decided to organize a symposium on the problems of Victimology. It took place at the Tokyo Medical and Dental Unviersity on 14th November 1959. The programme was as follows: (1) Introduction – Prof. Dr. T. Furuhata, president of the Japanese Association of Criminology. (2) Prospect of Victimology – Dr. O. Nakata, Associate Professor of Tokyo Medical and Dental University. (3) On the Victim of Female Homicide – Dr. K. Hirose. (4) Victimology from the viewpoint of Crime Prevention – T. Onojima, Chief of the Section of Crime Prevention, Tokyo Metropolitan Police. (5) On the Concept of Victimology – Prof. Dr. S. Yoshimasu, University of Tokyo. These studies were published in the Japanese Journal of Legal Medicine and Criminology, Tokyo, Vol. 25, No. 6/1959, Prof. Dr. Shûfu Yoshimasu published a study called *Studien über 200 Morder von ihren kriminellen Lebenskurven aus gesehen*, in the review Folia Psychiatria et Neurologica Japonica (1958) Tokyo, in which Victimology is taken into consideration.

Dr. Tetsuya Hirose, collaborator of Professor Dr. Yoshimasu in the Institute of Mental Research of the University of Tokyo, *Psychiatrische Untersuchungen an den Mörderinnen. Beobachtungen an den 50 strafgefangenen Mörderinnen und Totschlägerinnen und ihre kriminelle Katamnese.* The doctrine of Victimology is taken into consideration.

Dr. Yoshiske Ikeda of the Institute of Mental Research of the University of Tokyo (Prof. Dr. Shufu Yoshimasu), *Industrial psychiatric study on the human factors in the causation of accidents.* The doctrine of Victimology is considered.

Federal Republic of Germany: Klaus Bermann (University of Heidelberg) is preparing his doctoral thesis on Victimology in the Law Faculty of Mainz. Edgar Lenz, Assessor Frankfurt/Main, *Der Betrogene,* thesis for the degree of doctor in the Law Faculty of Mainz (Referent: Prof. Dr. Mergen, Co-referent: Prof. Dr. Klug, lithographed work, 192 pages).

Israel: *The delinquent and his victim* (Haavarian Vekorbano) appeared in the daily paper 'Haaretz' on May 28th, 1962. It was from the pen of Mr. Menahem Horovitz (Jerusalem), member of the committee of the Israelian Society of Criminology, who completely accepts the doctrine.

In regard to research in this field we have been greatly impressed by the promising studies by Dr. Reuben Rothenberg of Tel Aviv, psychiatrist. He deals with especially the psychiatric and psycho-analytical aspects of the problems of Victimology. He intends shortly to give a lecture on the subject with a presenta‑ tion of cases before the Neurological Society under the title of *The relations between victimology and psychiatry.* The following are the main points he will take up:

1. Victimology as a social doctrine: a. Its history. b. The founder, his experience, his researches. The researches of psychiatrists, psychologists and jurists. c. The importance of the epoch of social cataclysm provoked by Hitlerism; the Eichmann trial.
2. Two mutually opposed positions – positive and negative – concerning the victim: a. In crimes against life: Murders – examples. b. In crimes of finan‑ cial character: fraud. c. Treatment: hypnosis or suggestions.
3. The problems of the persecuted-persecutor in Freudian cases. The author of the crime becomes the victim and vice versa.
4. Rape in victimology; the problem of the Oedipus complex.
5. The relations to other doctrines.

Conclusions: A separate science or only a section of a science? An important contribution to Victimology has been made by Professor Baruk, who, with his characteristic foresight, has written articles and given lectures in national and international conferences on this conception and its perspectives. He says: (letter of 1.7.1957.) '. . . Victimology in the end will win general assent'.

In summary, the following aspects of the opinions expressed about the conception of Victimology are emphasized:

a) The specialists who expressed their points of view on Victimology, whether in articles in the scientific or the daily press, or in correspondence with me, were unanimous in recognizing the fact that the bio-psycho-social and legal aspects of the victim have been neglected and that a fundamental change of opinion is taking place.

b) The majority — almost the unanimous opinion — is in favour of Victimology, but solely within the bounds of Criminology.

c) The minority — which is becoming less of a minority — supports my view that Victimology should be a separate and autonomous science, should have its own institutions and should be allowed to develop for the well-being and progress of humanity.

2

The Notion of Victimology in Criminology

Willem H. Nagel

(1) The above article by Mr. Mendelsohn is of the greatest merit. This author, after all, has been the first to call attention to the victim in criminal events. While we do not want to lessen the importance of the fact that he has thrown light on an hitherto neglected aspect, we nevertheless want to ask ourselves objectively whether the concept of victimology, as a science in its own right besides criminology and penology, is indeed accurate.

Let us first compare the two. One might postulate that both sciences are erroneously distinguished as being separate. Some authors in fact make no distinction at all; this is especially the case in American manuals and textbooks. Penology, however, has by its special importance and its manifold connections with other arts and sciences, such as paedagogics and psychiatry, become a special branch of penal law, and rightly so. For ciminology the need for distinction was even greater. On the one hand, because its relationships to other sciences are even more extensive and intensive, and on the other hand, because the scope of criminology is far wider than that of the actual penal law.

Only if criminology were taken as the science dealing with the criminal would there be a need for a separate science dealing with the victim of the crime. This concept of criminology is far too restricted, however, and may even be radically wrong. But, classic aetiological criminology is so one-sided a science (and often, regrettably a quasi-science or even pseudo-science), and concerned with the delinquent only, that the need for a special consideration of the victim, as advocated by Mendelsohn, is fully justified.

In my opinion we should become so aware of the inadequacy of the classic 'euclidic' criminology that there is no longer a need of victimology. At first classic criminology studied criminality and delinquents in a numerical fashion. It seemed an improvement when the individual delinquent became the focus of interest. We thought we were well on the road of progress when everything regarding the offender that could be measured, weighed and counted, and when we classified the criminal by using real or invented systems. But the main point was neglected, viz. the relationships in which the delinquent commits his crime. Re-

Reprinted from *Excerpta Criminologica* (Abstracts on Criminology and Penology), 1963, 3 (3):245-247 by permission of *Excerpta Criminologica* and the author.

cently Professor Hellmuth Mayer made it clear once again what the anthropological principle of the new criminology is based on. This is that man is an open structure.[1]

His acts are not unequivocally determined by proclivity and environment. He lives in continuous relationships with others. These relationships form the context of his possible criminality. There are 'lateral' relationships with a mob, a group, a gang, companions, congenials, accomplices. The consideration of these relationships in criminology is a recent development. There is also the 'forward' relationship, which at present demands our particular attention: the relationship between the delinquent and the victim, and that between the victim and the delinquent. This distinction may need some explanation. The 'victim' may be: either the community (as a whole or in part) or individuals. Let us, for the sake of simplicity, limit ourselves to the latter case. Here the relationship can be assessed from the offender's point of view. The person he wishes to damage, thinks he is damaging or actually does damage, may then be called the victim.

Another, more obvious, point of view is to call those people victims who know or feel that they are the victims of a punishable act. The supposed offender can be unaware of the offence ascribed to him.

The most existential victimological situation doubtlessly occurs when the person the offender intends to damage does indeed feel victimized.

If in a general way we are to define modern criminology, I should prefer to call it the 'criminology of relationships'. In such a modern criminology of relationships, the victimological relationship is of such a paramount importance that there is no longer a need for a separate victimology.

(2) Before I continue, I should like to prevent the possibility of a deplorable misunderstanding. In the first place, we could never do without 'classic criminology', as I have ventured to call it. The work of the Gluecks has shown what can be accomplished in this field. Classic criminology is to criminology what radiology is for medical science. Without classic criminology, the twilight in which we are groping around would rapidly become darkness.

In the second place — and this may seem in contradiction to what has been said above, but actually only adds to it — it should be remembered that if the personality of the victim should only be considered in the old, criminological-aetiological way, there would be no progress. The counting, measuring, weighing, determing and comparing of victims, the collecting of victimological determinants, factors, associations and correlations will never acquire great importance. Modern criminology ought to study criminal behavior, the offender, and the victim (whether this be a person or not) ontologically and, if one so desired, in the *zeitüberbrückende Gegenwart* the time bridging present of the conflict.

(3) Criminal policy, inspired by classic criminology, consists in the removal of causes, factors, determinant conditions and whatever other aetiological concepts considered to have been traced. The only really effective criminal policy would be, at least, the removal of the conflict situation and, at best, the appeas-

ing between the victim and the offender. This aim cannot simply be reached by removing the factors, etc. as mentioned above. If the basic discontent consists, for instance, in discontent with a less personal or personifiable *Gegenüber,* with fate or nature or the essence of things, appeasement can hardly be obtained by the removal of a 'factor'. In practice, the remedy man often finds in such a situation of conflict consists in his search for a more definite opponent in his frustration, or fatalistic acceptance of the state of affairs. If another person is chosen as a substitute in the conflict, crime is obviously at hand. Fatalistic acceptance is, perhaps, adaptation, but then only in the most fruitless and empty sense: submission. This, regrettably, is the maximum that can be obtained in a great number of cases of penal treatment. The more personal the conflict, be it with God, society or an individual opponent, the greater the chance that the conflict situation may be removed by appeasing. By this I mean that the victim shows that the offence has been forgiven and that, as far as he is concerned, a good relationship has been re-established, with the sometime offender accepting this re-establishment. Our penal treatment should be directed towards such an appeasing. To this end it should be based on the victimological situation. How this should, and could be done may perhaps be illustrated by this example: if we want to weld the flaw in a steel band we have first to separate both ends of the flaw, so that the site and manner of breaking can be seen. This is also a matter of hygiene if there has been a breach of the law. The offender should be helped to discern his opponent as distinctly as possible. If, for instance, his opponent is not the neighbour he has hit, but fate, God or society, he should become aware of this. The actual victim should be as distinguishable as possible in the lawsuit, the damage should be determined as well as possible, and the possible indemnification should be considered as carefully as possible. Therefore, in the example given, both ends of the flaw will have to be heated if welding is to succeed. If there is a breach of law, warmth will be needed from the victim's as well as the offender's side, if appeasing is to be obtained.

(4) The victimological situation, therefore, tells us that it is not always the offender that requires attention with the aim of readaptation of the delinquent. I should like to make some restrictions however. In the first place, it should be recognized that material compensation is often impossible in view of the nature and the extent of the damage. If the material extent of the damage can never be compensated for by one person, I think that the community should take on this burden, since otherwise the victim runs the risk of traumata and criminogenic consequences. A second restriction concerns our respect for the feelings of the victim. He may be in good faith, but also in bad faith, or only partially in good faith. As Boven says: 'comme il y a parmi des "coupables" des normeaux et des anormaux, de même il y a parmi les "victimes ' des innocents et des coupables'.[2] The innocent victim might be called 'zurechnungsfähig', capable of being held responsible. However, this capability may undergo hypertrophy. To analyse the consequences of this I should first like to deal briefly with the offender and his

possible need for appeasement or atonement, his *Sühnebedürfnis.*

The concept of *Sühnebedürfnis* is rarely used, at least in the Netherlands. Perhaps the concept of *Strafbedürfnis* is more usual, but nevertheless the two should be distinguished.[3] *Sühnebedürfnis* is normal and has a positive meaning. *Strafbedürfnis* is more limited, may be pathological and may have a negative meaning. Neurotic and psychopathic offenders who feel only the need for punishment will be inclined to force the legal authorities to pay attention to them. Thus, this need for punishment may be very criminogenic. The two concepts therefore should be clearly distinguished. If we talk about *Sühnebedürfnis,* we usually think of the offender only. Indeed this *Sühnebedürfnis* may play an important part for him, and we should seriously take it into account in penal procedure. However, this need also plays a part as far as the victim is concerned. It does not only concern the compensation for the damage inflicted. It is a normal wish of the victim that the offender should be tried, that justice be done, apart from compensation. A legal verdict on the crime is a necessary element in the restitution ad integrum. In this sense, the *Sühnebedürfnis* of the victim should be considered a positive attitude.

This is not diminished by the fact that the victim, as well as the offender, may exaggerate his *Sühnebedürfnis.* We have stated that the offender who shows *Strafbedürfnis* only appears to be pathological. This also applies to the victim. If he has only *Strafbedürfnis,* we might rather use the term 'lust for revenge'. It is one of the principal tasks of the judge to examine the *Sühnebedürfnis* both of the offender and the victim as carefully as possible, and satisfy it, if necessary, with the greatest moderation only.

Notes

1. Dr. Hellmuth Mayer, "Strafrechtsreform für heute und morgen," *Kriminologische Forschungen,* Band 1 (1962).
2. *Archives de Neurologie et de Psychiatrie* 1943, p. 18
3. See Dohna, *Das Strafprozessrecht,* 2rd ed. 1929, p. 65.

3

The Beginnings of "Victimology"

Stephen Schafer

The Founders of "Victimology"

The revival of the victim's importance tends to involve among other things, the criminal-victim relationship as a partial answer to the crime problem. While compensation or restitution refers to the victim's role and the possibility of correction of the criminal in the postcrime situation, the criminal-victim relationship may point to the genesis of a crime and to a better understanding of its development and formation. "That the victim is taken as one of the determinants, and that a nefarious symbiosis is often established between doer and sufferer, may seem paradoxical. The material gathered, however, indicates such a relation." If this relation can be confirmed, and if the criminal-victim interactions and personal relationships can be observed in the "functional interplay of causative elements," crime can be seen and understood in a broader perspective. Revival of the victim's role in criminal proceedings not only means participation in his own behalf, but also may indicate his share in criminal responsibility.

Hans von Hentig might not have been the first to call attention to criminal-victim relationships, but, in the postwar period, his pathfinding study made the most challenging impact on the understanding of crime in terms of doer-sufferer interactions and invited a number of contributions to this aspect of lawbreaking. He seemed to be impressed by Franz Werfel's well-known novel, *The Murdered One is Guilty (Der Ermordete ist schuld),* and suggested that the victim himself is one of the many causes of a crime. Hentig hypothesized that, in a sense, the victim shapes and molds the criminal and his crime and that the relationship between perpetrator and victim may be much more intricate than our criminal law, with its rough and mechanical definitions and distinctions, would suggest.

Hentig suggested that a reciprocality exists between criminal and victim. He often found a mutual connection between "killer and killed, duper and dupe." "The mechanical outcome," writes Hentig, "may be profit to one party, harm to another, yet the psychological interaction, carefully observed, will not submit to this kindergarten label." A mutuality of some sort raises the question of the de-

From *The Victim and His Criminal: A Study in Functional Responsibility,* by S. Schafer, 1968, pp. 39-58. Copyright©by Random House, Inc. Reprinted by permission of the publisher.

17

pendability of external criteria, because, Hentig observes, the sociological and psychological aspects of the situation may be such as to suggest that the two distinct categories of criminal and victim in fact merge; it may be the case that the criminal is victimized.

Hentig backed his hypotheses with statistical data, documented fragments of experiences, and unstructured observations; but he did not support them by empirical research. However, his highly logical and vigorous speculations aided the revival of the victim's importance in the understanding of criminal problems. The concept of the "activating sufferer," who plays a part in "the various degrees and levels of stimulation or response" and intricate interacting forces, and who "is scarcely taken into consideration in our legal distinctions," is not original with Hentig, but his pioneering role and its great impact cannot be denied.[1]

B. Mendelsohn claims that he originated the idea.[2] He refers to his article, published a decade before Hentig's study, which, though not a study of the victim, led him to his "gradual evolution towards the conception of Victimology."[3] Mendelsohn, as a practicing attorney, had his clients answer some 300 questions. His findings from this questionnaire led him to the conclusion that a "parallelity" appears between the "biopsychosocial" personality of the offender and that of the victim. After he published his first impressions,[4] he concentrated his investigations on the victim, first of all on rape victims and on the extent of their resistence.

In his basic study of criminal-victim relationships[5] he proposes the term "victimology" in order to develop an independent field of study and perhaps a new discipline. Mendelsohn views the totality of crime factors as a "criminogen-complex," in which one set of factors concerns the criminal and another the victim. He objects to "the co-existence of two parallel ways" and asks that they be separated. This divorce of the "penal-couple" (as he terms the criminal and his victim) would lead to "a new branch of science," and this would be his victimology. He proposes new terms such as "victimal" as the opposite of "criminal"; "victimity" as the opposite of "criminality"; "potential of victimal receptivity" as meaning individual unconscious aptitude for being victimized. He suggests the broadest possible acceptance and implementation of his idea. Thus he recommends the establishment of a "central institute of victimology," "victimological cliniques," "an international institute for victimological researches in the United Nations," an "international society of victimology," and the publication of an "international review of victimology." In Mendelsohn's view victimology is not a branch of criminology but "a science parallel to it"; or, better, "the reverse of criminology."

Early Victim Typologies

Both Hentig and Mendelsohn attempted to set up victim typologies, but their classifications were speculative. Their work offers useful guidelines for research, but in the absence of systematic empirical observations it should be used with caution. In any case, the possibility of a spectacular variety of victim types is indicated, particularly by Hentig in his detailed list of such types. Mendelsohn distinguished between the guilt of the criminal and his victim; Hentig used a sociobiological classification.

In Mendelsohn's typology[6] the "correlation of culpability (imputability) between the victim and the delinquent" *(corrélation de culpabilité (imputabilité) entre la victime et l'infracteur)* is the focal point around which he gathered his victim types. In fact, Mendelsohn's victims are classified only in accordance with the degree of their guilty contribution to the crime. They are grouped in the following categories:

1. The "completely innocent victim." Mendelsohn regards him as the "ideal" victim, and refers first of all to children and those who suffer a crime while they are unconscious.
2. The victim with minor guilt" and the "victim due to his ignorance." Mentioned here as an example is the woman who "provokes" a miscarriage and as a result pays with her life.
3. The "victim as guilty as the offender" and the "voluntary victim." In explanation Mendelsohn lists the following subtypes:
   a. suicide "by throwing a coin," if punishable by law
   b. suicide "by adhesion"
   c. euthanasia (to be killed by one's own wish because of an incurable and painful disease)
   d. suicide committed by a couple (for example, "desperate lovers," healthy husband and sick wife)
4. The "victim more guilty than the offender." There are two subtypes:
   a. the "provoker victim," who provokes someone to crime
   b. the "imprudent victim," who induces someone to commit a crime
5. The "most guilty victim" and the "victim who is guilty alone." This refers to the aggressive victim who is alone guilty of a crime (for example, the attacker who is killed by another in self-defense).
6. The "simulating victim" and the "imaginary victim." Mendelsohn refers here to those who mislead the administration of justice in order to obtain a sentence of punishment against an accused person. This type includes paranoids, hysterical persons, senile persons, and children.

Hentig's typology is more elaborate and uses psychological, social, and biological factors in the search for categories. He distinguishes born victims from society-made victims. He also sets up a victim typology in thirteen categories.[7]

1. the young
2. the female

3. the old
4. the mentally defective and other mentally deranged
5. immigrants
6. minorities
7. dull normals'
8. the depressed
9. the acquisitive
10. the wanton
11. the lonesome and the heartbroken
12. tormentors
13. the blocked, exempted, and fighting

The young victim is an obvious type. Since the young are weak and inexperienced, they are likely to be victims of attacks. The young are easy victims not only because they are physically undeveloped, but because they are immature in moral personality and moral resistance. Though they are in the process of biological and cultural development, this cannot be fully complete in youth. However, the criminal's inner pressure to commit crime is normally a fully developed force against which the undeveloped resistance of the young is unable to compete on fair terms. Hentig suggested that since children do not own property, they are not usually victims of crimes for profit. However, a child may be murdered for profit if his life is insured. Kidnapping is an offense that usually involves the young. Further, children are frequently used by criminals to assist in committing crimes (mainly crimes against property).

In most countries laws are in force to protect children against involvement in moral turpitude; this indicates that they can be regarded even in this respect as victims. If the young person happens to be a girl, her victimization is well known with respect to sexual offenses. Leppmann, as cited by Hentig, pointed out that some young girls do not resist sexual assaults, and because of a mixture of curiosity, fear, physical inactivity, and intellectual challenge they do not try to escape from being victims.

The female is described by Hentig as a victim with "another form of weakness." Younger females sometimes become the victims of murder after suffering sexual assault; older women who are thought wealthy become victims of property crimes. The lesser physical strength of the female has greater significance than that of young people or children. While the criminal would find little point in committing a property crime against the propertyless young, this is not the case with regard to women. Women do have, or at least handle, things of financial value that may attract the criminal. Most offenders are men and therefore have the advantage of greater physical strength in crimes against women. Except in the case of rare homosexual offenses, women occupy a biologically determined victim status in sexual crimes.

The old are also likely to be victims in crimes against property. Hentig pointed out that "the elder generation holds most positions of accumulated wealth and wealth-giving power." At the same time old people are weaker physically and sometimes mentally. "In the combination of wealth and weakness lies the danger." Hentig suggests that old people are the ideal victims of predatory attacks. Their comparative weakness is behind proposed measures for their special defense, which would involve greater punishment for those who commit crimes against them.

The mentally defective and other mentally deranged persons are referred to by Hentig as a large class of potential and actual victims. It seems obvious that the insane, the alcoholic, the drug addict, the psychopath, and others suffering from any form of mental deficiency are handicapped in any struggle against crime. Hentig stated that of all males killed, 66.6 percent turned out to be alcoholics. He rarely found alcoholics among murder victims, but 70 percent of manslaughter victims were found to have been intoxicated. Often not only was the victim of manslaughter intoxicated, but the killer was also. Generally speaking, intoxicated persons are easy victims for any sort of crime, particularly property crimes. They are the targets of thieves, pickpockets, confidence men, gamblers, social criminals, and perhaps others. It has been demonstrated that crimes against persons in an intoxicated state are much greater than might be expected. As to the drug addict, Hentig refers to him as the "prototype of the doer-sufferer."

Immigrants are vulnerable because of the difficulties they experience while adjusting to a new culture. Hentig (not the first and probably not the last to experience it) points out that immigration is not simply a change to a new country or continent, but "it is a temporary reduction to an extreme degree of helplessness in vital human relations." Apart from linguistic and cultural difficulties, the immigrant often suffers from poverty, emotional disturbance, and rejection by certain groups in the new country. His competitive drive may evoke hostility. In these highly disturbing and conflict-producing situations the inexperienced, poor, and credulous immigrant, who desperately clutches at every straw, is exposed to various swindles. It takes many painful years for him to adjust to a new technique of living; only then can he escape from being victimized. It is amazing that while people in general cannot fully perceive the difficulties of the immigrant, one category of the population — its criminals — understands the immigrant's disturbed situation and takes advantage of it.

The minorities' position is similar to the immigrants'. Lack of legal equality with the majority of the population increases the chances of victimization. Racial prejudice may increase their difficulties and can involve them in a victim situation. This may lead to violent criminal-victim relationships.

The dull normals, says Hentig, are born victims. He attributes the success of swindlers not to their brilliance but to the folly of their victims. The characteristic behavior of the dull normal is similar to that of immigrants and minorities; all three may be included in one category.

The depressed, as opposed to the previous "general" or sociological classes, are psychological victim types. Depression is an emotional attitude that is expressed by feelings of inadequacy and hopelessness, and that is accompanied by a general lowering of physical and mental activity. Sometimes it is pathological. Hentig suggests that the reciprocal operation of affinities between doer and sufferer can be measured in degrees of strength. The depressed person's attitude is apathetic and submissive, lacking fighting qualities. Resistance is reduced and he is open to victimization. Often the depressed person is weak not only in his mental resistance, but also physically, and this increases the possibility of his becoming a victim.

The *acquisitive* person is called "another excellent victim." Desire may not only motivate crime, but may also lead to victimization. Criminal syndicates, racketeers, gamblers, confidence men, and others exploit the victim's greed for gain, which makes their work easier. These victims can be found in almost every social strata: the poor man struggles for security, the middle-class man takes a chance in order to obtain luxuries, the rich man wants to double his money. It is well known that the latter category is the most vulnerable acquisitive victim.

The *wanton* is also one of Hentig's types, though he thinks of him as "obscured and dimmed by the rough generalization" of laws and social conventions.

The *lonesome and the heartbroken* are also seen as potential victims. Both are reminiscent of the acquisitive type, with the difference that it is not gain or profit but companionship and happiness that are desired. Hentig cites well-known mass murderers: Henri Désiré Landru, Fritz Haarmann, even Jack the Ripper; all took advantage of the loneliness and heartbroken feelings of their victims. Such credulous persons are not only victims of murder but are also, and more frequently, victims of theft, fraud, and other swindles.

The *tormentor* is a victim type who is found in family tragedies. Hentig gives the example of an alcoholic or psychotic father who tortured his family for a long time and who was finally killed by his son. Doubtless the latter was provoked by the father. This type of victim seems to be characterized by a lack of a normal prognostic sense. Consequently he strains a situation to such an extent that he becomes a victim of the tense atmosphere he himself creates. One may suppose that most of the time this kind of person is a male.

The *blocked, exempted, and fighting* victims are Hentig's last category. By the blocked victim is meant "an individual who has been so enmeshed in a losing situation that defensive moves have become impossible or more injurious than the injury at criminal hands." Such is the case of a defaulting banker who has swindled in the hope of saving himself. Hentig refers here also to persons who are blackmailed; they are in a situation where the assistance of the police does not seem desirable. Hentig also refers to crimes of violence in which the victim fights back. In contrast to the "easy victims," this is the "difficult victim." Actually it would be better to exclude the fighting victim from the victim categories. Fighting back indicates resistance, thus this victim is less a victim type than the one whose resistance is overcome by the superior strength of the criminal.

Barnes and Teeters mentioned another victim type, the *negligent or careless*. [8] This type was later mentioned by others in connection with the problem of victim compensation. Barnes and Teeters referred to cases in which the victim's negligent or careless attitude toward his belongings makes it easy for the criminal to commit his crime. Inadequately secured doors, windows left open, unlocked cars, careless handling of furs and jewelry — these and other instances of negligence are an invitation to the criminal. They mention the theft of jewelry valued at $750,000 from the late Aga Khan. And they mention bank robberies in which the victims were "responsible." An FBI survey reported that bank robbers were apprehended by guards in seven of the twenty-six institutions that employed guards; in two instances the guard was either at lunch or not on duty at the time of the robbery. The same survey revealed that too few employees take advantage of the protective devices that are available to them. In one instance the teller pressed the alarm, but it did not work. It was learned afterward that the alarm system had not been checked for eighteen months. [9]

Another victim type, the *reporting or nonreporting* victim, is mentioned by Walter C. Reckless. [10] Here the victim is unwilling to report because he fears the social consequences of doing so. Reckless referred to blackmail and attempted suicide cases that remain invisible because of the nonreporting attitude of the victim. Henri Ellenberger, too, tried to classify victim types, but because his contribution is abstract, mention of it will be reserved for the section on speculative soundings about the victim.

This list of victim types could be extended but would not serve any purpose. Personal frustration has many forms, and negligence can be split into several types. Persons who are lonesome, heartbroken, or blocked may be reacting to certain situations and may not be types of victims. These situations may, however, serve as instructive examples of the important interactions and relations between the criminal and his victim. Thus, they can enlighten social situations, can call attention to victim risks, and may assist in determining responsibility; but they may fail to develop a general victim typology.

Victim typologies try to classify the characteristics of victims, but actually they often typify social and psychological situations rather than the constant patterns of the personal makeup of victims. The "easy" victim and the "difficult" victim appear according to the balance of forces in a given criminal drama. The lonesome are prey to the criminal only when they are lonely. The heartbroken are easy victims only when they suffer a temporary disappointment. On this basis hundreds of victim "types" could be listed, all according to the characteristics of a situation at any given moment.

However, there are indeed biological types of victims who, compared with temporary "situational" victims, seem to be continuously and excessively prone to becoming victims of crime. To be young, to be old, or to be mentally defective are not "situations" but biological qualities that indicate a more or less lasting vulnerability to crime. Apart from them, a typology of criminal-victim relationships — along with the patterns of social situations in which they appear — might hold more promise. It might increase the defense of those who cannot compensate for their weakness through their own efforts; it might elucidate and explain characteristics of victimizations; it might evaluate victim risks and accommodate crime control and social defense to them; it might develop a selective and universalistic rejuvenation of the responsibility concept.

Speculative Soundings about the Victim

Before empirical studies started to reveal the hidden realities in criminal-victim relationships, a number of speculative soundings were made, most of them based on abstract thought.

Iturbe agreed with Mendelsohn that a science of victimology should be created;[11] but Paul Cornil suggested that this is not a new departure and that the term "victim," mainly as it appears in German and Dutch translation* seems to have some background as a religious reference to the sacrifice of a human being or of an animal to the divinity.[12]

In an early article,[13] Hentig suggested that the reality of life "presents a scale of graduated interactivities between perpetrator and victim, which elude the formal boundaries, set up by our statutes and the artificial abstractions of legal science, that should be heeded by a prevention-minded social science." In his view there is a reciprocal action between perpetrator and victim. But, as mentioned before, chronologically Hentig was not the first in the field, nor was Mendelsohn. Prior to their studies, Jules Simon, among others, discussed the consent of the victim,[14] and Jean Hemard, too, approached criminal-victim relationships from the same angle.[15] Kahlil Gibran was talking about victim-precipitated crimes when he called attention to the fact that "the guilty is oftentimes the victim of the injured."[16] Ernst Roesner analyzed the statistical profile of murderer-victim relationships;[17] and Bòven discussed the victim's role in sexual crimes.[18] Also before Hentig and Mendelsohn provocation of homicide had been recognized as victim-precipitated by Rollin M. Perkins[19] and by Herbert Wechsler and Jerome Michael.[20]

In the 1950s interest in the criminal-victim relationship increased. Rhoda J. Milliken asked that the postcrime sufferings of the victim be considered. Too often, she wrote, the victim suffers not only from the crime at the time it is committed but also from a series of events that "serve to scar deeply and sometimes damage irreparably the human being for whose protection the public clamors."[21] Tahon also focused attention on the problem of the victim's con-

*The German, Dutch, and French words for victim are "Opfer," "Schlachtoffer," and "Victime."

sent to a crime.[22] Henri Ellenberger discussed the broader psychological aspects of the victim's relationship with his criminal,[23] and suggested that, in the common sense understanding, criminal and victim, though interrelated, are as different as black and white. In his somewhat psychoanalytic approach he emphasizes the importance of considering the doer-sufferer aspect *(le criminel-victime concept),* the problem of the potential victim *(la victime latente),* and the special subject-object relation *(la relation spécifique criminal-victime).* He set up a list of psychological victim types, among others the murderer (criminal) of himself (victim): in other words, the person who commits suicide. Another of his types is the victim of "reflexoid" actions (discussed a half-century before by Hans Gross). Also, he called attention to the "deluded" or "fascinated" (from the German *Verblendung)* easy victims and, among others, to the "born" victim. In Ellenberger's view special attention should be paid to "victimogen" factors and "future victims," since all individuals have the right to know the dangers to which their occupation, social class, or physical condition may expose them. He urges an investigation of the fundamental mechanisms of the criminal-victim relationship. His message is not so much for a better understanding of crime as for more crime prevention. As a result Ellenberger became one of the pioneers in directing attention to the practical importance of victim risks. A similar line is followed by Werner.[24]

After many attempts at understanding criminal-victim relationships through psychological investigations, Erwin O. Smigel tried to explore a segment of this field from more or less of a sociological viewpoint. He was concerned with theft as related to the size of the victim organization;[25] socioeconomic status, sex, religiosity, and group membership served as his variables in testing attitudes toward stealing of victim organizations of different sizes. Ehrlich analyzed fraud, its method and its victim, primarily from the preventive point of view.[26] David Reifen discussed sexual crimes and their victims.[27] Hans Schultz[28] and Souchet[29] made general remarks on victimology and on the criminological and legal relevance of criminal-victim relationships.

The Belgian publication *Revue de Droit Pénal et de Criminologie* devoted one number[30] to the problems of victimology and published several articles on understanding the criminal and his victim. One of the contributors, Willy Calewaert, discussed victimology in relation to cases of fraud.[31] Aimée Racine discussed the specific behavior of child victims and suggested psychiatric examination or at least social casework for young victims in certain instances.[32] Bray distinguished three phases of victim attitudes: those before, during, and after the crime.[33] René Dellaert wrote about the dynamics of the criminal-victim relationship from a "cinéramique" view. He observed the relationships from the angles of psychotechnique, clinical psychology, social psychology, mental pathology, preventive measures, and education.[34]

Noach tried to open up a new aspect of victimology, and focused his attention on the interaction between the criminal and a collectivity as his victim.[35]

It is unfortunate that his idea has not been elaborated upon: the history of mankind, even of recent times, can offer a great many illustrations. Leroy Schultz turned to an obvious and well-known example of criminal-victim relationships when, in commenting on interviews with the victims of sex offenders, he suggested that a "portion of guilt" may be attributable to the victim.[36] Edwin D. Driver investigated the victim's role in crimes in India and found that it is often possible for an affectionate or friendly relationship to end in homicide.[37] Gibbens and Joyce Prince analyzed the child victim of sex offenses. However, they seemed interested primarily in the defense and protection of children, and contributed little to the intricate relationship to the criminal.[38] Albert G. Hess, some two decades before, analyzed a similar topic and offered data on the age, sex life, intelligence, and social circumstances of the victimized children.[39]

Nagel meditates on the boundaries of "criminology" and suggests that if it were redefined as "criminology of relationships," victimology could not be justified as a separate discipline. He calls attention to the fact that criminology is often misidentified with criminal etiology; if it could be so identified, victimology would be justified. However, Nagel proposes, the "counting, measuring, weighing, determining and comparing victims" — and also the "collecting of victimological determinants, factors, associations and correlations" — will never achieve any great importance. Instead, he suggests, "the removal of the conflict situation" between criminal and victim should be the goal of criminal policy.[40] Reckless does not argue about the justification of "victimology," but he does call attention to "victim proneness"; many victims tend to be victimized and are in a sense responsible for provoking criminal behavior. He goes on to say that forgetfulness or absent-mindedness may provoke crimes.[41] Abdel Fattah analyzed "victimological" problems from a legalistic point of view. He questions the existence of harmony between the penal codes and scientific progress. His approach to the victim's responsibility refers largely to the legal position of the crime participants.[42]

Justification of "victimology" as an independent science or discipline may indeed be a questionable objective, but only adherents of the formalistic-individualistic interpretation of crime can oppose or devalue the victim's involvement in the understanding of responsibility, the measuring, weighing, and analysis of the criminal-victim relationship, and the need for intensive attention to victim risks. The judgment of crime *is* formalistic, and necessarily so, unless one were to advocate anarchy; and it *is* individualistic, unless the human being were to be dissolved in a collective whole. But formalism and individualism cannot be goals in themselves, and should be understood from the viewpoint of all participants in crime and from that of the societal context of criminal justice. Criminal, victim, and their society: one comprehensive concept should embrace all.

The Empirical Study of the Victim

The studies that we have just reviewed concerning the problem of "victimology" or, better, the problem of the criminal-victim relationship indicate the growing interest in aiding the revival of the victim's importance. However, all these studies, convincing and promising though they may seem, and though supported now and then by examples of crimes, criminals, and victims, suffer from the absence or insignificance of empirical evidence. In addition to studies of this kind there are a few research studies, in essence empirical, but even these seem to miss the central issue of the criminal-victim relationship. This issue is the functional responsibility for crime.

Marvin Wolfgang's study of the patterns of criminal homicide,[43] in which "the relationship of the antagonists to one another"[44] has been systematically researched, involves 588 homicide cases in Philadelphia, Pennsylvania, between 1948 and 1952. Race, sex, and age differences; methods and weapons of inflicting death; temporal and spatial patterns; alcohol and violence; previous police records; motives; personal relationships between victims and offenders; victim-precipitation — these and other aspects were subjects of the research. The findings provoked a great deal of thought.

Evelyn Gibson and S. Klein, members of the English Home Office Research Unit, presented an analytic survey of murders known to the police in England and Wales from 1952 to 1960.[45] The important changes in English law that were made by the Homicide Act of 1957 through the virtual redefinition of murder prompted a report on court proceedings and on victims and offenders in murder cases. The report was in the form of a purely statistical study based mainly on absolute figures, averages, and percentages.

Hunter Gillies made sixty-six psychiatric examinations of persons accused of murder between 1953 and 1964 in the Glasgow area in Scotland.[46] His examinations usually took place in a prison a few days or weeks after the arrest; but on seven occasions the interview was held at a police station a few hours after the arrest, and on three occasions it was held in a mental hospital. Gillies examined fifty-nine male and seven female offenders; no one else was present during any interview.

Stephen Schafter examined criminal-victim relationships in violent crimes in Florida.[47] A definition of violent crimes was based on a United Nations' report. The United Nations' International Group of Experts regarded the following crimes as major violent offenses:

1. criminal homicide, including first and second degree murder
2. aggravated assault: the unlawful, intentional disturbance of the physical well-being of a person, causing harm to the body or to health, if it results in a grievous, long-lasting, or permanent injury.

3. theft with violence, including robbery and burglary: robbery is a completed
    theft that involves violence or threat, or that involves violence or threat
    when the offender is caught *flagrante delicto,* either while in the act of
    stealing or while attempting to escape; burglary is a completed theft that in-
    volves the use of force on things (not persons), or that involves unlawful
    entry, hiding on the premises, or the unlawful use of keys or other imple-
    ments.[48]

However, these definitions had been designed only to furnish a convenient
basis for a planned uniform international crime reporting system. Thus, because
they are rather arbitrary and deal in generalities, the author adapted them only
as guides to the understanding of violent crime. In view of that, in this research
the investigation of criminal-victim relationships in violent crimes was confined
to Florida, and the definition of the three major violent offenses was accepted
according to the provisions of Florida law; that is to say, the law of the place
where the research was done, and as interpreted and applied by the courts. It
was assumed and hoped that these crimes of violence would offer the best possible chance for observing the victim's positive or active participation in crime.
During the investigation, however, this assumption and hope often failed. This
was due partly to the almost complete absence of relevant data in official files
and records, and partly to the reluctance of victims to reveal their roles in lawbreaking. One of the most important and instructive findings of the inquiry was
the fact of official disregard of the victims' participation in crimes.

Notes

1. Hans von Hentig, *The Criminal and His Victim, Studies in the Sociology of
    Crime* (New Haven, 1948).
2. B. Mendelsohn, "The Origin of the Doctrine of Victimology," *Excerpta
    Criminologica,* Vol. 3, No. 3 (May-June 1963).
3. B. Mendelsohn, "Method To Be Used by Counsel for the Defense in the
    Researches Made into the Personality of the Criminal," *Revue de Droit
    Pénal et de Criminologie* (August-October 1937), p. 877.
4. B. Mendelsohn, "Rape in Criminology," *Giustizia Pénale* (1940).
5. B. Mendelsohn, "The Victimology," *Etudes Internationales de Psycho-
    Sociologie Criminelle* (July-September 1956), pp. 25-26 (essentially the
    same in French under the title "Une nouvelle branche de la science
    biopsycho-sociale, la victimologie").
6. *Ibid.* (French), pp. 105-07, 108.
7. Hentig, *op. cit.,* pp. 404-38.
8. Harry Elmer Barnes and Negley K. Teeters, *New Horizons in Criminology*
    (3rd ed., Englewood Cliffs, 1959), pp. 595-96.
9. "Profile of a Bank Robber," *FBI Law Enforcement Bulletin,* 34 (November
    1965), 22.

10. Walter C. Reckless, *The Crime Problem* (3rd ed., New York, 1961), p. 24.
11. M. O. Iturbe, "Victimologia," *Revista Penal y Penitenciaria,* Ministerio de Educacion y de la Republica Argentina, XXIII, No. 87-90 (1958).
12. Paul Cornil, "Contribution de la 'Victimologie' aux sciences criminologiques," *Revue de Droit Pénal et de Criminologie,* 38 (April 1959), 587-601.
13. Hans von Hentig, "Remarks on the Interaction of Perpetrator and Victim," *Journal of the American Institute of Criminal Law and Criminology,* XXXI (May-June 1940, March-April 1941), 303-09.
14. Jules Simon, "Le Consentement de la victime justifie-t-il les lesions corporelles?" *Revue de Droit Pénal et de Criminologie* (1933), pp. 457-76.
15. Jean Hemard, "Le Consetement ed la victime dans le délit de coups et blessures," *Rev. crit. de législ. et jur.* (1933), pp. 292-319.
16. Kahlil Gibran, *The Prophet* (New York, 1935), p. 45.
17. Ernst Roesner, "Mörder und ihre Opfer," *Monatschrift für Kriminologie und Strafrechtsreform,* 29 (1938), 161-85, 209-28.
18. W. Boven, "Délinquants sexuels. Corrupteurs d'enfants. Coupables et victimes," *Schweizer. Archiv für Neurologie und Psychiatrie,* 51 (1943), 14-25.
19. Rollin M. Perkins, "The Law of Homicide," *Journal of Criminal Law and Criminology,* 36 (March-April 1946), 412-27.
20. Herbert Wechsler and Jerome Michael, "A Rationale of the Law of Homicide," *Journal of Criminal Law and Criminology,* 36 (March-April 1946), 1280-82.
21. Rhoda J. Milliken, "The Sex Offender's Victim," *Federal Probation,* 14 (September 1950), 22-26.
22. R. Tahon, "Le Consentement de la victime," *Revue de Droit Pénal et de Criminologie* (1951-1952), pp. 323-42.
23. Henri Ellenberger, "Relation psychologiques entre le criminel et la victime," *Revue Internationale de Criminologie et de Police Technique* (1954), pp. 103-21.
24. E. Werner, "Das Opfer des Mordes," *Kriminalistik* (1956), pp. 2-5.
25. Erwin O. Smigel, "Public Attitudes toward Stealing as Related to the Size of the Victim Organization," *American Sociological Review,* 21 (February 1956), 320-27.
26. C. Ehrlich, "Der Betrüger, sein Handwerkszeug und seine Opfer," *Kriminalistik* (October 1957), pp. 365-67.
27. D. Reifen, "Le délinquant sexuel et sa victime," *Revue Internationale de L'Enfant* (1958), pp. 110-24.
28. Hans Schultz, "Kriminologische und Strafrechtliche Bemerkungen zur Beziehung zwischen Täter und Opfer," *Revue Pénale Suisse* (1958), pp. 171-91.
29. C. R. Souchet, "La Victimologie," *La Vie Judiciaire* (December 15, 1958).
30. *Revue de Droit Pénal et de Criminologie* (April 1959).
31. Willy Calewart, "La Victimologie et l'escroquerie," ibid., pp. 602-18.
32. Aimee Racine, "L'Enfant victime d'actes contraires aux moeurs commis sur sa personne par ascendant," ibid., pp. 635-42.
33. L. de Bray, "Quelques Observations sur les victimes des delits de vol," ibid., pp. 643-49.

34. René Dellaert, "Première confrontation de la psychologie criminelle et de la 'victimologie'," ibid., pp. 628-34.
35. W.M.E. Noach, "Het Schlachtoffer en de Strafrechtspraak," in W.P.J. Pompe and G. Th. Kempe, eds., *Strafrechtspraak, Crimologische Studiën* (Assen, 1959), pp. 29-41.
36. Leroy G. Schultz, "Interviewing the Sex Offender's Victim," *Journal of Criminal Law, Criminology and Police Science,* 50 (May-June 1959), 448-52.
37. Edwin D. Driver, "Interaction and Criminal Homicide in India," *Social Forces,* 40 (October 1961), 153-158.
38. T.C.N. Gibbens and Joyce Prince, *Child Victims of Sex Offenses* (London, 1963).
39. Albert Günter Hess, "Die Kinderschädung unter besonderer Berücksichtigung der Tatsituation," in Franz Exner, ed., *Kriminalistische Abhandlungen* (Leipzig, 1934), pp. 41-46.
40. W. H. Nagel, "The Notion of Victimology and Criminology," *Exerpta Criminologica,* Vol. 3 (May-June 1963). Similar views appear in the author's "Victimologie," *Tijdschrift voor Strafrecht* (Leiden, 1959), pp. 1-26.
41. Reckless, op. cit., pp. 21-22.
42. Ezzat Abdel Fattah, "Quelques Problèmes posés à la justice pénale par la victimologie," *International Annals of Criminology* (2nd sem., 1966), pp. 335-61.
43. Marvin E. Wolfgang, *Patterns in Criminal Homicide* (Philadelphia, 1958).
44. Ibid., Thorsten Sellin's Foreword.
45. Evelyn Gibson and S. Klein, "Murder," *Home Office Studies in the Causes of Delinquency and the Treatment of Offenders,* 4 (London, 1961).
46. Hunter Gillies, "Murder in the West of Scotland," *British Journal of Psychiatry,* III (1965), 1087-94.
47. Stephen Schafer, "Criminal-Victim Relationships in Violent Crimes" (unpublished research, *U. S. Department of Health, Education, and Welfare,* July 1, 1965, MH-07058).
48. United Nations, *Criminal Statistics; Standard Classification of Offenses* (New York, March 2, 1959), pp. 6-23.

4

Victim Survey Research: Theoretical Implications

Daniel Glaser

Traditionally the volume of crime in any area is measured by tabulating the crimes reported to or by its police departments. Victim survey research, by asking a representative sample of the population whether they have suffered from any of various types of crime in a recent period, provides a new type of evidence on the volume of crime. This creates new ways of testing hypotheses deduced from prior criminological theory. However, it may be even more important as a basis for theory and research on agencies for social control. Let us consider first the comparisons and contrasts such surveys can promote in the concepts by which we classify crime.

Classification of Crimes by Conception of the Victim

Assuming we define "victim" as the person or organization injured by a crime, victim survey research immediately forces us to differentiate acts designated by law as "crime" according to how definitely their victims can be specified. On the one hand, there are those acts in which there is clearly a deliberately injured individual or corporate victim: the persons or organizations whose money or other property a criminal takes or damages, or whom the criminal consciously seeks to injure. We may call offenses with such intended victims "predatory crimes." They include theft, burglary, forgery, fraud, assault, rape, and murder, as legally defined. In comparison with other types of offenses, there is relatively little difficulty in identifying the victims in these acts, either by studying persons named as victims in police and court records (as von Hentig, Wolfgang, Schafer, and others in the new specialty of "victimology" have done), or by discovering victims through asking samples of the general population if specific offenses have been committed against them (as is done in victim survey research). Sometimes research is hampered because the victim is not immediately or ever aware that he has been deliberately injured, as in much shoplifting and fraud, but we have

D. Glaser, "Victim Survey Research: Theoretical Implications," in A.L. Guenther (ed.), *Criminal Behavior and Social Systems: Contributions of American Sociology,* pp. 136-146, ©1970 by Rand McNally and Company, Chicago. Reprinted by permission of Rand McNally College Publishing Company.

relatively little conceptual difficulty in defining the victim whenever we know of the occurrence of such crimes.

Crimes that are not clearly predatory form a scale with respect to the problem of defining a victim. Perhaps closest to predatory offenses are "public disorder crimes," where there is generally someone who complains because he is an unwilling audience to the disorder, or the police act as sole complainants. These offenses include such misdemeanors as public drunkenness, excessive noisemaking, and indecent exposure. Here there is usually no allegation of intent to injure a victim, and often no clear injury. Although they are the most frequent basis for arrest in the United States, they generally are not considered a serious social problem because the damage done any victim usually is considered negligible in comparison with the damage from predatory crimes.

A second marginal category consists of "negligence crimes," where no intent to injure is alleged, although they create either injured victims or an increase in the probability of unintentional victimization, as in reckless driving, speeding, and some other acts which are illegal on grounds that they endanger the public. These crimes, especially those involving autos, are a serious social problem, for the injuries to persons and property are several times as great as those clearly ascribed to predatory crimes. However, conceptually they are a relatively distinct category because of the presumption of no intent to victimize.

Further from predatory offenses, in terms of the clear existence of a victim, is any crime in which, instead of someone taking another's possessions or intentionally injuring him, the person whom the law defines as criminal is selling a commodity or a service to a willing purchaser. These "service crimes" include such things as sale of moonshine liquor or narcotics and sale of illegal services, such as prostitution and gambling. In these criminal transactions, as in legitimate economic exchanges, all participants usually gain satisfaction and do not consider themselves victims: the purchaser gets what he wishes to buy, at a price he is willing to pay, and the seller receives the payment which he requests. Insofar as being a customer of such services is also a crime, we have what might be called "consumption crimes," the extreme opposite of predatory crimes in our scale of victimization.

Thus, the first valuable contribution we can gain for criminological theory from victim research is more lucidity for the murky concept of crime. Victim research, of necessity, narrows our focus to predatory offenses. Criminologists still concern themselves with public disorder, negligence, and service or consumption crimes, and even in international and historical comparative research with "treason" and "illegal status" offenses. However, each of these other types of crime also has less universality, as types of individual behavior punishable by the state, than predatory crime. At any rate, victim research forces us to observe and to think about predatory crimes separately from other types of crime.

Epidemiological Research: The Interaction
of Methodology and Theory

Cressey has suggested that criminological theory has two distinct problems: to account for the development of individual cases of crime, and to account for the epidemiology of crime, particularly the trend, the density, and the geographic and demographic distribution of various types of crime.[1] Let us consider first the most publicized finding of the first national victim survey research project, the one conducted by the National Opinion Research Center (henceforth called NORC) in 1965 for the President's Commission on Law Enforcement and the Administration of Justice.[2] I refer to the finding that over twice as much major crime was reported by victims as had been reported to the police and tabulated in the *Uniform Crime Reports*. This will be the first of several illustrations of the difficulty of separating theoretical implications of survey research from the methodological implications with which they interact.

Data on the frequency of crime, or on any other phenomenon, are significant for theory only if they can be correlated with something else. However, even viewing the NORC total alone, without correlating it with anything, we find that, like much previous research in criminology, it is significant for the doubts it casts on many prevailing beliefs. For example, the FBI's *Uniform Crime Reports* for 1967 indicates that major crimes have increased 71 percent in the past seven years. This poses tremendous theoretical problems, for there has not been nearly a 71 percent increase in these seven years in anything generally designated as a cause of crime, such as urbanization, lack of opportunity, cultural deprivation, social isolation, family disorganization, the proportion of the population that is youthful, or the proportion that is youthful and has these various other problems. However, the NORC evidence is that less than 45 percent of major crime was covered in the 1965 *Uniform Crime Reports'* findings of very large percent increases in crime each year during the 1960's.

A 71 percent increase in the completeness of crime reporting by police forces to the FBI between 1960 and 1967 would create a 71 percent increase in the *Uniform Crime Reports'* total, even if the actual crime rate stayed constant. The NORC survey concluded that FBI data on major crimes in 1965 were 45 percent complete. Let us assume that for 1967 they were 50 percent complete. If they were only 29.2 percent complete in 1960, the increase to 50 percent complete in 1967 would be a 71 percent increase. That the current FBI coverage may represent an appreciable increase in completeness from preceding years is suggested by the success of many organizations, notably the FBI, in promoting growth in the size and training of police forces. There has also been a modernization of police data collection and tabulation systems . . . . Regularly repeated victim survey research should indicate how much fluctuation occurs in the actual crime rate, independently of changes in the adequacy of police data collection.

Therefore, such surveys would indicate how much of the increase in official crime rates is due merely to increases in completeness of coverage.

It follows that, in the interest of both theory and practice on social control, victim survey research should not be viewed as a replacement for police reports on the volume of crime, but as a continually necessary supplement to police figures. If both police and victim survey crime rates are tabulated, information on the difference between these rates may be just as valuable as either rate alone. For maximum scientific and practical utility, victim surveys should be repeated regularly by a permanent national staff, in a standardized manner, and the FBI's current *Uniform Crime Reports* should also be continued. Repeated victim survey research would not only reveal more accurately than the police figures the trend of predatory crime rates in this country, but in conjunction with tabulations like those now made by the FBI it would also show the proportion of the total volume of crime which comes to the attention of law-enforcement agencies. Variations in the discrepancy between victim survey and police tabulations could be a major guide for the comparative study of police systems with a view to identifying factors related to differences in their effectiveness.

In addition to providing a standard for the assessment of police effectiveness, victim survey data may be useful for testing theory on the ecological correlates of crime . . . Therefore, in appraising theoretical implications of victim research, we are bound to consider also the methodological question of the scope and correlates of error in both victim survey and police-reported crime rates.

A striking feature of the NORC victim survey data is that the discrepancy between their figures and the police-reported figures published in the *Uniform Crime Reports* varies markedly according to type of offense. The victim-reported burglary is over three times as frequent as police-reported burglary, victim-reported rates for grand larceny and for aggravated assault are over twice as high as police-reported rates, and victim-reported rates of robbery are about 50 percent above police-reported rates. On the other hand, victim-reported car theft is only four-fifths of police-reported rates, and victim survey rates for homicide are only three-fifths of official rates.

Let us consider the probable validity of the NORC figures by offense. It is a built-in consequence of the household sampling procedure alone that the burglary, larceny, and robbery figures of the NORC victim survey, although much more frequent than police data, still underrepresent crimes of this type, by omitting many crimes against corporations. With respect to larceny, Cameron found that stores report only a small fraction of the shoplifters whom they apprehend, and it is probable that they never are aware of most of the shoplifting and pilfering that is conducted in their premises.[3] The University of Michigan survey for the President's Commission more rigorously confirmed this.[4] In reporting the Bureau of Social Science Research survey for the President's Commission, Biderman has analyzed a variety of evidence of error in victim research; they were predominantly errors of underreporting property offenses.[5]

Automobile theft, unlike other property offenses, is reported not as frequently by the NORC survey as by police reports, although this discrepancy is small enough to be a function of sampling error, as is suggested by the fact that its direction varies by region. The high value of autos, the pressure to report car theft because of registration and insurance, and the high police recovery rate for stolen autos apparently make police-reported auto-theft rates sufficiently complete that victim survey research will not yield appreciably more accurate data on this offense. However, burglary and larceny other than auto theft are two-thirds of major offenses according to the FBI and three-fourths of major offenses according to the NORC survey. Actual rates of these offenses, including offenses against corporations and undetected shoplifting and pilfering, apparently exceed police-reported rates to an even greater extent than the NORC data suggest.

For crimes against persons, the relative discrepancy between victim survey and official crime rates by type of crime is a more complex function of reporting variables. For example, the NORC figures indicate about one rape per 1,250 females per year, while the FBI figures indicate about one per 4,300 females. Yet confidential interviews by sociologists Kirkpatrick and Kanin with 291 coeds at a midwest university indicated that about one in 15 suffered "aggressively forceful attempts at sex intercourse in the course of which menacing threats of coercive infliction of physical pain were employed."[6] This implies rape or attempted rape, yet none of these episodes had been reported to authorities. Since rape is an offense of which the victim is usually ashamed, the proportion which would be reported by the victims to survey interviewers probably is less than the proportion reported to university health-service specialists in an office interview under conditions more conducive to frank revelation of sex experiences.

This university research suggests that underreporting of rape — certainly of rape attempts — remains extensive in both police and NORC statistics. Yet of the rape incidents reported to NORC, three-fourths were said by the respondents to have been reported to the police. Since police-reported rape rates were only a fourth of the NORC rates, the three-fourths-reporting claims of NORC respondents suggest that even that fraction of rape reported to the police is underreported by them, perhaps reflecting definitional problems with this offense. Indeed, while improved knowledge of sexual offense rates will depend upon victim survey research, optimum field methods probably would resemble those of the Kinsey Foundation more closely than those of NORC. It is noteworthy that the Bureau of Social Science Research survey in Washington, D.C., used different questions and received more reporting of sex offenses than the NORC national survey. In summary, probably all available statistics on sex-offense rates are too questionable to warrant efforts at epidemiological generalization. It is quite possible that any correlates of sex-offense rates are as much a function of interviewing personnel and procedures as they are of the actual occurrence of these offenses.

Only one homicide was reported in the NORC survey, perhaps because an inquiry as to whether there were any murders in the household in the past year is not the best way to measure the frequency of this offense. The certificates on cause of death prepared by physicians, and tabulated in U.S. Public Health Service *Vital Statistics* reports, probably yield more accurate data on homicide than are likely to be gathered by either victim survey or police reports.

The borderline between simple and aggravated assaults and the borderline between simple assaults and altercations not considered crime are both vague. Accordingly, it is quite probable that variations in the customarily tolerated vigor of expressing interpersonal opposition may greatly affect variations in the reporting of assaults both to the police and to victim surveyors. In "polite society" a shove or a slap may be conceived as assault, while in high-violence groups only an intensive effort to beat up or to wound would be either reported to the police or recalled in a household survey. . . The major advantage of the victim survey in assault tabulation is revealed by the fact that in a third of the aggravated-assault cases and over half the simple assaults the victims did not report their assaults to the police, most often on the grounds that they considered it a private matter. Indeed, probably many intrahousehold assaults are also not reported to survey interviewers. However, we can assume that, despite lingering omissions and definitional problems, victim survey research probably provides much more complete and accurate statistics on the frequency and distribution of assault than are available from police reports.

The first section of this paper suggested that victim survey research is clearly applicable only to predatory offenses. This section concluded that such research would not improve our knowledge on rates of homicide, rape, or auto theft. These comprise approximately one-fourth of all major predatory crimes according to the FBI, but scarcely more than one-tenth according to the NORC survey.

The New Victimology

Our discussion thus far has dealt with victim survey information on crime rates. These differ not in kind, but in being more complete and therefore presumably more accurate than crime rates collected by the police. Victim survey research, of course, by covering crimes more completely, also enhances the completeness of statistics on attributes of victims, but data on victims also are available from police and court records, and led to the growing field of "victimology."[7] In general, the NORC data confirm leading conclusions on victims developed previously from police data, such as the predominance of Negro victims among crimes by Negroes, and the predominance of white victims among crimes by whites. . . There is also little not previously indicated by police figures in the survey data on the ecology of risk, such as their finding that middle- and upper-class persons, of either race, are victimized most if they live near the slums. However, much more important is the distinctly new kind of victimology data which survey research adds to the police-record information. These new data are concerned with victim attitudes.

The hardest data on attitudes toward the police yielded by victim surveys are not the verbal opinions they compile regarding the police, but the reports they collect on whether or not crime victims notify the police. These reports on actions express the attitudes of the respondents better than their evaluative words. For property crimes, at least, the hypothesis which survey data seem to support is simply: *The proportion of total crimes that are reported by victims to the police varies directly with the proportion of reported crimes on which the police act effectively.* Vicious circles obviously can develop here: the less successfully police cope with crimes reported to them, the smaller will be the proportion that is reported to them, and hence the less successfully they can cope with them. Beneficient circles, however, can also occur: the more successfully the police cope with crime, the larger the proportion of offenses of which they will be told. This may be one reason why improved police work leads to higher police-reported crime statistics: more crime is reported to good police forces, in addition to better records being kept by them. Regularly collected victim survey crime rates could break this particular circle of higher apparent crime rates with improved policing, due to lower discrepancy between police-reported rates and actual rates.

Attitudes toward the police reported by victims in evaluative language reflect primarily the intervening variable in reporting offenses or not reporting them, which is perceived probability of police effectiveness. The most frequent reason given for not reporting property crimes to the police is simply doubt that the police will do anything about them. With crimes against persons the intervening variables are more complex: the most frequent reasons given for not reporting assault and rape to the police were belief that these offenses were personal matters, not of police concern; doubts of police effectiveness were only the second most frequent reason for not reporting these offenses.

In addition to probing reasons for nonuse of the police by crime victims, the survey technique permits inquiry on the satisfaction obtained by those who call the police. The NORC findings suggest that retribution by punishment of the offender remains the ultimate objective of those who have suffered from a crime, despite predominant growth in public support for nonpunitive approaches to changing offenders. However, these data also show that punishment does not really get to be an issue in almost nine-tenths of the cases. This is because, according to the victims, the police did not even come when called in a quarter of the cases; in a quarter of those in which they did come, they did not treat the offense as a crime; and they made an arrest in only a fifth of the cases which they did define as crimes. Obviously, data on the variation of these percentages by police system, by offense, by attributes of the victim, and by neighborhood will be a tremendous asset for identifying the differential effectiveness of various police forces, and for guiding theory and research to account for such variations.

. . . . The tremendous potential utility of public knowledge and opinion surveying has hardly begun to be realized by law-enforcement agencies, despite the
fact that police and court effectiveness depends so much on community support.

The NORC survey confirmed prior impressions that a less favorable attitude
toward the police prevails among nonwhites than among whites. It was surprising
only in finding relatively little relationship of these orientations to income within racial groups, but distinctly more negative orientations toward the police in
nonwhite women than in nonwhite men. There is no breakdown by age. The
University of Michigan survey was highly detailed and specific in its probes on
types of illegal action that the respondents actually saw police commit or believed they committed. There would certainly be merit in analysis of these attitudes
by integration indices for communities and for police forces, and by many other
attributes of communities and of police policy and procedure.

Notes

1. Donald R. Cressey, "Epidemiology and Individual Conduct: A Case from
   Criminology," *Pacific Sociological Review, 3,* no. 2 (Fall 1960): 47-58.
2. Phillip H. Ennis, "Crimes, Victims, and the Police," *Trans-action, 4,* no. 7
   (June 1967): 36-44; Phillip H. Ennis, *Criminal Victimization in the U.S.:
   A Report on a National Survey,* Field Surveys II of the President's Commission on Law Enforcement and Administration of Justice (Washington, D.C.:
   U.S. Government Printing Office, 1967).
3. Mary Owen Cameron, *The Booster and the Snitch* (New York: Free Press,
   Macmillan, 1964), chap. 1.
4. Albert J. Reiss, Jr., and associates, *Studies in Crime and Law Enforcement
   in Major Metropolitan Areas,* vols. 1 and 2, Field Surveys III of the President's Commission on Law Enforcement and Administration of Justice
   (Washington, D.C.: U.S. Government Printing Office, 1967). This is
   hereafter referred to as the University of Michigan survey, as it was administered by the Survey Research Center and other units of the University
   of Michigan.
5. Albert D. Biderman and associates, *Report of a Pilot Study in the District
   of Columbia on Victimization and Attitudes Toward Law Enforcement,*
   Field Survey I of the President's Commission on Law Enforcement and
   the Administration of Justice (Washington, D.C.: U.S. Government
   Printing Office, 1967).
6. C. Kirkpatrick and E. Kanin, "Male Sex Aggression on a University Cam-
   pus," *American Sociological Review, 22* (1957): 52-58.
7. For systematic reviews of this literature, see Albert Morris, "What About
   the Victims of Crime?" *Correctional Research,* United Prison Assn. of
   Massachusetts bulletin no. 16 (November 1966); Stephen Schafer. *The
   Victim and His Criminal: A Study in Functional Responsibility* (New York:
   Random House, 1968); President's Commission on Law Enforcement and
   the Administration of Justice, "Victimology," *Technical Papers* (Washing-

ton, D.C.: U.S. Government Printing Office, 1967); Ezzat Abdel Fattah, "Quelques problemes posés à la justice pénale par la victimologie," *Annales Internationales de Criminologie,* 5, no. 2 (1966): 335-361.

Part I Bibliography

Abdel-Fattah, E.   "Q'est-ce qu'est la Victimologie et quel est son Avenir," *Revue Internationale de Criminologie et de Police Technique* 1967, 21 (2, Avril–Juin): 113–124; 21 (3, Juillet-Septembre): 193–202.

Biderman, A. D.   "An Overview of Victim Survey Research." A paper presented at the Annual Meeting of the American Sociological Association, 1967.

Caplan, N., and   "On Being Useful: The Nature and Consequences of Psycholo-
S. D. Nelson   gical Research on Social Problems," *American Psychologist* 1973, 28 (3): 199–211.

Cornil, P.   "Contribution de la Victimologie aux Sciences Criminologiques," *Revue de Droit Pénal et de Criminologie* (Bruxelles) 1959 (7, Avril): 587–601.

De Castro, L. A.   *La Victimologia.* Maracaibo: Centro de Investigaciones Criminologicas, Universidad del Zulia, 1969.

Dellaert, R.   "Première Confrontation de la Psychologie Criminelle et de la Victimologie," *Revue de Droit Pénal et de Criminologie* 1959, 39 (7): 628–634.

Fuentes, Gonzales C.   "Victimologia," *Policia Cientifica* (Caracas) 1955 (June), 10.

Gasser, R.   "Victimologie." Thesis, University of Zürich, Coire 1965.

Iturbe, O.   "Victimologia: Nuevo Enfoque Criminologica de la Victima del Delito," *La Revista Penal y Penitenciaria* 1959, 24 (87–90, Enero-Diciembre): 199–223.

Jimenez, D. A.   "La Llamada Victimologia," *Estudios de Derecho Penal y Criminologia,* I. Buenos Aires, Editores-Libreros, 1962, 19–41.

Kaplan, B.   "Victimology: Analysis, Evaluation, and Potential." New York: John Jay College of Criminal Justice, 1970. Unpublished master's thesis.

Karoly, E.   "A Viktimologia" (Victimology, the New Line of Modern Criminology), *Acta Facultatis Politico-Iuridicae,* Tomus XI, Budapest, 1969.

Marx, I.   "A Propos de la Victimologie," *Revue de Science Criminelle et de Droit Pénal Comparé* (Paris) 1958.

Mendelsohn, B.   "Une Nouvelle Branche de la Science Bio-Psycho-Sociale: La Victimologie," *Revue Internationale de Criminologie et de Police Technique* 1957, 11 (2): 95–109.

————.   "La Victimologie: Science Actuelle," *Revue de Droit Pénal et de Criminologie* (Bruxelles) 1959, 39 (7): 619–627.

Mannheim, H.   *Comparative Criminology.* Boston: Houghton-Mifflin, 1965 (esp. pp. 670–676).

Paasch, G.   "Grundprobleme der Viktimologie." Doctoral thesis, Faculty of Law and Political Science, Westphalian University, Muenster, 1965.

President's Commission   *Field Survey I.* Report on a Pilot Study in the District
on Law Enforce-   of Columbia on Victimization and Attitudes toward Law
ment and the   Enforcement. Washington, D.C.: U. S. Government
Administration   Printing Office, 1967.
of Justice.

————.   *Field Survey II.* Criminal Victimization in the United States. A Report of a National Survey (National Opinion Research Center). U. S. Washington, D.C.: U. S. Government Printing Office, 1967.

————.   *Field Surveys.* Report of Research Studies submitted to the President's Commission on Law Enforcement and the Administration of Justice. Washington, D.C.: U. S. Government Printing Office, 1967.

Šelih, A.   "Viktimologija in njena vloga v boju zoper Kriminaliteto" (Victimology and Its Role in the War on Crime), *Revija za Kriminalistiko in Kriminologijo* (Ljubljana) 1967, 18 (1–2): 37–42.

Souchet, C. R.   "La Victimologie," *Etudes Internationales de Psycho-Sociologie Criminelle* (Paris), 1958, 4: 13–14. Also in *Excerpta Criminologica* 1960, 1: 24.

Van Der Kwast, S.   *Seksuele Criminaliteit.* Leiden, 1968, ch. 4.

Von Hentig, H.   *The Criminal and His Victim: Studies in the Socio-biology of Crime.* New Haven: Yale University Press, 1948.

Weinstock, N.   "Daniel Defoe, Observateur du Milieu Criminel," *Revue de Droit Pénal et de Criminologie* (Bruxelles) 1965, 45 (9): 935–953.

Wertham, F.   *The Show of Violence.* New York: Doubleday, 1949.

Wolfgang, M. E.   "Analytical Categories for Research on Victimization,"
                  Kriminologische Wegzeichen Festschrift für Hans Von Hentig.
                  Hamburg, 1967.

Part II
The Victim-Offender Relationship

Introduction

The administration of justice presupposes a clear distinction between the criminal and his victim. But in reality the line separating the protagonists of the criminal situation is at times blurred and overlapping. While many believe that the role of the criminal and that of the victim are totally different, there is a growing evidence that such conceptual model must be revised to reflect more realistically the varieties of the relationship between the offender and the victim. Thus, in order to reach a just evaluation and assessment of the penal responsibility in a criminal circumstance, it is necessary to examine both parties, their personalities, their interrelationship and interaction, and to study the role that each has played while the crime was committed.[1]

Von Hentig, in his article published in 1941 and reprinted here, was among the first scholars to comment on the interaction of perpetrator and victim. While discussing the "scale of graduated inter-activities between perpetrator and victim which elude the formal boundaries set up by our statutes and the artificial abstractions of legal science," he formulated a typology of victims.

Victim typologies are critically reviewed by Silverman. He examines victim classifications undertaken by Von Hentig, Mendelsohn, Abdel-Fattah, Sellin, and Wolfgang. Finally, he offers his own reformulation.

The selection by Dynes and Quarantelly adds an interesting dimension to the study of the victim-offender relationship. They examine some of the patterns and conditions associated with organizations as victims in mass civil disturbances from an interactional perspective.

The articles by Wolfgang and by Agopian, Chappell, and Geis apply the methodology of empirical research to the question of the interaction between the criminal and the victim in cases of homicide and of forcible rape. Wolfgang collected the data for his analysis of victim-precipitated homicides from the files of the Philadelphia Police Department. The Agopian, Chappell, and Geis data consist of instances of interracial rape involving black offenders reported to the police in Oakland, California during 1971. Their study qualify, and at times contradict, some of the results reported from Philadelphia by M. Amir in his study, *Patterns of Forcible Rape*.

In his paper, R. Quinney makes the argument that "the victim" is a social construction. In other words, criminologists and others choose certain kinds of persons, and not others, as being the victims of crime, in accord to a particular theory of reality. More often than not such theory supports the existing social order and excludes from being considered as victims those who may threaten it or who suffer because of it. Quinney calls for a critical re-examination of the theories of reality each one of us holds, lest we blindly accept the official version of what reality is, and — consequently — of who the victims are.

Notes

1. Abdel Fattah, "La Victimologie: Qu'est-elle et quel est son avenir?" *Revue Internationale de Criminologie et de Police Technique* 1967, 21 (2): 113.

5

Remarks on the Interaction of Perpetrator and Victim

Hans von Hentig

I.

We are want to regard crime as an occurrence which falls upon the victim without his aid or cooperation. It is true, there are many criminal deeds with little or no contribution on the part of the injured individual. You may be wounded, killed, robbed or swindled without your own conduct affecting or modifying the final detrimental outcome. In other cases the relation between offender and offended person is only slight and general, and pertains to the common facts of life. Possession of money has certainly to do with robbery, and prettiness or youth are contributing factors in criminal assaults. There is some reciprocal action between perpetrator and victim in such cases; this juncture, however, is not specific, and therefore presents no changeable and preventive relation.

On the other hand we can frequently observe a real mutuality in the connexion of perpetrator and victim, killer and killed, duper and dupe. Although this reciprocal operation is one of the most curious phenomena of criminal life it has escaped the attention of socio-pathology.[1] There is a new form of grouping, casual or permanent. When these elements meet, it is likely that a novel compound is set up in the world of human relations, explosive and big with ruinous conflicts.

There is probably a corresponding relation among beasts of prey and preyed creatures in the animal world.[2] The difference rests upon the fact, that the attributes of the beasts of prey are adjustments to the foibles of their booty, whereas the human victim in many instances seems to lead the evildoers actively into temptation. The predator is—by varying means—prevailed upon to advance against the prey. If there are born criminals, it is evident that there are born victims, self-harming and self-destroying through the medium of a pliable outsider.

That the behavior of culprit and injured are often closely interlocking can be noticed in a multitude of crimes. Many tricks of the pick-pocket, for instance, are only applicable to human types of a certain psychological responsiveness. We shall restrict ourselves to three major crimes: rape and confidence game, since they permit us to exemplify most evidently our theory.

Reprinted by special permission of the *Journal of Criminal Law, Criminology, and Police Science* 1941, 31 (March-April): 303-309, Copyright©1941 by Northwestern University School of Law.

II.

The bulk of the perfect murder victims is formed by four types which we shall examine briefly; although some more categories could be set up, we are concerned in this paper only with main classifications.

The *depressive* type heads the group. Obviously, the dejected individual lacks ordinary prudence and discretion. There is no doubt that we would find a good many depressive persons among the people who are killed in accidents. Some scholars have gone further and contended that the depressed is dominated by a secret and subconscious desire to be annihilated, and there are certainly some murder cases in which the victim seemed to encourage the slayer to have the slain dispatched. However this may be, it is evident that the saddish individual may easily be induced to approach doubtful persons and to venture into risky situations. His instinct of self-preservation being weakened he is not bold but simply unsuspecting and careless.[3]

We mention but one typical case of this sort:

The Belgian lawyer Guillaume Bernays (the trial occurred in 1881 in Antwep) had marital troubles. He suspected a former intimate friend of his to be in love with his wife.

Shortly before driving to Brussels where he was murdered, Bernays had written to a friend and had touched on the frictions in his home. He had confessed "his secret longing to withdraw from the world, and . . . to live, forgotten by everybody, as a missionary in a far cut-off country where he might be devoured by cannibals or carried away by the yellow fever." [4]

Not keeping with the legal etiquette the lawyer was drawn into the ambush of a vacated house in Brussels for a consultation and slain by the brother of his rival.

The *greedy of gain* is another type who shows an inclination to be victimized. The expectance of easy money acts on certain individuals like a drug, removing all normal inhibitions and deadening any well-founded suspicion. The Scottish murder case Slater[5] brought an illustrative example to the attention of the public.

The victim, an 82 year old woman, was found to have had jewelry to the value of about $15,000 in her possession. Unknown "business men" used to visit her. She was believed to be a resetter of jewelry.

We have described a similar type, this time a male, some years ago:[6]

In 1917 an illicit sugar trader, X, was found murdered in a deserted wood near the city of Dresden. At this time sugar was strictly rationed in Germany, but there were some possibilities to obtain sugar at an exorbitant price from illegal traders.

X had received a letter, telling him that he could have a vast amount of smuggled sugar, if he would meet the owners in a lonely wood at night where the sugar was supposed to be hidden. They were ready to strike the bargain, if he could pay in cash.

In the hope of a substantial and easy gain X went alone to the place with several thousand marks in his pocket. There he was slain and robbed by three youngsters.

We are already here on the borderline of homicide and confidence game and shall meet the same type again in discussing the victim of buncos. Sometimes several imperiling factors combine which are met in an avaricious disposition: female sex, old age, solitary life, the business of a pawnbroker or an usurer. We have known many cases where there was no initial murderous intention. The perpetrator contemplated robbing the old woman, stunning her with a blunt instrument and leaving her alive. However the skull, weakened by old age, was fractured and death ensued. The robber had become a murderer.

The *wanton type*. In discussing the sex of his homicide victims Brearley[7] has wondered why in the United States more than four times as many males as females were homicide victims, whereas in England "two out of every three persons murdered are women."

This apparent discrepancy can easily be explained.[8] The legal concept of murder differs widely in England, Germany, France and all of Europe from the American notion. It corresponds somewhat to the first degree murder of our statutes and is even more restricted than that. We erroneously, therefore, try to draw a parallel between two incompatible magnitudes.

Where the legal notions coincide, we arrive at similar results. Thus 56 per cent of 135 murder victims which were slain in 1928, 1929 and 1930 in Germany, were females.[9] Some Chicago figures point in the same direction: During the years 1926 and 1927 the ensuing family murders occurred:[10]

Husbands killed ... 13 .. 23.6 per cent
Wives killed. ...... 42 .. 76.4 per cent

Total of family
murders. ..... 55. . 100.0 per cent

All these observations are meant to answer one purpose. They prove that serious murder criminality recruits mostly women as victims. Female foibles[11] therefore, might play a role in ther interaction of slain and slayer.

In naming this group the "wanton" type a subdivision does not seem to be out of place. The practice at least presents again and again the youthful victim and the middle-aged woman, who, approaching the climacteric period, falls a victim of an aggressor and her own critical condition.

Such a wanton type was Irene Munro who was murdered in 1920 in the English sea-resort of Eastbourne.

Neither her mother nor her employee could but give the 17 year old girl an excellent character. The mother described her as quiet, reserved, neat, fond of reading and unsuspecting. But some girl-acquaintances of Irene told the court another story: "She had been extremely attractive to the opposite sex, and in the habit of boasting about "picking up" unknown male admirers who took her to expensive restaurants and entertainments and gave her costly presents."[12] Irene Munro followed two young unemployed whom she had met casually to an unfrequented part of the shore where she was beaten to death and buried under shingles.

The sensuality of a girl is often intensified by climatic influences (high altitude, marine surroundings, etc.), by the isolation of a solitary trip, and the fact that the girl is just indisposed.[13] The climacteric specimen which comes next is perhaps more noteworthy still[14] than the young sensual type. The cases of Landru who was tried in 1921 in Versailles and that of Johann Hoch who faced the Chicago jury in 1905 come back to our memory.

On December 4, 1904, Hoch had inserted in a newspaper an advertisement wishing the acquaintance of a widow without children. "Object: matrimony." A Mrs. Julia Walker, divorced, 46 years old, answered. Hoch paid her a visit. The result of this one visit was that they were married on December 12.

Events then were going fast.

"The bridegroom seems to have been able to explain to his bride the need of ready money, for he persuaded her to sell out her little shop for 75 dollars, to withdraw three hundred dollars from a savings bank, and to turn all this, her total wordly capital, over to him for use or safe-keeping."[15]

She suddenly became ill on December 20. On January 12, a month after the wedding, she died, from poison, as the later trial proved. Four days after the death of his wife, Hoch married her sister whom he had conquered on the ride back from the cemetery.

There is a final class of victims which might be called the *tormentor-type*. In these cases some form of oppression, parental, marital or other has lasted for a long time. It grows more and more tyrannical and insufferable. Often the age-relation, being slowly displaced by the course of time, favours a rearing rebellion and the final explosion.

The normal man has the choice of many legal ways to get rid of a tormentor.

The son may leave the unbearable father's house. Separation or divorce may keep husband and wife asunder. It is the most primitive way of solving a personal conflict to annihilate physically the cause of the trouble, and we should not wonder that the percentage of insanes killing their wives is much larger than that of the normal wife-slayers.[16] The lawyer Armstrong who poisoned his tormentor wife, is a very illustrative instance of this type: he was of subnormally small stature, physically and emotionally immature in spite of his advanced age and had submitted to her tyranny silently for many years.

In examining parricides more closely, we again meet frequently the tormentor-type.[17] The father, often an alcoholic or an insane, goes on worrying wife and children unhampered. When the son grows up, the conflict is ripe for a violent explosion. The same murderous disposition, represented in father as well as in son, clashes and ends in murder, and it is difficult to say—for the psychologist, not for the omniscient lawyer—who is culprit and who is victim. No one of them is guiltless and both cooperated eagerly in bringing about the fatal outcome.

III.

Already in law the step from an accomplice to a victim is rather short in some sex crimes. Some courts have referred to the victim of seduction, for instance, as a "quasi particeps criminis." In American law all women participating in the crime of incest are regarded as accomplices, if she was not forced or deceived. In most European laws, however, descendants under 18 years are not punishable. After having reached this age they proceed from the category of victim to the higher rank of an accomplice.

But it is not the law with its facile and definite classifications we are concerned with here, we are interested in the factual, psychological and sociological relations of perpetrator and victim.

Confining ourselves to two representative sex-crimes, rape and incest, we see that the best experts emphasize again and again the element of seduction which emanates from many victims. Friederich Leppmann[18] who happened to examine thousands of sex criminals in Berlin courts points out that many defendants come forth with the excuse, that the child had requested the criminal deed. Many times this excuse is lame. In other cases, however, the plea should be checked closely. Leppmann relates a series of occurrences which cast light on the incredible depravity of many half-grown-up girls.

The writer has related the case of a child who very actively debauched her own father by stepping over his bed every morning in a narrow room in which they were herded together. Another daughter slipped into the bed of the father who, after the death of the wife, was gravely ill and unable to move in his feverish state.[19]

IV.

The felony of false pretenses as a rule includes the cooperation of the victim. By means of the false pretenses the defrauded person is tempted to act in the direction of his own detriment. As in rape, abduction and seduction the personal qualities of the victim have played a large role in the requirements of the statutes.[20] The victim could be held unworthy of being protected by the law, either not being a female "of previous chaste character" or succumbing to false pretenses which would not deceive "a man of ordinary intelligence and caution." This doctrine however appears to die out slowly and the offended person is regarded as a victim, whatever his points, good or bad, may be.

Since the bunco is a cooperative exertion of energies and therefore justly called a confidence "game," there is perhaps no crime in which the interaction of swindler and defrauded stands out in more bold relief. The victim not only contributes amply to the commitment of the crime, but his way of cooperation is often such that it prevents him from having the felon reported and prosecuted effectively in court. After having rendered himself a victim he obstructs the course of justice and grants the criminal immunity.

It is agreed among confidence-men that the sucker must possess two virtues: He must have sufficient money and "be willing to use dishonest methods of making money."[21] It is impossible to beat an honest man in a confidence game. All professionals concur in the rule.[22] The interaction of perpetrator and victim could not come more distinctly to light than in the felony of fraud, at least in many successful variations of confidence-game.

It is not the lack of intelligence and caution which makes a perfect bunco victim. It is more a specific emotional set-up, the life of urges and impulses that is important. Let us listen to a criminal of vast experience and considerable insight in the labyrinth of criminality:[23]

> Strange as it seems, the best meat for the confidence man's teeth is the hard-boiled business man. The business man is just as easy to deceive as anybody else, and there are two things about him that make him the best choice. In the first place he is glad of a chance — or what looks like a chance—to make money, and in the second place he hates to be shown up as a fool in money matters. When he finds himself caught in a trap and when he realizes that the way out will entail publicity . . . he usually decides to call the loss a bad debt and discreetly forget about it. At a guess I should say that out of ten "goldbricks" sold to business men, only one gets reported in the papers.[24]

The same picture is given by a prominent practitioner in the field of crime detection:

> In bunco operations the same psychology, based upon certain fundamental principles, is applied as in legitimate selling. The "sucker" as a rule believes in his own superior intelligence and knows that certain things are possible. He has heard of others who have made large sums through similar operations. He will therefore listen very readily to the smooth proposals of the buncos. Professional men, reputable business

men, and even bankers, are their victims. Police executives have also been listed[25] as victims, yet these men seldom succumb virtuously, for while the operations may appear to be those of legitimate business enterprise, the victim is seldom deceived on the point and really knows that he is in some manner gaining an unfair advantage.

MacDonald[26] says "unfair advantage," but looking at his book we note at once that in many buncos illegal gains are suggested, as in the "money-making machine,"[27] in the trade of stolen, smuggled, or lost objects. This bearing of an unlawful character is often somewhat obliterated by the introduction of emotional appeals: the desperately coughing old man, the deceased mother, the starved and fainting woman in the "flop-racket," the lost and bewildered miner in the "stranded prospector" racket and so forth. By emphasizing the affiliation with a specific national or ethnical group another powerful sentimental cord is touched. Cautious prudence is overcome by an emotional assault and cool intellectual capacity cannot prevail against the superior power of instincts and impulses.

MacDonald quotes[28] the words of a certain bunco who has ably summarized the perpetrator-victim problem as far as this felony is concerned. "An honest man will not allow himself to be a party in any scheme in order to gain sudden riches. A man must have larceny in his mind to become a perfect victim."

V.

Are we permitted to say that in some cases criminality is a self-consuming process of antisocial elements in which criminals prey on criminaloids, killers on suicides or other killers, oversexed on oversexed, dishonest individuals on dishonest? We think that any generalization should be avoided and that our formulation might be somewhat overdrawn. The reality of life, however, presents a scale of graduated inter-activities between perpetrator and victim which elude the formal boundaries, set up by our statutes and the artificial abstractions of legal science, that should be heeded by a prevention-minded social science. By separating in time the fatally "harmonizing" parties, the formation of an explosive social compound can be averted. Remaining would be a potential perpetrator without a victim and a potential victim without a partner to whom he or she could turn to be victimized.

Notes

1. Sutherland in his *Criminology* (J.B. Lippincott, Chicago, 1939, pages 24-26) has discussed the victim from a different point of view.
2. See my distinction of terrorizers and terrorized specimen in my paper "Limits of Deterrence," *Journal of Criminal Law and Criminology,* 1938 (XIX), p. 555.

3. We think that melancholic murderers are caught with less trouble by the police and easier induced to plead guilty.

4. Gerard, Harry: *The Case Peltzer,* New York, Charles Scribner's Son, 1928, p. 36.

5. William Roughead: *Trial of Oscar Slater,* Edinburgh, William Hodge and Company, 1932, pages 10 and 50.

6. "Das gezeichnete Gestaendnis." *Monatsschrift fuer Kriminalpsychologie* XVIII (1927), pages 514-526.

7. H.C. Brearley: *Homicide in the United States,* Chapel Hill, University of North Carolina Press, 1932, p. 81.

8. Another point is the altered sex-ratio in the population of the United States. If there are less females, there must be less female victims, setting aside the colonial respect for the rare, and therefore dominating female.

9. Computed from figures in *Kriminalstatistik fuer das Jahr 1931,* Berlin, 1934, p. 36

10. *The Illinois Crime Survey,* Chicago, 1929, p. 610.

11. Evidently males too sometimes take the bait of their sensual disposition. The monk Rasputin was lured into the house of his murderers by the prospect of meeting a beautiful young countess. See Frederic A. Mackenzie, *Twentieth Century Crimes,* Boston, Little Brown and Company, 1927, p. 83. From all we know the famous monk was among those hypersexed men who, by that very nature, are as close to failure as they are to success.

12. Winifred Duke: *Trial of Field and Gray,* Edinburgh, William Hodge and Co. 1939, p. 13.

13. "She was menstruating." Finding of the medical expert in the case of Irne Munro. Ib. p. 7.

14. Frequently various components can be met. Thus a combination of the greedy and the climacteric victim is of no rare occurrence. In the murder case Holste (Hamburg, 1910) a 55 year old woman, managing a pawn shop, fell in love with the 22 year old perpetrator. Her way of showing her liking was somewhat commercial. She granted him higher loans than to other people and permitted him to enter her apartment after shutting up her shop. In the midst of a common reading of the evening-paper he killed her with a hammer. Richard Wosnik: *Beitraege zur Hamburgischen Kriminalgeschichte.* Hamburg, 1927. p. 132.

15. Edward H. Smith: *Famous Poison Mysteries.* The Dial Press, New York, 1927, pages 112-114.

16. "16 per cent of the sane and 29 per cent of the insane homicides killed their wives." William Norwood East: *Medical Aspects of Crime.* London, 1936, p. 370.

17. The writer has reported three such cases of parricide: "Drei Vatermordfaelle" in *Monatsschrift fuer Kriminalpsychologie,* 1930, pages 613-618.

18. F. Leppman: Der Sittlichkeitsverbrecher, *Vierteljahrsschrift fuer gerichtliche Medizin.* XXIX, p. 26.

19. Hans von Hentig und Theodor Viernstein: *Untersuchungen ueber den Inzest,* Heidelberg, 1925, p. 207.

20. See May's *Law of Crimes,* rewritten and revised by Kenneth C. Sears and Henry Weihofen, Boston, Little, Brown and Company, 1938, p. 373.
21. *The Professional Thief,* annotated and interpreted by E.H. Sutherland, University of Chicago Press, 1937, p. 57.
22. Ib. 69.
23. James Spenser: *Limey Breaks In,* London, Longmans, Green and Company, 1934, p. 239.
24. On the elimination of forgery-fraud cases in the preliminary hearing see: Morse and Beattie: *Survey of the Administration of Criminal Justice in Oregon,* Eugene, 1932, p. 57. The *Colorado Crime Survey* has established that fraud has an enormous "disposed without conviction" rate which rises to 42.2 per cent in the United States and up to 49.2, in the state of Colorado (average of the three years 1934-36).
25. The so-called "Simple Simon" racket is worked exclusively on police officers.
26. John C.R. MacDonald: *Crime is Business,* Stanford University Press, 1939, p. 1.
27. On this racket, see MacDonald, p. 26-36.
28. Id. p. 2.

6

Victim Typologies: Overview, Critique, and Reformulation

Robert A. Silverman

There have been several victim typologies discussed in the criminological literature to date (Schafer, 1968; Sand, 1970). These have ranged from rather straight
victim categorization to those that attempt explanation through typification.

In examining these typologies, we are searching for a typology that will
meet the following criteria. Any typology should offer categories that are exhaustive of the variable under consideration (that is, all possible types of victims
should be included). And the categories should, of course, be mutually exclusive.
Further, we would like a typology to be useful in empirical research no matter
what type of data are available (interview, survey, police or court records and
so forth). In the following pages, we critically review four victim typologies
with these criteria in mind.

Summary[1]

Hans von Hentig was a pioneer in the study of victims. He classified victims by
"general classes" and by "psychological types" of victim (Hentig, 1948). Hentig
abandons any legal criteria which might distinguish "doers and sufferers" in favor
of social, psychological, and biological factors which offer indications for classification. A summary of his final categorization as it appears in *The Criminal and
His Victim* (1948, p. 438) constitutes eleven categories:

1. *The Young* — "The weak specimen, in the animal kingdom and in mankind,
   is the most likely to be a victim of an attack."
2. *The Female* — "Female sex is another form of weakness recognized by law."
3. *The Old* — "The aging human being is handicapped in many ways."
4. *The Mentally Defective and Other Mentally Deranged* — "The feeble-minded,
   the insane, the drug addict, and the alcoholic form another large class of potential and actual victims."

Paper presented at the Interamerican Congress of Criminology, Caracas, Venezuela,
November 1972. Printed by permission of the author. This paper is a revised version of
work done for a larger empirical study conducted by the author (Silverman 1971).

55

5. *Immigrants, Minorities, Dull Normals* — An "artificial disadvantage" is imposed on these three groups of potential victims. The immigrant is likely to be poor and inexperienced in the ways of his new land.

6. *The Depressed*[2] — "Among all maladies there is no graver or more dangerous disease than a disturbance of *the instinct of self-preservation.*"

7. *The Acquisitive* — "The greedy can be hooked by all sorts of devices which hold out a bait to their cupidity."

8. *The Wanton* — This type refers to cases of sexual assault or adultery where the female plays as much of a seducing role as the male.

9. *The Lonesome and Heartbroken* — These victims lower their defenses while they seek companionship. These types may be victims of crimes ranging from murder to fraud.

10. *The Tormentor* — The tormentor is generally found in "family tragedies."

11. *Blocked, Exempted, and Fighting Victims* — "The blocked victim [is] . . . an individual who has been so enmeshed in a losing situation that defensive moves have become impossible or more injurious than injury at criminal hands."

B. Mendelsohn has constructed a six-part typology that is characterized by the amount of guilt a victim contributes to the event.

Stephen Schafter has given us an excellent summary of Mendelsohn's typology in *The Victim and His Criminal* (1968, pp. 42-43). Schafer's summary is presented below:

1. The "completely innocent victim." Mendelsohn regards him as the "ideal" victim, and refers first of all to children and those who suffer a crime while they are unconscious.

2. The "victim with minor guilt" and the "victim due to his ignorance." Mentioned here as an example is the woman who "provokes" a miscarriage and as a result pays with her life.

3. The "victim as guilty as the offender" and the "voluntary victim." In explanation Mendelsohn lists the following subtypes:
   a. suicide "by throwing a coin," if punishable by law
   b. suicide "by adhesion"
   c. euthanasia (to be killed by one's own wish because of an incurable and painful disease)
   d. suicide committed by a couple (for example, "desperate lovers," healthy husband and sick wife)

4. The "victim more guilty than the offender." There are two subtypes:
   a. the "provoker victim," who provokes someone to crime
   b. the "imprudent victim," who induces someone to commit a crime

5. The "most guilty victim" and the "victim who is guilty alone." This refers to the aggressive victim who is alone guilty of a crime (for example, the attacker who is killed by another in self-defense).
6. The "simulating victim" and the "imaginary victim." Mendelsohn refers here to those who mislead the administration of justice in order to obtain a sentence of punishment against an accused person. This type includes paranoids, hysterical persons, senile persons, and children.

Mendelsohn says that his interests are centered on what he calls the biopsychosocial contact which characterizes a delinquent event. However, the typology itself indicates a concern for legal categories. Guilt is the major component typifying victims.[3]

In "Towards a Criminological Classification of Victims," Abdel Fattah (1967) offers a rather complex scheme which has five major types of victims and eleven subgroups. We offer here the five major types.

1. *Nonparticipating Victims* – This type has two distinguishing features: (a) an attitude of denial or repulsion toward the offense and the offender, and (b) no contribution to the origin of the offense.
2. *Latent or Predisposed Victims* – The term latent victim is used to designate people who, because of peculiar predispositions or traits of character, are more liable than others to be victims of certain types of offenses. They are also more likely to be victims of the same type of offense more than once.
3. *Provocative Victims* – The provocative victim plays a definite role in the etiology of crime, either by inciting the criminal to commit it or by creating or fostering a situation likely to lead to crime. This type of victim can be said to "provoke" the crime by his own actions.
4. *Participating Victims* – We have seen that provocative victims play an important part in the origins of crimes and setting off the criminal process. Participating victims, on the other hand, play their part while a crime is being committed, either by adopting a passive attitude or making the crime possible or even making it easier, or else by assisting the criminal.
5. *False Victims* – The false victim is someone who is not really the victim of a crime committed by another person. He may not be a victim at all or he may be a victim of his own actions. (Fattah 1967, pp. 162-169)

The subcategories of these five groups help to illuminate the exact meanings of these categories. Generally they are founded upon sociological and psychological traits of the victims.

In *The Measurement of Delinquency* (1964) Thorsten Sellin and Marvin Wolfgang introduced the following typology.[4]

1. *Primary victimization* is used to refer to a personalized or individual victim, who may be directly assaulted or injured in a vis-a-vis offense, who is threatened, or has property stolen or damaged.
2. *Secondary Victimization* generally refers to establishments such as department stores, railroads, theaters, chain stores, churches and the like. The victim is impersonal, commercial and collective . . . .
3. *Tertiary victimization* . . . includes offenses against the public order, social harmony and the administration of government. Regulatory offenses and violations of city ordinances are typical.
4. *Mutual victimization* . . . refers to those cases in which the participants engage in mutually consensual acts, such as, fornication, adultery or statutory rape.
5. *No victimization* in the Sellin-Wolfgang delinquency study was used as a category for offenses that could not be committed by an adult . . . . (Wolfgang 1967, pp. 1-3).

Critique

The categories displayed in Hentig's typology are neither exhaustive nor are they mutually exclusive. Hentig admits a deficiency with respect to exhaustiveness (Hentig 1948, p. 433). It is also easy to see instances where the categories overlap (for example, an old, depressed, acquisitive victim). Further, the psychological types suggested by Hentig do not easily lend themselves to use with most sources of sociological data.

Much of Mendelsohn's typology is based on the amount of guilt divided between victims and offenders. However, guilt is never defined to the point where researchers are given guidelines for placing events into categories. Further, this typology deals only with personal (individual) victims which indicates that it is not exhaustive of all victims.

Fattah's categories may be mutually exclsuive but they are not exhaustive — they are only usable with crimes against the person. In the latter case, they suffer from the same types of problems encountered by Hentig (1948). Fattah does not consider his typology a completed work. He says that it is part of a larger work which was in progress at the time (Fattah 1967, p. 169).

Of the four typologies reviewed, only the classification scheme suggested by Sellin and Wolfgang fit the criteria outlined earlier. The categories are both mutually exclusive and exhaustive. The categories are based on victim-offender relationships and this categorization will serve as a basis for our reformulation.

Research Needs and Category Modifications

While the Sellin-Wolfgang typology best fits the criteria suggested, the categories may seem too broad for some researchers. Certainly the aim of other researchers

(Mendelsohn, Hentig, Fattah) was to get very specific subcategories within personal offenses. In the following pages, I will attempt to show that the general categories suggested in *The Measurement of Delinquency* (1964) may be divided into logical subcategories that retain the original intention of the typology (a basis in victim-offender relationships). At the same time, I hope to offer researchers the desired specificity for particular types of research. The following reformulation is not to be considered final. Rather, these are suggestions that may be built upon as specific needs arise. Many of the suggestions are based on the work of Hentig (1948), Mendelsohn (1956a), and Fattah (1967).

Each of the five categories will be treated individually. The needs for future research and possible modifications to the categories will be indicated.

No Victimization. Few researchers have felt it necessary to deal with offenders who fall into this category. Offenders in this category have no immediately discernable victims and the offenses involved are of a relatively minor nature.

Depending on how one perceives this category there may or may not be victims involved. Some researchers may want to think in terms of victims of broken homes; victims of incorrigible children, and so forth. In other words, we can see "sufferers" in this category if we wish to do the type of research that will illuminate these types.

Criminologists have had good reason not to study juveniles in this category, but to those who are interested in victims, they make an interesting subgroup. It is left to future research to determine who these victims are and what their relationship is to other forms of criminality.

Mutual Victimization. The mutual victimization category is perhaps the most clearcut of all the categories. Among juvenile and adult offenders, it takes in a small proportion of offenses known to the police. Because they involve consensual acts, the crimes in this category are rarely discovered and are rarely reported. The only problem here is determining who the victim is in a consensual act. The rule of thumb to be followed is that the victim is the person other than the (charged) offender; but this does not always work. In a statutory rape case, it is easy to assign an offender and victim role, but not so with homosexual acts. If both members voluntarily participate in homosexual acts, then properly they should be charged with the act. Then in the case of mutual victimization, our concept of the victim must change. For here there really is no victim, or alternately, all offenders are also victims. We need not be too concerned with this group and the problem of defining the victim here. The rubrics set down by Schur (1965) in *Crimes without Victims* apply well. It should be obvious that victims in mutual crimes are quite distinct from the other types and should be analyzed separately.

Tertiary Victimization. The tertiary category is made up of an amorphous group of crimes said to be "against the public order." This category has also been unexplored. The crimes that make up the group have only the fact in common that they offend against a certain type of statute or law. We would not expect that narcotics offenders, weapons offenders, or those who are disorderly or drunk in public necessarily have much in common, and yet they all perform acts which the public has deemed to be against its own best interests. In a way, the public is the corporate victim of these crimes. We feel that the way we can best deal with the notion of tertiary victims is to understand the motivations for having each law which is violated in this class of crime. For example, who is the public attempting to protect in each instance? We propose the following answers as examples of hypotheses which may be tested in some future research:

1. In the case of narcotics, the law is meant to protect the offender from what is considered to be an evil substance and from victimizing himself. It is further meant to protect the public from being victimized by users of said substances.
2. Laws concerning weapons (specifically carrying a concealed deadly weapon) are meant to protect the public from the potential use of such weapons.
3. Disorderly conduct and drunk laws are meant to protect urban dwellers from invasions of privacy. They are also meant to keep people who are considered undesirable out of "respectable" areas.

One could go on and on with such constructs. It should be obvious from these examples that we are interested in a perceptual rather than a legal definition of the law. What is important is whether, and how, people feel victimized by these actions. The question is: Does the public feel victimized or threatened by these events or have we a situation in which a violation of the law exists with no victim? We are asking future researchers who examine this category to examine the question from the perspective of the relationship between the offender and the victim (the public). We have suggested that this relationship involves a certain type of perception on the part of the public.

Secondary Victimization. Secondary victimization involves a corporate organizational victim (for example, church), or a privately or publicly owned enterprise victim. The offenses usually involve theft, damage, or a combination of the two. There are several ways to differentiate the types of victims. One is the size of the enterprise that is victimized (that is the "mom and pop" corner store and the large warehouse or department store). However, because we are concerned with the victim-offender relationship, we prefer a different focus for differentiation. We want to know who is the real victim of the attack. The attack may have been consciously levied against the proprietor of a small or large enterprise by the offender. The offender may have perpetrated the offense because of a dislike of the owner or because the organization represents something that the offender wishes to attack. On the other hand, a large store may have been chosen simply because it is a relatively easy target. Small stores may be victimized because they are close by and easy to break into or because the offender knows where the proprietor keeps his cash.

What we are suggesting here is a knowledge of the interpersonal relationships between victims and offenders in secondary offenses. The first step to getting at this is to determine whether an attack is aimed at an individual in an organization, at the organization as representative of something else, or simply at the property involved.

Our suggested modifications indicate the need for interview data in order that we might fully explore this category. This is an important category that is virtually unexplored in the literature (in terms of victimization). Knowledge of victim-offender relationships in this category will offer insights into motivations that have never before been obtainable.

Primary victimization. Primary victimization is divided into two categories — face-to-face and non-face-to-face. Face-to-face indicates that the victim has at least visual contact with the offender during the event. Non-face-to-face indicates that there is no visual or physical contact between offender and victim.

Face-to-Face. The face-to-face category is the most important one from the point of view of the public. The actions which make up this category are those which cause the public to fear victimization most. In some instances, having all of one's valuable goods stolen through burglary may not be as traumatic as having to confront a thief in a face-to-face encounter. The offenses in this category run the gamut from taking a victim's watch to taking his life. These are the actions which the urban dweller fears most because they impinge upon his privacy in a most personal way. The individual who walks down a street carries with him his "egocentric territory," and infringement upon his space is analogous to trespassing on his property.[5] The urban environment is at least partially characterized by fear of such infringement. We lock our doors, stay in after dark, and even in daylight we walk on "safe" streets. After dark, the prudent man may be seen walking on the part of the sidewalk nearest the gutter, thus avoiding possible attack from the dark areas and alleys near buildings.

Because the face-to-face category is so important, we reexamine it here. We find the category to be quite robust, with few problems of classification or definition of the victim. We have only two minor suggestions for researchers who may want to use it in the future.

First, given the public fears, it is wise for research to distinguish between the types and frequency of actual physical contact. The researcher may grasp more fully the interaction taking place between offenders and victims. To further this understanding, one might also inquire into the degree of injury victims perpetrate on offenders. In a study conducted by the author, victims injured offenders in 8 percent of the face-to-face actions (Silverman 1971).

Second, the researcher might consider using two subcategories of face-to-face victim. That is, within the face-to-face category there are individual victims per se who are attacked by offenders, but there are also individuals who represent corporate bodies. For example, a teller in a bank may be robbed in a face-to-face action, but he looses none of his personal goods. This class of crime, committed against a commercial agency through an individual, may be an interesting subclass of face-to-face action to be studied. If the teller is injured, the matter is complicated, for the injury is considered against him as an individual but the theft is committed against the bank whose agent is the teller. To obtain an accurate description of the relationships, we want to know why an offender chose a particular bank and why he chose a particular teller. We expect that relationships found here will be closer to those found in secondary crime rather than in other types of face-to-face events.

Non-Face-to-Face. Second only to face-to-face events in the fear they invoke in the public are "non-face-to-face" events. In these events the victim does not see the offender, but he is likely to have some property taken, damaged, or both. The American ethos dictates a pride in a value of personal possessions. The offender violates the victim's right to call possessions his own. This too is a violation of privacy in the form of private property. Here at least the victim is spared the ordeal of facing the individual who intends to violate his rights.

By asking the question, Who are the victims of non-face-to-face actions, one can easily see how this category might be subdivided to offer the researcher his desired specificity. We offer the following suggestions to serve as a preliminary basis for future research utilizing this category.

1. There is one type of non-face-to-face victim that is solitary. That is one person who has goods taken or damaged, and he is the only person who is harmed by the loss of the object.
2. More than one victim may own an object. All who suffer from the loss should be counted.
3. There may be corporate bodies who are the victims of non-face-to-face action. For example the theft of an automobile may result in a loss to a whole family.
4. There may be cases where there is essentially no victim in a non-face-to-face event. For example, an abandoned building (owned by an individual) is about to be torn down and is vandalized by offenders. Because nothing of value has been destroyed or taken, we do not consider the owner to be a victim.

We consider the most important distinction to be between the corporate, solitary, and multiple victim. Solitary and multiple victims should be similar in characteristics, but in the corporate victim there is an interesting and new subgroup. Perhaps, used in this sense, the corporate victim will turn out to be an intellectual construct not found in the empirical world. However, the construct offers the researcher many interesting avenues of exploration. Does the corporate victim feel the loss as a group or do the individuals who make up the corporate entity feel the loss as individuals—each concerned only with his special interests in the loss? If the latter is the case, the group could be treated as multiple victims.[6]

We want to know, from the offender's point of view, who his victim is. Is it the property or the property owner? The answer to this question will not be of too much interest to the victim of the crime, but it should be to the researcher interested in victim-offender relationships. We are interested in interactions, but the perceived victim of a crime may be different for victims and offenders in the same offense. If we are to discuss victim-offender relationships in non-face-to-face events, then we should be aware of the offender's perception as well as the victims. To the offender, there may be no personal victim involved.

Conclusion

The above discussion and reformulation was based on an empirical study that incorporated the original typology (Silverman 1971). We do not consider our suggested modifications of the typology to be a definitive statement, rather, we mean the extended discussion to add to a fuller understanding of the potential uses of this typology.

In one sense we have, by our suggestions, detracted from the use of the typology. Originally, and in the author's research, the typology was used with so-called hard data—data derived from court and police records. The typology is certainly equal to that task. Many of our modifications could not be incorporated with the use of that type of data. Those suggestions would require interview data. Our suggestions are of little value to the researcher with only police data.

One thing is clear: the use of the Sellin-Wolfgang typology has already been successful in empirical research. For use with hard data, it is well suited. Further and perhaps as important, we believe the typology is a flexible instrument that may be molded to specific research needs. Given interview data concerning offenders and victims of crimes, it offers many possibilities. The only provision in use of the typology in the way described is that the researcher must fully state the modifications of the basic typology that he has made. In using modifications, the researcher must be certain that the categories remain mutually exclusive and exhaustive of the data under consideration.

Notes

1. Because of space limitations, we have not considered typologies that deal exclusively with sexual offenses.
2. This is the first psychological type. Thus far Hentig has been dealing with "general classes."
3. Of course, guilt may be a psychological state, but we feel that Mendelsohn's usage indicates the legal criteria of guilt.
4. For a complete understanding of the development of this classificatory scheme, the reader is directed to *The Measurement of Delinquency* (Sellin and Wolfgang 1964).
5. This notion is taken from Erving Goffman and was discussed in a seminar held at the University of Pennsylvania in 1969.
6. The discussion here is developed from ideas presented by M.E. Wolfgang in "Analytical Categories for Research in Victimization" (1967).

References

Fattah, E.A.,   "Towards a Criminological Classification of Victims."
1967   *International Criminal Police Review* 209.

Hentig, Hans von   "Remarks on the Interaction of Perpetrator and Victim."
1940   *Journal of Criminal Law, Criminology and Police Science*
                31 (Sept.-Oct.): 303–309.

1948   *The Criminal and His Victim.* New Haven: Yale University
                Press.

Mendelsohn, B.   "Victimologie." *Rev. Int. Criminal. Police Tech.* 10/2, April–
1956a   June.

1956b   "The Victimology." *Etud. Int. Psycho-Soc. Crim.* 1 (July-
                Sept.): 23–26.

1963   "The Origin of the Doctrine of Victimology." *Excerpta
                Criminologica* 3:239–245.

Sand, H.   "The Victim and His Students: A Review and Critique of
1970   Selected Victimological Literature and Thought." Unpublished
                Manuscript, Philadelphia. Mimeograph.

Schafer, S.   "The Victim and His Criminal – 'Victimology' ". Paper pre-
1966   pared for the President's Commission on Law Enforcement
                and the Administration of Juvenile Justice.

1968   *The Victim and His Criminal.* New York: Random House.

Schur, E.   *Crimes without Victims.* Englewood Cliffs, N.J.: Prentice-Hall.
1965

Sellin, T. and   *The Measurement of Delinquency.* New York: John Wiley
M. E. Wolfgang   and Sons.
  1964

Silverman, R.A.   "Victims of Delinquency." Unpublished Doctoral Dissertation.
  1971   University of Pennsylvania, Philadelphia.

Wolfgang, M.E.   "Analytical Categories for Research on Victimization."
  1967   *Kriminologische Wegzeichen Festschrift für Hans von Hentig,*
                      Hamburg, 167–185.

Wolfgang, M.E.,   *Delinquency in a Birth Cohort.* Report to NIMH. (University
R. Figlio, and   of Chicago Press, 1972).
T. Sellin
  1971

7 Organizations as Victims in Mass Civil Disturbances

Russell R. Dynes and
E.L. Quarantelli

From 1964 through 1969, there were at least 325 separate massive civil disturbances in American urban ghettos.[1] The figure arrived at depends upon the definition used, and the sources of information employed, but it is in that general vicinity if the deployment of extra police forces is taken as the major criterion of identification. This count includes only disturbances that involved mass activities in the streets, and excludes the more recent and numerous disorders generally confined to high school and college buildings.

In most of these major civil disturbances, vandalism, looting, arson and sniping occurred. At a minimum, 212 of these events were marked by vandalism. Looting took place in around 150 of these situations, and arson in 227 of them. Sniping was less frequent, with only 51 communities reporting it in the context of a mass disturbance.

The overall losses to particular communities were substantial. Over 175 persons were killed and at least 8,500 injured in the course of these mass disturbances. Apart from huge indirect losses in trade, tourist business and delayed production of goods, the dollar cost in direct property damage alone was in the millions — Watts, 45 million; Detroit, 64 million; Newark, 15 million; Chicago, 10 million, and so on.

The figures are impressive and the events themselves are the stuff of history. However, it is not this that interests us. Neither is it the face that vandalism, looting, arson and sniping are clearly criminal offenses. Rather our attention is focused on the fact that these illegal acts were committed not against individuals, but organizations. In other words, that is criminal behavior where an organization is victim. As such, the legal violations involved provide a series of challenges, not only to conventional views of law enforcement, but also to current approaches in criminology. This paper examines some of the patterns and the conditions associated with the organization as victim in mass civil disturbances.

Reprinted from "Organization as Victim in Mass Civil Disturbances," by R.R. Dynes and E.L. Quarantelli, published in *Issues in Criminology* 1970, 5 (2): 181-193, by the graduate students of the School of Criminology at the University of California, Berkeley. Also, by permission of the authors.

The Literature

. . . Very few studies have taken specific aspects of organizations into account
in understanding the victim-offender relationship.[2] Cameron (1964) alludes to
certain characteristics of organizations, such as the spread of self-service, in her
study of shoplifting. In a more systematic fashion, Camp (1967) suggests that
both banks and bank robbers define their situations as ones in which each, for
different reasons, believes he has nothing to lose by committing a bank robbery
or by being the victim of a robbery. While banks rely on formal agents of control
to prevent and control robberies, the bank robber sees these agencies as being
ineffectual and thus the bank becomes an easy victim. Using a slightly different
approach, Smigel (1955) probed public attitudes toward stealing as related to the
size of the organization. While he evidently dealt with an all-white sample he
did find that lower class people were less disapproving of stealing than were higher status persons and that size of organization seemingly made a difference in
these attitudes. Generally, there was greater disapproval of pilfering and thievery
from small business, more approval for stealing from large business. In their attitudes toward theft from government, the effect of size was somewhat mitigated
by conceptions of loyalty and patriotism.

The point in all this is that the existing literature in the area of victimology
provides scant clues to analytical variables, other than those which relate to persons. There are few guidelines when property crimes are involved or when an organization is a victim. All of the widespread offenses common to mass civil
disturbances have an organization as victim. While this is most obvious of the
three involving property — vandalism, looting and arson — we would contend that
it is also true of sniping since, in many instances, the victim is "chosen" because
he somehow represents an organization. In order to explore further the organizational variables involved in civil disturbances, it is necessary to discuss the context in which the offenses take place.

The Nature of Mass Civil Disturbances

We have spoken so far in general terms of mass civil disturbances. This terminology is specifically being used to distinguish the events in the American urban
ghettos in the middle and late 1960's from the earlier — one might say classic —
riot pattern of confrontation between collectivities of whites and blacks, as in
Chicago in 1919 (Chicago Commission, 1922) or Detroit in 1943 (Lee and Humphrey, 1943). The Watts outbreak in 1964 was a turning point. It initiated a pattern that prevailed for about five years.[3] Manifest most clearly in Detroit and
Newark in 1967, and in Chicago, Pittsburgh and Washington in 1968, the pattern
took the form of massive police and military activity in the face of widespread
looting and arson and sometimes sniping. No actual confrontation of groups of

blacks and whites occurred, except as it was evident in police action. In other words, this kind of conflict situation was not a direct clash of two groups, but the attack of one group against the symbols or representatives of the larger society.

In these kinds of disturbances, there was also a range in the scope of involvement. That is, different numbers of persons participated in the various criminal acts. Sniping clearly involved the fewest people, seemingly a handful of individuals in most instances. Vandalism and arson were undertaken by more, mostly young men and male adolescents. Looting clearly was far more inclusive in involvement, engaging both men and women, and practically the whole age range possible. Thus, in major outbreaks (the primary focus of our attention), as much as a fifth of the total ghetto population may have actively participated in the various illegal behaviors. (Fogelson and Hill, 1968: 217-244). In this sense, these were mass civil disturbances. They were not the handiwork of a handful of individuals.

Most observers recognize that the urban disorders in the middle and late 1960's did not take the form of "classic riots" and that they involved large numbers of persons, but there are some misconceptions about other aspects. These have to be clarified here because otherwise they imply that a consideration of the "victim" is irrelevant to understanding such behavior. That is, they suggest that the criminal behavior is almost independent of the perceived characteristic of the object of attack.

In particular, two widespread views of the urban disorders have to be examined. These views are relatively common among the "lay" public but are also prevalent in academic circles, although in the latter case they generally are disguised in more sophisticated terms. First, much of the discussion of criminal activities during such disturbances emphasizes the fact that such offenses occur in a context in which social control mechanisms are weak or non-existent. Much is made of the difficulties in deploying police and extra-community law enforcement agencies, such as the National Guard. The implicit assumption underlying this is that, given temporary difficulties in traditional social control agencies, certain kinds of criminal offenses are predictable, if not expectable. In short, illegal behavior is to be expected when formal police groups can not operate in their usual manner.

These expectations are linked to a second view that man's baser tendencies come to the fore where external social control is absent or lacking. In situations of mass civil disturbance, it is supposed that the thin coating of human qualities is ripped off, and man is revealed as a malicious savage. It is asserted that the same kind of anti-social behavior is manifested in natural disaster situations (Banfield, 1968, and Oberschall, 1968 but see Quarantelli and Dynes, 1970). In brief, not too deep down, human beings are predatory and aggressive creatures.

Given these conceptions about man's inherent criminality and the necessity of external social control, the criminal behavior seen in the mass disturbances is assumed to be random in expression and "irrational" in form. Such assumptions are especially likely to be confirmed by the destruction of property through vandalism or arson. To many people, crimes involving personal gains are at least understandable, but not destruction or seemingly meaningless behavior such as sniping. Even the looting is bewildering to many observers, for it is assumed to be undertaken with little discrimination as to object of attack.

If these two views of civil disturbances are valid, they make consideration of the organization as victim irrelevant. But the fact of the matter is that there is a selective pattern. As we shall show, there was discrimination in selection of objects for attack, whether this be by way of vandalism, looting, arson or sniping. Furthermore, the behavior during urban disturbances, even criminal acts, is collective rather than individualistic, partly socially supported rather than totally condemned, and public rather than private. Elsewhere, this has been illustrated in the case of looting behavior, (Dynes and Quarantelli, 1968), and the same could be done for vandalism, arson and sniping. In varying degrees they are marked by the same characteristics. However, our emphasis here is on the selective focus of the different illegal acts, and the indication that they can be interpreted as communicating a message instead of being meaningless (Quarantelli and Dynes, 1970). If so, an examination of the organization as victim is not only possible but necessary for a full understanding of the phenomena.

Objects of Attack

It is apparent that the pattern of damage in mass disturbances centered on small, retail business establishments. For example, industry-wide insurance figures for the Newark outbreak show that the categories with over 100 reports were liquor stores and bars, clothing and small department stores, groceries, commercial multiple occupancies, cleaners and furniture stores. These made up over two-thirds of the damage reports. On the other hand, dwellings, both apartments and one and two family houses, constituted only about 2-1/2 percent of all buildings damaged or destroyed in some way. Institutional and public properties, such as schools and churches, made up less than one-quarter of one percent of the full total. In Detroit, the same type of retail stores constituted 55 percent of the damaged property; dwellings of all kinds less than 10 percent. Not even one-half of one percent of all buildings affected were public or institutional in nature. In Watts, of the 600 buildings burned, over 95 percent were retail outlets. Elsewhere, the pattern was the same. Ghetto dwellers did not burn their own homes. They were not indiscriminate in their attacks: some categories of objects were clearly more victims than others.

The direct, interactional explanation for choice of victim, a seemingly valid account when applied to much personal, violent crime, does not seem fully applicable in mass civil disturbances. In many cases, it does not appear that the participants in looting or arson had prior, major contact with the specific stores attacked. Certainly the stores were not the focus of attack because of any immediate confrontation. In almost all instances, they were looted and burned while closed as a result of curfew, management decision or normal working schedules.

To the extent that a selective pattern has been noted, different explanations for it have been provided by the popular press, academicians, ghetto residents, the police and arrested participants in the disturbances. Most of the attempts to account for the selectivity have had the underlying theme of direct retaliation for economic exploitation or the notion that "the poor pay more" (Caplovitz, 1963). For example, it has been frequently suggested that supermarket chains charge differential prices in ghetto located outlets (Marion et al., 1969: 8-14). White ownership of ghetto stores likewise has sometimes been singled out as a major factor in the selective attacks during outbursts. Some explanations have also been advanced attempting to make a case in terms of impersonal economic exploitation by gigantic corporate structures. Finally, the selective pattern has at times been accounted for by the allegation that certain commercial enter prises charge exorbitant rates for credit or do not grant it at all (National Advisory Commission on Civil Disorders, 1968).

There may be an element of truth in all of these explanations. However, there is also much evidence which contradicts each. Some studies have not revealed any differential pricing in chain supermarkets or even neighborhood stores in the ghetto areas (Marion et al., 1969). In many mass disturbances, also, outlets of certain chains have been attacked whereas those of other companies, presumably as impersonal, have been ignored. Certain kinds of businesses such as used car dealers, have generally been untouched during the disturbances despite their very heavy reliance on credit operations. Likewise, enough black owners and managers have been affected to raise questions about the importance of white ownership as a major variable in the selective attacks.

The contradictory nature of many of these explanations is well symbolized in an observation made by one of the authors during the Watts disturbance. A very large, discount outlet of a national chain, with huge display windows stood intact across the street from a number of iron-barricaded, small shops (some locally owned) that had all been attacked, looted and burned. In a situation of equivalent opportunity for attack, less accessible and seemingly less lucrative targets were struck.

In seems, then, that the selection of organizations as victims cannot be easily understood by using simple "objective" characteristics. That is, other factors appear to be more influential in the selective process than whether the objects of attack do or do not actually have certain objectionable features. More important is how organizations, especially classes of them, come to be perceived. In essence, what appears to be involved is best described as a collective definitional process.

In another context, it has been suggested that looting in civil disturbances can best be explained as temporary redefinitions of property rights within the ghetto areas (Quarantelli and Dynes, 1968). This is so particularly if property is conceived of as normative definitions of the right to use community resources, rather than as material objects. Widespread looting in mass disturbances is a manifestation of an extensive reversal of traditional definitions of property. Established procedures are rejected, including the mechanism of distribution and pricing.

We suggest that this process of collective definitions and redefinitions is not operative solely at a time of disturbance. Rather, it is always going on, especially among dissatisfied groups such as those in American ghetto areas. In the course of the process, certain types of stores come to symbolize economic exploitation, whether they actually exhibit it or not. Retail stores are particularly vulnerable to being so defined. They are for many ghetto dwellers where economic realities become apparent. It is there that the weekly pay check and its inelasticity is driven home. Limited income may also result in restrictions being placed by these stores on credit allowances. Such stores likewise highlight the potential availability of goods within the larger society which could be obtained if property rights were defined differently. Certainly, as the Campbell-Schuman survey (1968) showed, many blacks *feel* that they are overcharged or given inferior or spoiled goods in neighborhood ghetto stores.

The development of a collective definition about "imagined" economic exploitation can be buttressed by experience. However, this experience is neither necessary nor essential. As a consequence, some "innocent" victims may be selected. Given a strong definition of exploitation by a grocery chain, many outlets of this company may be attacked. Also, certain stores may be "saved" from destruction by a positive general evaluation. Something of this symbolic nature might explain the fact that in the 1968 disturbances in Washington, D.C., for example, 19 out of 50 outlets of one supermarket chain were attacked while none of the stores of another company in the same neighborhoods were touched.

Turner (1964), talking of the development of collective behavior in general, notes that "the rumor process serves to bring symbols into selective salience and to reconstitute their meanings in relation to shared requirements for action." We are essentially saying the same thing with respect to what leads up to certain objects becoming the focus of attack in civil disturbances. Furthermore, in the context of the milling of many people, the symbols and definitions that develop may appear to have overwhelming local support.

However, these collective definitions may change quickly. This is particularly likely to occur when other, higher values enter into the situation. This can be easily seen in the two following instances known to the authors. In one, fire department personnel were attempting to put out fires in a series of small stores. They were being harassed by what is usually described as an "angry" crowd. A wall collapsed in a building, burying two firemen. Members of the "angry" crowd immediately started to help the firemen rescue their co-workers. What moments before had symbolized the white community, now became "our" firemen needing "our" help.

In another disturbance, units of a fire department battling a major blaze were being subjected to verbal abuse and threats by the surrounding ghetto dwellers. The wind conditions changed, raising the possibility that the fire would leap over into the next block, which was composed primarily of private homes. For very complicated reasons, totally at variance with the realities of the situation, the companies fighting the fires were ordered to withdraw from the scene by police officials. The residents of the threatened homes pleaded with the firemen to stay, offering to provide armed protection for the units that would remain.

Such rapid transformations from harassers and hecklers to helpers and protectors shows that some of the definitions that develop are very volatile. Thus, the redefinition of property, for example, setting the stage for vandalism or looting can come about very rapidly in a collective context. In the same fashion, there can be quick redefinitions sometimes back to earlier conceptions.

The previous illustrations suggest another point. While retail stores evoke images of economic exploitation, the police apparently evoke images of political exploitation.[4] Police organizations symbolize varying types of real and felt oppression within the ghetto. Most other local, public agencies seem to be somewhat immune to this kind of definition. Public buildings are notably absent in statistics. While part of this can be explained by their relative absence within the ghetto, still schools, welfare offices, health clinics, and so on, do exist but are seldom the object of attack. The fire department is in a somewhat intermediate position. For example, from 1966 to 1967, harassment of firemen occurred in 67 out of 101 major disturbances. It is our impression that such harassments tend to be primarily verbal in nature and, as the previous illustrations indicate, are subject to dramatic reversals. By contrast, the image of the police is much more negative and inflexible. This is documented in a number of studies (Boesel et al., 1969). In one sense, then, the police are the major target and the focus of ghetto hostility toward political exploitation.[5] They are also a primary focus of the most serious, but also by far the most infrequent offense, sniping.

Reports of sniping, of course, have sometimes been descriptions of random shooting by uneasy security forces in the disturbance areas. In some instances at least, "snipers" have turned out to be policemen and National Guardsmen shooting at one another. It seems, however, that when sniping has occurred, it has been more often directed toward organizational equipment rather than personnel. Police cars and fire trucks have been usual targets. Organizational personnel are naturally often near this kind of equipment.

We do not wish to imply that public officers have never been targets. In Newark, both a policeman and fireman were killed, and their deaths were attributed to snipers. In Detroit one fireman was thought to have been killed by sniper fire. Nevertheless, it is a fact that practically all the deaths in mass civil disturbances are likely to be ghetto residents. For example, in Newark, 26 persons died, only 2 of which were white. In Watts, only three of the 34 dead were white. Of the 43 killed in Detroit, 33 were Negro. Thirty-eight of the 43 killed died from gunshot wounds, but only 5 were thought to have been killed by sniper fire and only one sniper was convicted on confirmed evidence. This is the historical pattern of many societies in different time periods where in most cases the formal control agencies have done almost all of the killing instead of the supposedly murderous "crowd," "rioters" or "demonstrators" (Couch, 1968). However, what is important about the extremely low loss of life from snipers in American mass disturbances is that it indicates that such shootings that did occur were symbolic rather than instrumental in nature. As Boskin (1969) has noted, the low casualty rates can hardly be attributed to poor marksmanship.

Class, Status, and Power Aspects

The major organizational victims in civil disturbances are retail stores and the symbols of authority, notably the police. These targets can best be explained by noting that these are the key points of contact between the ghetto and the larger white society. Perhaps increased insight into the selectivity involved is achieved by using Max Weber's conception of class, status and power (1946). As he indicated, these variables are never perfectly correlated and all might be present in a specific situation. We might suggest that all of these interests are present in major civil disturbances. Within the ghetto community, they perhaps are more closely correlated than elsewhere in the society. Ghetto residents are obviously low in the possession of economic goods and lack opportunities for income. Color caste is indicative of a lack of social prestige or status. The acquisition of political power by those in the ghetto is minimal.

The reaction to this low status consistency is seldom expressed in ideological terms but through action in what have come to be called civil disturbances.[6] Reaction to economic position is most clearly revealed in looting, which temporarily, at least, redistributes the wealth. Response to low status and the ghetto style of life which is part of it is seen in the smoke of the arsonist. The ghetto style of life has such low value that there can be little loss. Political powerlessness is reacted to by attacking the symbols of power which indicate repression and control. These various interests combine and recombine in a number of ways. Retail stores symbolize both lack of economic resources and despised style of life. The police symbolize political and repressive power. To many middle class persons, the resultant criminal offenses seem senseless. There is the old saying that possession is nine-tenths of the law, but ghetto residents have neither the possession nor the law. The mass civil disturbances reflect this; and retail stores and the police serve as the victims, less because of particular discriminatory or repressive behavior on their part, but more because they symbolize for the ghetto residents their comparative and enduring deprivations.

Notes

1. Unless otherwise documented, all the figures used or cited in this article were computed from unpublished data provided by the American Insurance Claims Bureau, or from material in the files and archives of the Disaster Research Center at The Ohio State University.
2. For example, the most recent work in the field by Schafer (1968) focuses exclusively on personal crimes.
3. Since 1969 massive disturbances have been a rarity. Reasons for this are discussed by Quarantelli and Dynes (1970). Becoming more prominent are incidents involving small groups of ghetto militants engaging in firearm fights with the police. One of the first such incidents is described in Masotti and Corsi (1969).
4. Sears and Tomlinson (1965) in their survey study of Watts found that the objects of hostility were primarily white merchants and almost any symbol of constituted authority.
5. As Boskin (1969) notes, the police became a main focal point of attack not only because of their actions and attitudes toward ghetto blacks, but chiefly because they came to symbolize the hated but not visible white power structure.
6. Thus, Murphy and Watson (1969) found that those Watts residents who most experienced discrimination on the part of the police and felt exploited by the white merchants were more likely to have participated in the disturbance than those ghetto dwellers who evidenced little concern about these two matters.

References

Banfield, Edward C.   "Rioting Mainly for Fun and Profit." James Q. Wilson,
1968   editor. *The Metropolitan Enigma: Inquiries into the Nature and Dimensions of America's Urban Crisis.* Cambridge, Mass.: Harvard University Press: 284–308.

Boesel, David et al.   "White Institutions and Black Rage." *Trans-Action* 6
1969   (March): 24–31.

Boskin, Joseph   "The Revolt of the Urban Ghettos, 1964–1967." *Annals*
1969   *American Academy of Political and Social Science* 382 (March): 2–14.

Cameron, Mary O.   *The Booster and the Snitch.* New York: Free Press.
1964

Camp, George M.   "Nothing to Lose: A Study of Bank Robbery in America."
1967   Yale University. Unpublished Ph.D. dissertation.

Campbell, Angus and   "Racial Attitudes in Fifteen American Cities" Supple-
Howard Schuman   mental Studies for The National Advisory Commission on
      1968   Civil Disorders. Washington, D.C.: U.S. Government Printing
                    Office: 1-67.

Caplovitz, David *The Poor Pay More.* New York: Free Press.
      1963

Chicago Commission *The Negro in Chicago.* Chicago: University of Chicago
on Race Relations Press.
      1922

Couch, Carl   "Collective Behavior: An Examination of Some Stereotypes."
      1968   *Social Problems* 15: 310-322.

Dynes, Russell and   "What Looting in Civil Disturbances Really Means."
E. L. Quarantelli   *Trans-Action* 5 (May): 9-14.
      1968

Fogelson, Robert M.   "Who Riots? A Study of Participation in the 1967 Riots."
and Robert B. Hill   Supplemental Studies for The National Advisory Commis-
      1968   sion on Civil Disorders. Washington, D.C.: U.S. Government
                    Printing Office: 217-248.

Lee, Alfred M. and *Race Riot.* New York: Dryden.
N. D. Humphrey
      1943

Marion, B. W. et al *Food Marketing in Low Income Areas: A Review of Past
      1969   Findings and a Case Analysis in Columbus, Ohio.* Columbus,
                    Ohio: Cooperative Extension Service, The Ohio State Univer-
                    sity.

Masotti, Louis H. *Shootout in Cleveland. Black Militants and the Police.* Washing-
Jerome R. Corsi   ton, D.C.: U.S. Government Printing Office.
      1969

Murphy, Raymond J.   "Levels of Aspiration, Discontent, and Support for
and James Watson   Violence: A Test of the Expectation Hypothesis." Paper
      1969   presented at the 1969 annual meeting of the American Socio-
                    logical Association in San Francisco, California.

National Advisory *Report.* New York: Bantam Books.
Commission on Civil Disorders
      1968

Oberschall, Anthony   "The Los Angeles Riot." *Social Problems* 15 (Winter):
      1968   335-338.

President's Commission   *The Challenge of Crime in a Free Society.* Washin-
on Law Enforcement   ton, D.C.: U.S. Government Printing Office.
and Administration
of Justice
    1967

Quarantelli, E. L. and   "Looting in Civil Disorders: An Index of Social
Russell R. Dynes   Change." *American Behavioral Scientist* 7 (1968): 7-10.
    1968

    1970   "Property Norms and Looting: Their Patterns in Community
                  Crises" *Phylon* 31 (Summer): 168-182.

Schafer, Stephen   *The Victim and His Criminal: A Study of Functional*
    1968   *Responsibility.* New York: Random House.

Sears, David and   "Riot Ideology in Los Angeles: A Study of Negro Attitudes."
T. M. Tomlinson   *Social Science Quarterly* 49 (Dec.): 485-503.
    1968

Smigel, Erwin D.   "Public Attitudes Toward Stealing as Related to the Size of
    1955   the Victim Organization." *American Sociological Review* 21
                  (1955):320-327.

Turner, Ralph   "Collective Behavior." Robert Faris, editor. *Handbook of*
    1964   *Modern Sociology.* Chicago: Rand McNally.

Von Hentig, Hans   *The Criminal and His Victim.* New Haven, Conn.: Yale
    1958   University Press.

Weber, Max   *Essays in Sociology.* New York: Oxford.
    1946

Wolfgang, Marvin E.   *Patterns of Criminal Homicide.* Philadelphia: University
    1958   of Pennsylvania Press.

8 Victim-Precipitated Criminal Homicide

Marvin E. Wolfgang

In many crimes, especially in criminal homicide, the victim is often a major contributor to the criminal act. Except in cases in which the victim is an innocent bystander and is killed in lieu of an intended victim, or in cases in which a pure accident is involved, the victim may be one of the major precipitating causes of his own demise.

Various theories of social interaction, particularly in social psychology, have established the framework for the present discussion. In criminological literature, however, probably von Hentig in *The Criminal and His Victim,* has provided the most useful theoretical basis for analysis of the victim- offender relationship. In Chapter XII, entitled "The Contribution of the Victim to the Genesis of Crime," the author discusses this "duet frame of crime" and suggests that homicide is particularly amenable to analysis.[1] In *Penal Philosophy*, Tarde[2] frequently attacks the "legislative mistake" of concentrating too much on premeditation and paying too little attention to motives, which indicate an important interrelationship between victim and offender.

And in one of his satirical essays, "On Murder Considered as One of the Fine Arts," Thomas DeQuincey[3] shows cognizance of the idea that sometimes the victim is a would-be murderer. Garofalo,[4] too, noted that the victim may provoke another individual into attack, and though the provocation be slight, if perceived by an egoistic attacker it may be sufficient to result in homicide.

Besides these theoretical concepts, the law of homicide has long recognized provocation by the victim as a possible reason for mitigation of the offense from murder to manslaughter, or from criminal to excusable homicide. In order that such reduction occur, there are four prerequisites.[5]

1. There must have been adequate provocation.
2. The killing must have been in the heat of passion.
3. The killing must have followed the provocation before there had been a reasonable opportunity for the passion to cool.

Reprinted by special permission from the *Journal of Criminal Law, Criminology and Police Science,* Copyright©1957 by the Northwestern University School of Law, 1957, 48 (1): 1-11.

4. A casual connection must exist between provocation, the heat of passion, and the homicidal act. Such, for example, are: adultery, seduction of the offender's juvenile daughter, rape of the offender's wife or close relative, etc. Perkins claims that "the adequate provocation must have engendered the heat of passion, and the heat of passion must have been the cause of the act which resulted in death."[6]

Definition and Illustration

The term *victim-precipitated* is applied to those criminal homicides in which the victim is a direct, positive precipitator in the crime. The role of the victim is characterized by his having been the first in the homicide drama to use physical force directed against his subsequent slayer. The victim-precipitated cases are those in which the victim was the first to show and use a deadly weapon, to strike a blow in an altercation — in short, the first to commence the interplay or resort to physical violence.

In seeking to identify the victim-precipitated cases recorded in police files it has not been possible always to determine whether the homicides strictly parallel legal interpretations. In general, there appears to be much similarity. In a few cases included under the present definition, the nature of the provocation is such that it would not legally serve to mitigate the offender's responsibility. In these cases the victim was threatened in a robbery, and either attempted to prevent the robbery, failed to take the robber seriously, or in some other fashion irritated, frightened, or alarmed the felon by physical force so that the robber, either by accident or compulsion, killed the victim. Infidelity of a mate or lover, failure to pay a debt, use of vile names by the victim, obviously means that he played an important role in inciting the offender to overt action in order to seek revenge, to win an argument, or to defend himself. However, mutual quarrels and wordy altercations do not constitute sufficient provocation under law, and they are not included in the meaning of victim-precipitated homicide.

Below are sketched several typical cases to illustrate the pattern of these homicides. Primary demonstration of physical force by the victim, supplemented by scurrilous language, characterizes the most common victim-precipitated homicides. All of these slayings were listed by the Philadelphia Police as criminal homicides, none of the offenders was exonerated by a coroner's inquest, and all the offenders were tried in criminal court.

A husband accused his wife of giving money to another man, and while she was making breakfast, he attacked her with a milk bottle, then a brick, and finally a piece of concrete block. Having had a butcher knife in hand, she stabbed him during the fight.

A husband threatened to kill his wife on several occasions. In this instance, he attacked her with a pair of scissors, dropped them, and grabbed a butcher knife from the kitchen. In the ensuing struggle that ended on their bed, he fell on the knife.

In an argument over a business transaction, the victim first fired several shots at his adversary, who in turn fatally returned the fire.

The victim was the aggressor in a fight, having struck his enemy several times. Friends tried to interfere, but the victim persisted. Finally, the offender retaliated with blows, causing the victim to fall and hit his head on the sidewalk, as a result of which he died.

A husband had beaten his wife on several previous occasions. In the present instance, she insisted that he take her to the hospital. He refused, and a violent quarrel followed, during which he slapped her several times, and she concluded by stabbing him.

During a lover's quarrel, the male (victim) hit his mistress and threw a can of kerosene at her. She retaliated by throwing the liquid on him, and then tossed a lighted match in his direction. He died from the burns.

A drunken husband, beating his wife in their kitchen, gave her a butcher knife and dared her to use it on him. She claimed that if he should strike her once more, she would use the knife, whereupon he slapped her in the face and she fatally stabbed him.

A victim became incensed when his eventual slayer asked for money which the victim owed him. The victim grabbed a hatchet and started in the direction of his creditor, who pulled out a knife and stabbed him.

A victim attempted to commit sodomy with his girlfriend, who refused his overtures. He struck her several times on the side of her head with his fists before she grabbed a butcher knife and cut him fatally.

A drunken victim with knife in hand approached his slayer during a quarrel. The slayer showed a gun, and the victim dared him to shoot. He did.

During an argument in which a male called a female many vile names, she tried to telephone the police. But he grabbed the phone from her hands, knocked her down, kicked her, and hit her with a tire gauge. She ran to the kitchen, grabbed a butcher knife, and stabbed him in the stomach.

The Philadelphia Study

Empirical data for analysis of victim-precipitated homicides were collected from the files of the Homicide Squad of the Philadelphia Police Department, and include 588 consecutive cases of criminal homicide which occurred between January 1, 1948 and December 31, 1952. Because more than one person was sometimes involved in the slaying of a single victim, there was a total of 621 offenders responsible for the killing of 588 victims. The present study is part of a much larger work that analyzes criminal homicide in greater detail. Such material that is relevant to victim-precipitation is included in the present analysis. The 588 criminal homicides provide sufficient background information to establish much about the nature of the victim-offender relationship. Of these cases, 150, or 26 percent, have been designated, on the basis of the previously stated definition, as VP cases.[7] The remaining 438, therefore, have been designated as non-VP cases.

Thorough study of police files, theoretical discussions of the victim's contribution, and previous analysis of criminal homicide suggest that there may be important differences between VP and non-VP cases. The chi-square test has been used to test the significance in proportions between VP and non-VP homicides and a series of variables. Hence, any spurious association which is just due to chance has been reduced to a minimum by application of this test, and significant differences of distributions are revealed. Where any expected class frequency of less than five existed, the test was not applied; and in each tested association, a correction for continuity was used, although the difference resulting without it was only slight. In this study a value of P less than .05, or the 5 percent level of significance, is used as the minimal level of significant association. Throughout the subsequent discussion, the term *significant* in italics is used to indicate that a chi-square test of significance of association has been made and that the value of P less than .05 has been found. The discussion that follows (with respect to race, sex, age, etc.) reveals some interesting differences and simi‚ larities between the two (Table 8-1).

Race

Because Negroes and males have been shown by their high rates of homicide, assaults against the person, etc., to be more criminally aggressive than whites and females, it may be inferred that there are more Negroes and males among VP victims than among non-VP victims. The data confirm this inference. Nearly 80 percent of VP cases compared to 70 percent of non-VP cases involve Negroes, a proportional difference that results in a *significant* association between race and VP homicide.

Sex

As victims, males comprise 94 percent of VP homicides, but only 72 percent of non-VP homicides, showing a *significant* association between sex of the victim and VP homicide.

Since females have been shown by their low rates of homicide, assaults against the person, etc., to be less criminally aggressive than males, and since females are less likely to precipitate their own victimization than males, we should expect more female *offenders* among VP homicides than among non-VP homicides. Such is the case, for the comparative data reveal that females are twice as frequently offenders in VP slayings (29 percent) as they are in non-VP slayings (14 percent) — a proportional difference which is also highly *significant*.

The number of white female offenders (16) in this study is too small to permit statistical analysis, but the tendency among both Negro and white females as separate groups is toward a much higher proportion among VP than among non-VP offenders. As noted above, analysis of Negro and white femals as a combined group does result in the finding of a *significant* association between female offenders and VP homicide.

Age

The age distributions of victims and offenders in VP and non-VP homicides are strikingly similar; study of the data suggests that age has no apparent effect on VP homicide. The median age of VP victims is 33.3 years, while that of non-VP victims is 31.2 years.

Methods

In general, there is a *significant* association between method used to inflict death and VP homicide. Because Negroes and females comprise a larger proportion of offenders in VP cases, and because previous analysis has shown that stabbings occurred more often than any of the other methods of inflicting death,[8] it is implied that the frequency of homicides by stabbing is greater among VP than among non-VP cases. The data support such an implication and reveal that homicides by stabbing account for 54 percent of the VP cases but only 34 percent of non—VP cases, a difference which is *significant*. The distribution of shootings, beatings, and "other" methods of inflicting death among the VP and non-VP cases shows no significant differences. The high frequency of stabbings among VP homicides appears to result from an almost equal reduction in each of the remaining methods; yet the lower proportions in each of these three other categories among VP cases are not separately very different from the proportions among non-VP cases.

Place and Motive

There is no important difference between VP and non-VP homicides with respect to a home/not-home dichotomy, nor with respect to motives listed by the police. Slightly over half of both VP and non-VP slayings occurred in the home. General

Table 8-1 Victim-Precipitated and Non-Victim-Precipitated
Criminal Homicide by Selected Variables,
Philadelphia, 1948–1952

	Total Victims		Victim-Precipitated		Non-Victim-Precipitated	
	Number	Percent of Total	Number	Percent of Total	Number	Percent of Total
Race and Sex of Victim						
Both Races	588	100.0	150	100.0	438	100.0
Male	449	76.4	141	94.0	308	70.3
Female	139	23.6	9	6.0	130	29.7
Negro	427	72.6	119	79.3	308	70.3
Male	331	56.3	111	74.0	220	50.2
Female	96	16.3	8	5.3	88	20.1
White	161	27.4	31	20.7	130	29.7
Male	118	20.1	30	20.0	88	20.1
Female	43	7.3	1	0.7	42	9.6
Age of Victim						
Under 15	28	4.8	0	— —	28	6.4
15–19	25	4.3	7	4.7	18	4.1
20–24	59	10.0	18	12.0	41	9.4
25–29	93	15.8	17	11.3	76	17.3
30–34	88	15.0	20	13.3	68	15.5
35–39	75	12.8	25	16.7	50	11.4
40–44	57	9.7	23	15.3	34	7.8
45–49	43	7.3	13	8.7	30	6.8
50–54	48	8.2	11	7.3	37	8.5
55–59	26	4.4	6	4.0	20	4.6
60–64	18	3.1	7	4.7	11	2.5
65 and over	28	4.7	3	2.0	25	5.7
Total	588	100.0	150	100.0	438	100.0
Method						
Stabbing	228	38.8	81	54.0	147	33.6
Shooting	194	33.0	39	26.0	155	35.4
Beating	128	21.8	26	17.3	102	23.3
Other	38	6.4	4	2.7	34	7.7
Total	588	100.0	150	100.0	438	100.0
Place						
Home	301	51.2	80	53.3	221	50.5
Not Home	287	48.8	70	46.7	217	49.5
Total	588	100.0	150	100.0	438	100.0
Interpersonal Relationship						
Relatively close friend	155	28.2	46	30.7	109	27.3
Family relationship	136	24.7	38	25.3	98	24.5
(Spouse)	(100)	(73.5)	(33)	(86.8)	(67)	(68.4)
(Other)	(36)	(26.5)	(5)	(13.2)	(31)	(31.6)

	Total Victims		Victim-Precipitated		Non-Victim-Precipitated	
	Number	Percent of Total	Number	Percent of Total	Number	Percent of Total
Acquaintance	74	13.5	20	13.3	54	13.5
Stranger	67	12.2	16	10.7	51	12.8
Paramour, Mistress Prostitute	54	9.8	15	10.0	39	9.8
Sex rival	22	4.0	6	4.0	16	4.0
Enemy	16	2.9	6	4.0	10	2.5
Paramour of Offender's mate	11	2.0	1	.7	10	2.5
Felon or police officer	6	1.1	1	.7	5	1.3
Innocent bystander	6	1.1	—	—	6	1.5
Homosexual partner	3	.6	1	.7	2	.5
Total	550	100.0	150	100.0	400	100.0
Presence of Alcohol during Offense						
Present	374	63.6	111	74.0	263	60.0
Not Present	214	36.4	39	26.0	175	40.0
Total	588	100.0	150	100.0	438	100.0
Presence of Alcohol in the Victim						
Present	310	52.7	104	69.3	206	47.0
Not Present	278	47.3	46	30.7	232	53.0
Total	588	100.0	150	100.0	438	100.0
Previous Arrest Record of Victim						
Previous arrest record	277	47.3	93	62.0	184	42.0
Offenses against the person	150	25.5 (54.2)	56	37.3 (60.2)	94	21.4 (50.1)
Other offenses only	127	21.6 (45.8)	37	24.7 (39.8)	90	20.5 (49.9)
No previous arrest record	311	52.7	57	38.0	524	58.0
Total	588	100.0	150	100.0	438	100.0
Previous Arrest Record of Offender						
Previous arrest record	400	64.4	81	54.0	319	67.7
Offenses against the person	264	42.5 (66.0)	49	32.7 (60.5)	215	45.6 (67.4)
Other offenses only	136	21.8 (34.0)	32	21.3 (39.5)	104	22.1 (32.6)
No previous arrest record	221	35.6	69	(46.0)	152	32.3
Total	621	100.0	150	100.0	471	100.0

altercations (43 percent) and domestic quarrels (20 percent) rank highest among VP cases, as they do among non-VP cases (32 and 12 percent), although with lower frequency. Combined, these two motives account for a slightly larger share of the VP cases (3 out of 5) than of the non-VP cases (2 out of 5).

Victim-Offender Relationship[9]

Intra-racial slayings predominate in both groups, but inter-racial homicides comprise a larger share of VP cases (8 percent) than they do of non-VP cases (5 percent). Although VP cases make up one-fourth of all criminal homicides, they account for over one-third (35 percent) of all inter-racial slayings. Thus it appears that a homicide which crosses race lines is often likely to be one in which the slayer was provoked to assaulty by the victim. The association between inter-racial slayings and VP homicides, however, is not statistically significant.

Homicides involving victims and offenders of opposite sex (regardless of which sex is the victim or which is the offender) occur with about the same frequency among VP cases (34 percent) as among non-VP cases (37 percent). But a *significant* difference between VP and non-VP cases does emerge when determination of the sex of the victim, relative to the sex of his specific slayer, is taken into account. Of all criminal homicides for which the sex of both victim and offender is known, 88 involve a male victim and a female offender; and of these 88 cases, 43 are VP homicides. Thus, it may be said that 43, or 29 percent, of the 150 VP homicides, compared to 45, or only 11 percent, of the 400 non-VP homicides, are males slain by females.

It seems highly desirable, in view of these findings, that the police thoroughly investigate every possibility of strong provocation by the male victim when he is slain by a female – and particuarly, as noted below, if the female is his wife, which is also a strong possibility. It is, of course, the further responsibility of defense counsel, prosecuting attorney, and subsequently the court, to determine whether such provocation was sufficient either to reduce or to eliminate culpability altogether.

The proportion that Negro male/Negro male[10] and white male/white male homicides constitute among VP cases (45 and 13 percent) is similar to the proportion these same relationships constitute among non-VP cases (41 and 14 percent). The important contribution of the Negro male as a victim-precipitator is indicated by the fact that Negro male/Negro female homicides are, proportionately, nearly three times as frequent among VP cases (25 percent) as they are among non-VP cases (9 percent). It is apparent, therefore, that Negroes and males not only are the groups most likely to make positive and direct contributions to the genesis of their own victimization, but that, in particular, Negro males more frequently provoke females of their own race to slay them than they do members of their own sex and race.

For both VP and non-VP groups, close friends, relatives, and acquaintances are the major types of specific relationships between victims and offenders. Combined, these three relationships constitute 69 percent of the VP homicides and 65 percent of the non-VP cases. Victims are relatives of their slayers in one-fourth of both types of homicide. But of 38 family slayings among VP cases, 33 are husband-wife killings; while of 98 family slayings among non-VP cases, only 67 are husband-wife killings. This proportional difference results in a *significant* association between mate slayings and VP homicide.

Finally, of VP mate slayings, 28 victims are husbands and only 5 are wives; but of non-VP mate slayings, only 19 victims are husbands while 48 are wives. Thus there is a *significant* association between husbands who are victims in mate slayings and VP homicide. This fact, namely, that *significantly* more husbands than wives are victims in VP mate slayings — means that (1) husbands actually may provoke their wives more often than wives provoke their husbands to assault their respective mates; or, (2) assuming that provocation by wives is as frequent, or even more frequent, than provocation by husbands, then husbands may not receive and define provocation stimuli with as great or as violent a reaction as do wives; or (3) husbands may have a greater felt sense of guilt in a marital conflict for one reason or another, and receive verbal insults and overt physical assaults without retaliation as a form of compensatory punishment; or, (4) husbands may withdraw more often than wives from the scene of marital conflict, and thus eliminate, for the time being, a violent overt reaction to their wives' provocation. Clearly, this is only a suggestive, not an exhaustive, list of probable explanations. In any case, we are left with the undeniable fact that husbands more often than wives are major, precipitating factors in their own homicidal deaths.

Alcohol

In the larger work of which this study is a part, the previous discovery of an association between the presence of alcohol in the homicide situation and Negro male offenders, combined with knowledge of the important contribution Negro males make to their own victimization, suggests an association (by transitivity) between VP homicide and the presence of alcohol. Moreover, whether alcohol is present in the victim or offender, lowered inhibitions due to ingestion of alcohol may cause an individual to give vent more freely to pent up frustrations, tensions, and emotional conflicts that have either built up over a prolonged period of time or that arise within an immediate emotional crisis. The data do in fact confirm the suggested hypothesis above and reveal a *significant* association between VP homicide and alcohol in the homicide situation. Comparison of VP to non-VP cases with respect to the presence of alcohol in the homicide situation (alcohol present in either the victim, offender, or both), reveals that alcohol was present in 74 percent of the VP cases and in 60 percent of the non-VP cases. The proportional difference results in a *significant* association between alcohol and VP homicide. It should be noted that the association is not necessarily a causal one, or that a causal relationship is not proved by the association.

Because the present analysis is concerned primarily with the contribution of the victim to the homicide, it is necessary to determine whether an association exists between VP homicide and presence of alcohol in the victim. No associa‧ tion was found to exist between VP homicide and alcohol in the offender. But victims had been drinking immediately prior to their death in more VP cases (69 percent) than in non-VP cases (47 percent). A positive and *significant* relationship is, therefore, clearly established between victims who had been drinking and who precipitated their own death. In many of these cases the victim was intoxicated, or nearly so, and lost control of his own defensive powers. He frequently was a victim with no intent to harm anyone maliciously, but who, nonetheless, struck his friend, acquaintance, or wife, who later became his assailant. Impulsive, aggressive, and often dangerously violent, the victim was the first to slap, punch, stab, or in some other manner commit an assault. Perhaps the presence of alcohol in this kind of homicide victim played no small part in his taking this first and major physical step toward victimization. Perhaps if he had not been drinking he would have been less violent, less ready to plunge into an assaultive stage of interaction. Or, if the presence of alcohol had no causal relation to his being the first to assault, perhaps it reduced his facility to combat successfully, to defend himself from retaliatory assault and, hence, contributed in this way to his death.

Previous Arrest Record

The victim-precipitator is the first actor in the homicide drama to display and to use a deadly weapon; and the description of him thus far infers that he is in some respects an offender in reverse. Because he is the first to assume an aggressive role, he probably has engaged previously in similar but less serious physical assaults. On the basis of these assumptions several meaningful hypotheses were established and tested. Each hypothesis is supported by empirical data, which in some cases reach the level of statistical significance accepted by this study; and in other cases indicate strong associations in directions suggested by the hypotheses. A summary of each hypothesis with its collated data follows:

(1) In VP cases, the victim is more likely than the offender to have a previous arrest, or police, record. The data show that 62 percent of the victims and 54 percent of the offenders in VP cases have a previous record.

(2) A higher proportion of VP victims than non-VP victims have a previous police record. Comparison reveals that 62 percent of VP victims but only 42

percent of non-VP victims have a previous record. The association between VP victims and previous arrest record is a *significant* one.

(3) With respect to the percentage having a previous arrest record, VP victims are more similar to non-VP offenders than to non-VP victims. Examination of the data reveals no significant difference between VP victims and non-VP offenders with a previous record. This lack of a significant difference is very meaningful and confirms the validity of the proposition above. While 62 percent of VP victims have a police record, 68 percent of non-VP offenders have such a record, and we have already noted in (2) above that only 42 percent of non-VP victims have a record. Thus, the existence of a statistically *significant* difference between VP victims and non-VP victims and the *lack* of a statistically significant difference between VP victims and non-VP offenders indicate that the victim of VP homicide is quite similar to the offender in non-VP homicide — and that the VP victim more closely resembles the non-VP offender than the non-VP victim.

(4) A higher proportion of VP victims than of non-VP victims have a record of offenses against the person. The data show a *significant* association between VP victims and a previous record of offenses against the person, for 37 percent of VP victims and only 21 percent of non-VP victims have a record of such offenses.

(5) Also with respect to the percentage having a previous arrest record of offenses against the person, VP victims are more similar to non-VP offenders than non-VP victims. Analysis of the data indicates support for this assumption, for we have observed that the difference between VP victims (37 percent) and non-VP victims (21 percent) is *significant;* this difference is almost twice as great as the difference between VP victims (27 percent) and non-VP offenders (46 percent), and this latter difference is not significant. The general tendency again is for victims in VP homicides to resemble offenders in non-VP homicides.

(6) A lower proportion of VP offenders have a previous arrest record than do non-VP offenders. The data also tend to support this hypothesis, for 54 percent of offenders in VP cases, compared to 68 percent of offenders in non-VP cases have a previous police record.

In general, the rank order of recidivism — defined in terms of having a previous arrest record and of having a previous record of assaults — for victims and offenders involved in the two types of homicide is as follows:

	Percent with Previous Arrest Record	Percent with Previous Record of Assault
(1) Offenders in non-VP Homicide	68	46
(2) Victims in VP Homicide	62	37
(3) Offenders in VP Homicide	54	33
(4) Victims in non-VP Homicide	42	21

Because he is the initial aggressor and has provoked his subsequent slayer into killing him, this particular type of victim (VP) is likely to have engaged previously in physical assaults which were either less provoking than the present situation, or which afforded him greater opportunity to defer attacks made upon him. It is known officially that over one-third of them assaulted others previously. It is not known how many formerly provoked others to assault them. In any case, the circumstances leading up to the present crime in which he plays the role of victim are probably not foreign to him since he has, in many cases, participated in similar encounters before this, his last episode.

Summary

Criminal homicide usually involves intense personal interaction in which the victim's behavior is often an important factor. As Porterfield has recently pointed out, "The intensity of interaction between the murderer and his victim may vary from complete non-participation on the part of the victim to almost perfect cooperation with the killer in the process of getting killed . . . . It is amazing to note the large number of would-be murderers who become the victim." [11] By defining a VP homicide in terms of the victim's direct, immediate, and positive contribution to his own death, manifested by his being the first to make a physical assault, it has been possible to identify 150 VP cases.

Comparison of this VP group with non-VP cases reveals *significantly* higher proportions of the following characteristics among VP homicide:

(1) Negro victims;
(2) Negro offenders;
(3) male victims;
(4) female offenders;
(5) stabbings;
(6) victim-offender relationship involving male victims of female offenders;
(7) mate slayings;
(8) husbands who are victims in mate slayings;
(9) alcohol in the homicide situation;
(10) alcohol in the victim;
(11) victims with a previous arrest record;
(12) victims with a previous arrest record of assault.

In addition, VP homicides have slightly higher proportions than non-VP homicides of altercations and domestic quarrels; inter-racial slayings, victims who are close friends, relatives, or acquaintances of their slayers.

Empirical evidence analyzed in the present study lends support to, and measurement of, von Hentig's theoretical contention that "there are cases in which they (victim and offender) are reversed and in the long chain of causative forces the victim assumes the role of a determinant."[12]

In many cases the victim has most of the major characteristics of an offender; in some cases two potential offenders come together in a homicide situation and it is probably often only chance which results in one becoming a victim and the other an offender. At any rate, connotations of a victim as a weak and passive individual, seeking to withdraw from an assaultive situation, and of an offender as a brutal, strong, and overly aggressive person seeking out his victim, are not always correct. Societal attitudes are generally positive toward the victim and negative toward the offender, who is often feared as a violent and dangerous threat to others when not exonerated. However, data in the present study — especially that of previous arrest record — mitigate, destroy, or reverse these connotations of victim-offender roles in one out of every four criminal homicides.

Notes

1. Hans von Hentig, *The Criminal and His Victim* (New Haven: Yale University Press, 1948), pp. 383-385.
2. Gabriel Tarde, *Penal Philosophy* (Boston: Little, Brown and Company, 1912), p. 466.
3. Thomas DeQuincey, "On Murder Considered as One of the Fine Arts," in Edward Bulwer-Lytton, Douglas Jerrold, and Thomas DeQuincey, *The Arts of Cheating, Swindling, and Murder* (New York: The Arnold Co., 1925), p. 153.
4. Baron Raffaele Garofalo, *Criminology* (Boston: Little, Brown and Company, 1914), p. 373.
5. For an excellent discussion of the rule of provocation, from which these four requirements are taken, see: Rollin M. Perkins, "The Law of Homicide," *Jour. of Crim. Law and Criminol.,* (March-April, 1946), 36: 412-427; and Herbert Wechsler and Jerome Michael, *A Rationale of the Law of Homicide,* pp. 1280-1282. A general review of the rule of provocation, both in this country and abroad, may be found in "The Royal Commission on Capital Punishment, 1949-1952 Report," Appendix II, pp. 453-458.
6. Ibid., p. 425. The term "cause" is here used in a legal and not a psychological sense.
7. In order to facilitate reading of the following sections, the *victim-precipitated* cases are referred to simply as VP cases or VP homicides. Those homicides in which the victim was not a direct precipitator are referred to as non-VP cases.

8. Of 588 victims, 228, or 39 percent, were stabbed; 194, or 33 percent, were shot; 128, or 22 percent, were beaten; and 38, or 6 percent, were killed by other methods.

9. Only 550 victim-offender relationships are identified since 38 of the 588 criminal homicides are classified as unsolved, or those in which the perpetrator is unknown.

10. The diagonal line represents "killed by." Thus, Negro male/Negro male means a Negro male killed by a Negro male; the victim precedes the offender.

11. Austin L. Porterfield and Robert H. Talbert, "Mid-Century Crime in Our Culture: Personality and Crime in the Cultural Patterns of American States", (Fort Worth: Leo Potishman Foundation, 1954), pp. 47-48.

12. Von Hentig, op. cit., p. 383.

9 Interracial Forcible Rape in A North American City: An Analysis of Sixty-three Cases

Michael W. Agopian, Duncan Chappell, and Gilbert Geis

Introduction

The crime of forcible rape, committed by a black man against a white woman, possesses a number of characteristics setting it apart from most offenses against the person. For one thing, interracial forcible rape sometimes has an ideological component, representing an explosion of hatred by the black male against his oppressors. Eldridge Cleaver, for instance, writing about the period after his release from prison, noted: "I became a rapist. To refine my technique and modus operandi, I started out by practicing on black girls in the ghetto . . . and when I considered myself good enough, I crossed the tracks and sought out white prey."[1] Cleaver cogently indicates the symbolic content of his behavior:

> Rape was an insurrectionary act. It delighted me that I was defying and trampling upon the white man's law, upon his system of values, and that I was defiling his women – and this point, I believe, was the most satisfying to me because I was very resentful over the historical fact of how the white man had used the black woman. I felt I was getting revenge.[2]

Thus, rape of white women by black men may be regarded at times as a particularly satisfying fracturing of a fundamental element of the mythology of American racial etiquette, one which placed high value on protecting white women from the presumed lust of black men. As Jesse Bernard has written: "[T]he white world's insistence on keeping Negro men walled up in the concentration camp [of the ghetto] was motivated in large part by its fear of their sexuality."[3] The use of capital punishment, particularly in southern states,for black-white rape further defined both terror and temptation into the behavior, and undergirded an extensive lore among blacks about compliant white females who, faced with discovery, maintained that they had been taken by force.

White male rape of black females has its own distinctive attributes, which would lead an investigator to believe that unless the cultural background items

---

Paper presented at the Interamerican Congress of Criminology, Caracas, Venezuela, 1972. Printed by permission of the authors.

unexpectedly balanced out, American society would show very different rates of interracial rape for black and for white offenders. Historically, black females were regarded as notably accessible to white men, if not by the choice of the female (for there were advantages to be gained from such liaisons), then by a coercion which involved little, if any, likelihood of subsequent penalty.

Today, such historical conditioning is overlaid with elements of the contemporary interracial ethos of the United States. There has been an increase in social interaction between black men and white women, especially among the young in the more cosmopolitan American cities. Black males gaining sexual access to white females might further frustrate their brothers who see more of such activity but who themselves are not participating in it. Black women, for their part, reportedly resent attention that black males sometimes give to white females. Traditional male initiative in such matters, among other things, precludes similar overtures to white males by black females, and also removes potential masculine partners from the realm of the black female — and often men who are especially desirable. These, and similar social conditions, all probably play a role in establishing and giving meaning to interracial forcible rape rates.

Numerical Perspective

Our study sample consisted of sixty-three instances of interracial rape involving black offenders reported to the police during 1971 in the city of Oakland, California. We know of no other work which has examined in detail the characteristics of cases of interracial rape, though there were several studies which provide information on the relative occurrence of rape in terms of the race of the offenders and the victims. In Table 9-1, we have compared our findings to the results reported in other investigations.

The varying distributions of intraracial and interracial rape indicated in the table may be a function of phenomena such as the location and culture of the jurisdictions surveyed, the racial demography of the sites examined, and the study populations involved. The work by Hayman and his colleagues, for instance, was concerned only with persons who reported to a hospital for treatment, a sample that represented about half of the cases in the District of Columbia. Our study, it can be seen from the table, found the largest percentage of black male-white female rapes among the reported inquiries, and represents the only investigation listed in the table in which white women constitute more than half of the total of rape victims. One other contribution to the literature on forcible rape, that by MacDonald, has noted that 60 percent of some 200 rape cases reported to the Denver Police Department in the late 1960s involved black offenders and white victims, while only one case in 29 had white offenders and black victims.[4] MacDonald maintains that blacks in Denver are more likely to rape white than black women, though he does not provide further numerical underpinning for this conclusion.

Table 9-1

**Reported Percentage of Forcible Rape by Race of Offenders
and Victims in Four Studies**

Type of Case		Hayman[a]	Amir[b]	NCCPV[c]	Our Results
	N	1243	646	465	192
Black male-Black female		76%	77%	60%	40%
White male-Black female		.4	4	.3	2
Black male-White female		21	3	10.5	33
White male-White female		3	18	30	19
Indian, Mexican male- Indian, Mexican female					7
Total		100.4%	102%	100.8%	101%
				(Errors Due to Rounding)	

[a]C. R. Hayman, C. Lanza, R. Fuentes, and K. Algor, "Rape in the District of Columbia." Paper presented to the American Public Health Association, October 12, 1971, p. 6. The study period was July 1969 through December 1970.

[b]M. Amir, *Patterns in Forcible Rape* (Chicago, University of Chicago Press, 1971) p. 44. The results are for Philadelphia for the years 1958 and 1960.

[c]National Commission on the Causes and Prevention of Violence, *Crimes of Violence* (Washington: Government Printing Office, December, 1969). The results are from a 10 percent random sample of cases drawn from 17 cities for the year 1967.

Perhaps the most interesting speculation deriving from Table 9-1 is that which suggests that the striking difference between the black offender-white victim forcible rape rate reported by us and that reported by Amir from Philadelphia in the late 1950s is a function not of the sites and the qualities of their populations (for both Oakland and Philadelphia have about the same proportion of black residents — 34 percent in the former, 41 percent in the latter) but rather represents a true increase in the amount of the behavior over time, and an index of a changing climate of race relations. The intermediate numbers reported by Hayman for the District of Columbia (with a relatively high black population) and by the Violence Commission, based on a nationwide sampling, would tend to provide support for such a hypothesis.

Further Findings

We had at first intended to analyze and to compare the white male-black female cases with those involving black offenders, but the small number of the former cases — only three — necessitated our discarding that approach and concentrating on the remaining sixty-three instances of interracial rape.

In terms of the age of perpetrators and victims, our findings contradict the result reported from Philadelphia by Amir. He had found that white offenders in interracial rape followed the usual pattern of selecting victims either of the same age bracket or one younger than themselves. Black offenders, to the contrary, in 44 percent of the cases chose victims who were ten or more years older than themselves. It was this finding in particular which led Amir to suggest that the dynamics of interracial rape might vary significantly from those of the intraracial offense. We found, however, that in about two-thirds of our cases the offender chose as his victim someone in the same ten-year age bracket as himself or someone younger. More than half of the cases of victims who were ten or more years older than offenders involved blacks of 19 or younger choosing victims in the 20-to-29-year-old bracket. Particularly interesting is the fact that only two rapes by blacks involved white victims above the age of 40. Most offenders — (62 percent) and most victims (71 percent) — fell in the 20-to-29 age grouping.

Table 9-2

Season of Year Rape Committed and Age of Offender

Age of Offender	Fall	Winter	Spring	Summer
19 or less	4 (20.0%)	5 (27.8%)	0 —	12 (54.5%)
20–29 years	6 (30.0%)	9 (50.0%)	16 (100.0%)	10 (45.5%)
30–39 years	10 (50.0%)	2 (11.1%)	0 —	0 —
40–49 years	0 —	2 (11.1%)	0 —	0 —
Total N	20	18	16	22
%	(100.0)	(100.0)	(100.0)	(100.0)

Note: $X^2 = 46.89$, $p < .001$
          Lamda (Asymmetric) .171 with age dependent; .333 with season dependent

Our study once more confirmed the finding of earlier research that warm weather months are the high season for the offense of rape.[5] Fifty-nine percent of the cases occurred in spring and summer, with the highest percentage for the four seasons — 33 percent — taking place during the summer. Especially interesting, though, was an analysis, the results of which are presented in Table 9-2, which took into account the relationship between the offender's age and the season in which the offense was committed. The results showed that 50 percent of the offenders were in the 30-to-39-year-age group during the fall season. For winter, the modal age dropped to 20-to-29. In the spring, all cases (N = 16) were in the 20-to-29 bracket, while in the summer the modal offender age dropped to 19 or less. School vacations and youthful sexuality associated with recess freedom, plus seasonal employment patterns, might partly account for this finding.

The Oakland interracial rape data differed from that in other general studies, both of rape and of homicide, which report that peak activity takes place during the weekends. The midweek period showed the largest amount of interracial forcible rape. Wednesday was the day with the greatest number of offenses (25.4 percent), and the combination of Monday, Tuesday, and Wednesday included 62 percent of the cases. The weekend days — Friday, Saturday, and Sunday — accounted for only one-quarter of the number of interracial rapes.

The location of the rape event provides some initial indication of the dynamics of the situation which led to its occurrence. Intraracial rape, studies have indicated, tend to take place indoors, quite often in the residence of one of the participants. The assumption may be made that out of fear or what would prove to be indiscretion the victim allowed herself to go, be taken, be visited, or be intruded upon by the offender. These findings do not hold up, however, for the Oakland interracial sample. Rather, most of the offenses — some 40 percent — took place in nonresidential settings, not including automobiles, which were the locus of an additional 22 percent of the cases.

While violent anger and hatred may underlie many of the interracial rapes, it does not manifest itself in severe beatings of victims by offenders. Only two of the victims, according to the police reports, suffered what could be classified as "brutal beatings," though 11 of the 63 victims were reported to have been beaten by their assailants in the course of the offense.

The victim's degree of submissiveness was closely related to the use of physical violence against her. Most of the victims — 57 percent — reported themselves submissive to the rape. Only four of these — out of a total of 36 — were beaten, and only one was beaten severely. Of the women who fought back, a matter we defined as one stage beyond a show of resistance, more than half — 7 of 13 — were physically beaten. The interactive chronological nature of these events cannot be determined from the reports, however. Victim belief that use of force was imminent may have led to heavy resistance, which in its turn could have triggered the latent violence of the offender.

In regard to the response to rape by the victim in terms of her age, we found that the younger the girl the greater the likelihood that she would be submissive. Young girls may have been frightened into submission, or reacted in a more acquiescent manner because they possessed fewer racial and moral scruples. Older women who, because of their longer exposure to sexual experience, might be expected to regard defilement more casually, in fact seemed to resist more frequently. This resistance may reflect a generation gap in moral attitudes toward sexual intercourse, or perhaps heightened racial prejudices which define assaults by blacks as more serious than those by a member of the same race.

The suggestion has been offered by Amir that rape offenses might be examined in terms of what he labels "sexual humiliation." This term embraces, rather indiscriminately (as well as in part invidiously and moralistically) repeated intercourse, fellatio, and cunnilingus. Such events might better be regarded for what they are in fact, without guessing at the motive of the offender or the feelings of the victim. In Philadelphia, Amir found that 44 percent of the black male-white female rapes involved repeated intercourse – that is, more than one act of intercourse, separated either by time or orgasmic response by the offender(s). Cunnilingus took place in 22 percent of the cases, and fellatio in the same proportion. In our sample, repeated intercourse was reported in only two cases. Fellatio occurred in 9 instances, while there were no reports of cunnilingus. The last finding is consistent with observations that black men are more reluctant than whites to engage in cunnilingus.[6]

Multiple offender rapes, though, were considerably rarer in the Oakland sample than they have been found to be elsewhere.[7] Fifteen percent of the offenses involving black men and white women were multiple offender cases, a figure that contrasts to more than half of the interracial rapes involving black men in Amir's Philadelphia study. We also found that in at least a third of the cases the rape was combined with another felony, usually robbery, a figure which is approximately similar to the result reported by Amir for interracial rape.

The prior relationship, if any, between the offender(s) and the victim in the Oakland sample proved to be at most slight. In a majority of instances, the victim and offender were unknown to each other until events very closely related to the rape began to unfold (such as the offering of a ride to a girl waiting for a bus). This finding is strikingly different for that reported elsewhere in regard to intraracial rape. Thus, Amir, for instance, noted that in 53 percent of the intraracial cases the victim and the offender were *at least* acquaintances. Using the same classificatory criteria as Amir employed, we found that in 90.4 percent of our interracial rape cases the victim and offender were strangers, and that for 96.8 percent the relationship was no deeper than that of acquaintances.

Equally interesting was the fact that we had only one case in which the matter of "ideological rape" found its way into the police reports. These reports, of course, tend toward the skeletal in terms of the information supplied, though there is some effort to establish a *modus operandi* which might aid in solving a coterie of offenses committed by one person or by a group of individuals.

The single ideological offense was marked by particular hostility toward the victim as well as a flurry of activity whose meaning is not at all clear to us. The victim was intercepted on her way to do her marketing at about 5 in the evening. She was first accosted in the street and was beaten and kicked. Then, when she escaped momentarily, she reported that her assailants followed her into the supermarket and dragged her out. She said she had been forced to walk to the apartment of one alleged offender, who repeated over and over again: "I want a white woman." She was, she maintained, subjected to a variety of sexual insults by two suspects involving, the police report notes rather coyly, "numerous positions" for 3 1/2 hours. The puzzling note in the report is the observation that the suspect told the complainant that "she was going to steal for him because he needed money," indicating perhaps a known status of the girl or a peculiar fantasy of the offender.

Another case history provides a flavor of the events that cannot be as readily transmitted by numerical summaries. The case is a felony-rape, in which the sexual assault appears almost as an afterthought, the consequence of a sudden catalytic realization that a potential object of rape is available and at the offender's mercy. The victim in this case was a 24-year old student; the offender a 16-year old:

> Complainant states she was riding her bicycle when she noticed another bicycle rider riding very close behind her and to her left side. She did not turn around and therefore did not see who it was. He turned off to her right. About 1/2 block further up the complainant hit a bump causing her to fall. She then noticed that her purse was missing from the basket mounted on the rear of her bike. She went back to where the other bike rider had turned off behind her and found suspect #1 with his bike. She asked him if he had seen her purse and he told her it was on the side of a hill which was part of the freeway foundation. She climbed up the hill and found her purse with its contents scattered. While she was picking it up, suspect attacked her and told her he wanted to screw her. She resisted but he overpowered her and succeeded in making penetration into her vagina with his penis. When he was finished she asked him for her money back, he gave her back the four one dollar bills she had had in her purse. He then grabbed three of them from her hand, ran to his bicycle and rode out of sight on a side street.[8]

The intriguing ambivalence of the offender, returning her money momentarily to the victim before grabbing most of it back, is somewhat indicative of a phenomenon which seemed to occur with unusual regularity in the series of police reports we examined. It involved the offender redefining the encounter after his use of force has achieved its sexual end. We had found similar kinds of behavior in intraracial rapes in Boston and Los Angeles, when we earlier studied the offense reports there, but such redefinition seemed particularly common in the Oakland cases, being noted in about 20 percent of the reports. Offenders surprisingly often made attempts to meet their victims at a future date, and went to some trouble to take the victim to her home rather than dropping her near the offense site. One report notes, for instance: "Complainant states that when suspect was finished, suspect dressed himself, being very nonchalant about what had just happened, making small talk as he dressed. Suspect then drove from scene to bus stop, gave complainant a dollar for bus fare, and left complainant there."

If, indeed, this kind of behavior is more common among black offenders dealing with white victims than in other offender-victim combinations, we would hypothesize that it represents in part a response by the offender to the acquiescent (translated into "approving") behavior of the victim, as well as an understandable attempt to redefine force into romantic seduction, to shore up a self-esteem that might likely find some difficulty in facing the fact that an imperative of masculine performance had been achieved not by female choice but rather against the will of the sex object.

Discussion

Interracial rape in Oakland, according to our data, is overwhelmingly a stranger to stranger crime. Unlike intraracial rape, where the offender and his victim frequently make initial contact in a social context, such as drinking at a bar together, the access of black offenders to white women is obviously restricted. The crossing of interracial boundaries takes place at those points at which the white victim is most readily available and vulnerable. The dominant sense of interracial rape in Oakland is of victims being seized in public places, as they await transportation, or walk in a street or park. That the majority of offenses occur on weekdays suggests that victims are more likely to be engaged in work-oriented tasks, involving unescorted movement in open urban areas. The victim will be a student on the way home from class, the housewife out shopping, the secretary leaving her office for home, and similar targets of opportunity.

Amir, seeking to account for intraracial rape in his study in Philadelphia, advances the thesis that rape of this type is primarily the culmination of a misfired attempt at seduction. In Amir's intraracial sample, many victims and offenders were acquaintances, Saturday evenings accounted for the highest frequency of rapes, and the majority of rapes took place indoors. While Amir reported that about one-third of the intraracial cases in Philadelphia involved alcohol, our reports showed that not a single victim was reported to be other than sober, and only one offender was said to be under the influence of alcohol.

Our data indicate, then, that the social interaction theory does not apply to interracial rape. The data also suggest that an important element of interracial rape reported by Amir and other investigators does not necessarily apply to different kinds of urban settings. We have noted earlier that in Oakland, unlike Philadelphia, for instance, we did not find a high incidence of multioffender interracial rape, did not show black offenders selecting victims significantly older than themselves, and, most strikingly, did not support the view that blacks are more often the victims of rape than whites.

Such variations, however, may reflect differences which involve not the event being studied but the manner in which it is dealt with. Police reporting and recording, and police-community relations, for instance, may seriously distort the data that becomes available.[9] For example, one informant we questioned about the very small number of white offender-black victim rapes in our sample remarked: "No black woman would report being raped by a white man to the police in Oakland. They might report it to the Panthers, but never the police."

Demographic factors and the relations between races may also condition findings. Race tensions between police and citizens are believed to be higher in Oakland than in most cities, with a militant black population seeking greater access to seats of power in the city. Under such conditions, cooperation with the police by blacks may be minimal, while white victims may more often than in other places take their reports of victimization to law enforcement officials. Similarly, the police may respond differentially — in terms of recording and investigating events — when the victim is white rather than black.

There are other factors too that bear upon the accuracy of any crime statistics, and which also influence the number of criminal events in one place compared to another. Rape, for instance, seems to be particularly responsive to climatic conditions, so that a city such as Oakland, with a relatively benign climate, will, all other things being equal, show a higher rape rate than a city in the midwestern or northeastern part of the country. The ecological distribution of ethnic groups, the age structure of the population, transportation systems, and similar variables also bear upon criminal behavior and its explanation.

Before any firm conclusions can be drawn about national patterns of interracial rape, we require more extensive research using uniform definitions of the offense, and involving homogeneous reporting forms and procedures. Such research may throw light on the "dark figures" of interracial rape, and upon variables which tend to elevate or lower the rate of this offense. At a time when forcible rape, alone among the index crimes, is increasing rapidly each year, the need for a much better understanding of the factors which produce such criminal behavior is preeminently clear.

Notes

1. E. Cleaver, *Soul on Ice* (New York: Dell Publishing Co., 1968), p. 26.
2. Ibid.
3. J. Bernard, *Marriage and Family among Negroes* (Englewood Cliffs, New Jersey: Prentice-Hall, 1966), p. 75.
4. J. M. MacDonald, *Rape Offenders and Their Victims* (Springfield, Illinois: Charles C. Thomas, 1971), p. 51.
5. Although a recent unpublished study of forcible rape in New York City has indicated that seasonal trends are not evident among offenses committed in that location. An examination of 389 cases of forcible rape in New York City committed over a two-year period (February 1970 through January 1972) revealed that 34 percent occurred between January and April, 33 percent between May and August, and 33 percent between September and December. D. Chappell and S. Singer "Rape in New York City: A Study of the Data in Police Files and Its Meaning."
6. R. Staples, "The Sexuality of Black Women," *Sexual Behavior,* 2, no. 6 (June 1972), p. 11
7. See G. Geis and D. Chappell, "Forcible Rape by Multiple Offenders," *Abstracts of Criminology and Penology* 11, no. 4 (July-August 1971), p. 431, and D. Chappell, G. Geis, S. Schafer and L. Seigel, "Forcible Rape: A Comparative Study of Offenses Known to the Police in Boston and Los Angeles," *Studies in the Sociology of Sex,* J. Henslin ed. (New York: Appleton-Century Crofts, 1971), p. 169.
8. Oakland Police Department files, Oakland, California. Reprinted by permission.
9. See, in particular, "Police Discretion and the Judgment That a Crime Has Been Committed — Rape in Philadelphia," *University of Pennsylvania Law Review* 117, no. 2 (December 1968), p. 277.

10 Who is the Victim?

Richard Quinney

A victim cannot be taken for granted. Which is to say, a victim is a conception of reality as well as an object of events. All parties involved in any sequence of actions construct the reality of the situation. And, in the larger social context, we all engage in commonsense construction of "the crime," "the criminal," and "the victim." In our own minds we know who or what is the victim in any situation. At the same time, we exclude other contenders from our image of the victim.

What I am arguing, then, is that although anyone or anything can be party to events, how we characterize these persons, collectivities, or properties is a matter of imagination. That our conceptions of victims and victimization are optional, discretionary, and by no means innately given is my concern in this paper. The conceptions we do hold, however, have consequences for our work as criminologists. And moreover, such conceptions affect the ways in which we all live our lives.

Definition of a Victim

By the social construction of law itself, *all crimes* have a victim. Acts, in fact, are defined as criminal because someone or something is conceived of as a victim. In this sense, the victim — that is, a conception of the victim — *precedes* the definition of an act as criminal. If a victim cannot be imagined, a criminal law is neither created nor enforced. A "victimless" crime can only be one that is defined after the fact by an outside observer.

That every crime has a victim is recognized in legal definitions of crime. Thus, Perkins (1957: 5) has noted that a crime is "any social harm defined and punishable by law." The "social harm," of course, can be a physical injury to an individual, *if* the state feels that such an injury *also* threatens its social order, to the most diffuse harm that in some way is regarded as hurting the body social.

Obviously, not all conduct which could conceivably result in social harm is regulated by law. Only those acts which cause harm to those who are able to make and enforce the law become crimes (Quinney, 1970: 29-42). And, similarly, when the social harms that are a part of the written law cease to be regarded by those in power as a harm to their interests, these laws are no longer enforced. While every act may conceivably involve a victim, only those acts that threaten the welfare of the ruling class become crimes. Social harm, no matter how abstract, is a reality decided upon by those in power.

The presence of a victim, then, the one officially designated, is an indication that the existing social order has been challenged. Which is also to say, the rhetoric of victimization is one more weapon the ruling class uses to justify and perpetuate its own existence. The victim, a concrete one, apart from the state itself, is held up as a defense of the social order.

Patterns of Victimization

The concrete victim is the objective of many of our criminal statutes. From the legalistic standpoint, the victim is often clearly specified. For example, someone is a victim when his property is stolen; rape is against someone in particular; fraud is committed against a person or an organization; and then there are those crimes that are against "nature." In all these crimes, a victim is the rationale for the law.

The conceptions of the victim become more complicated when removed from the criminal law. But it is in this realm of commonsense conceptions that gives meaning to the question, "Who is the victim?" It is these conceptions that affect the administration of the law and our everyday reactions to crime. They also influence the formulation of new laws and the way we regard and treat the victims among us.

From recent surveys, it is clear that the public is much more aware of vicimization than the official statistics would indicate. In a national sample of households, where persons were asked whether anyone in the household had been a victim of a crime during the preceding twelve months, their reporting of being victims of personal and property crimes was considerably higher than recorded in the official figures (Biderman and Reiss, 1967; Ennis, 1967). Forcible rape victimization was more than 3.5 times the recorded rate; burglary victimization was 3 times greater; assault and larceny victimizations were more than double; and robberies were 50% greater.

In spite of their knowledge of victimization, the respondents failed to officially report the crimes. Their refusal to report is in part a reflection of how they conceive of themselves as victims. While many felt the police would do nothing if the offenses were reported, the most frequent reason offered for failure to report an offense was that it represented a private matter or that the victim did not want to harm the offender. This explanation applied particularly to assaults, family offenses, and consumer frauds. Other studies (Smigel, 1956) have similarly shown that persons readily qualify either their own victimization or the victimization of others.

In other words, there are definite public conceptions of victims and victimization. These conceptions are likely patterned and vary from one segment of society to another. But most important to the formulation of public policy are those conceptions held by the ruling segments of society. These are the conceptions that ultimately regulate our lives.

Victimology

Criminologists have their own conceptions of the victim. These images are necessarily qualified, restricted, and limited to certain possibilities rather than others. Whatever the conceptions, they have consequences when the efforts of criminologists influence public policy.

In recent years, criminologists have discovered "victimology." Following the positivistic assumptions of causation, criminologists have investigated the role of the victim in the commission of offenses. For the most part, however, the criminal-victim relationship has been limited to a narrow range of crimes – primarily murder, aggravated assault, forcible rape, and robbery (President's Commission on Law Enforcement and Administration of Justice, 1967: 80-84; National Commission on the Causes and Prevention of Violence, 1969: 207-258). Alternative relationships have thus been ignored. Criminologists are reluctant to consider that victims are present in less dramatic offenses. Perhaps they refuse to admit there is in fact a victim in other types of crimes – in consumer frauds and war crimes, for example. Certainly, it is assumed, as Schafer (1968: 103) has noted, that "the more physical activity is involved in a crime, the better are the chances for observing the victim's eventual contribution to it."

The dominant image of the victim held by criminologists is that of the passive victim. The thrust of Von Hentig's (1948) argument was that victims are in some way *vulnerable* individuals. His categories of victims point to various personal characteristics, such as being apathetic, acquisitive, sensual, or lonesome. Others (Wolfgang, 1958) have sought to balance this image by investigating the more active role of victims. It is being suggested that victims range in the degree to which they precipitate an offense.

The victim may be deemed of such importance that types of crime can be delineated specifically in terms of the victim. Thus, a recent book (Smigel and Ross, 1970) is devoted to "crimes against bureaucracy." The interest here may not be so much that bureaucratic organizations – corporate and governmental – are the active agents of their own victimization, but rather that the criminologist abhors the victimization of these bureaucracies. No matter how unjust or criminal the bureaucracy may be, the focus is on their victimization. Personal and social values shape our conceptions of the victim.

Likewise, it is through our value assumptions that we can suggest that there are "crimes without victims." Schur (1965: v) has thus argued that abortion, homosexuality, and drug use are such crimes: "In each case the offending behavior involves a willing and private exchange of strongly demanded yet officially proscribed goods and services; this element of consent precludes the existence of a victim — in the usual sense of the word." Through similar qualifying procedures any offense situation could be defined as victimless. Such is the prerogative of the criminologist. But what we do is crucial, even moral, in that we are creating one reality at the expense of other realities.

Victim Compensation

The modern movement for compensation of victims also has its own conventional wisdom regarding the victim. The numerous proposals for victim compensation contain their own conceptions as to who is the victim. Moreover, these proposals are addressed to specific points regarding the victim, including ideas about the offender-victim relationship, responsibility, human nature, governmental functions, and the nature of society. "Who is the victim?" is not an innocent question.

Recent interest in victim compensation is attributed to the work of Margery Fry, an English penal reformer. Fry (1957) argued that the state ought to be liable for "criminally caused" injuries suffered by citizens. The debates and counter-proposals that have ensued reflect varying conceptions of victimization. Most of the presentations (e.g., Childres, 1964), nevertheless, restrict compensation to particular types of victims, to persons suffering injuries from criminal homicide, assault, and forcible rape.

Recognition of the need to compensate victims of these crimes is grounded on the notion that modern criminal law has evolved away from the victim's right to private redress. And since the state has taken upon itself the function of maintaining law and order, it is liable for the personal injuries of the victims of some forms of crime. Hence (Northwestern University Law Review, 1966: 91), "a compensation program would once again bring the victim's private interests in redress back into the law enforcement process." This form of reasoning emphasizes the responsibility of society. Departing from the laissez faire philosophy of individual responsibility and personal fault, the argument (Miller, 1959; Wolfgang, 1965) is that the state must aid the victim through public funds — just as the worker is compensated when he is unemployed.

There are, of course, disclaimers to this notion of the victim and his right to be compensated. Some writers (e.g., Mueller) stress more emphatically the role of individual responsibility and question welfare programs by the government. Fred Inbau (1959: 202) writes that "to compensate victims of violent crimes is to indulge in the kind of thinking that would lead us into an abandonment of all notions of individual responsibility and a resort to complete dependence upon government paternalism." And related to this notion of the victim and compensation is the idea (Starrs, 1965) that if the victim is to be compensated, the solution ought to be found in private insurance programs.

Those who argue against victim compensation or for extremely limited programs conceive of the victim as being responsible for his own victimization. A lawyer (Weihofen, 1959: 214, 215) writes: "Some people are born to be victims," and adds, "Others seem to be bent on making victims of themselves." Since the victim is seen as a perpetrator of the offense, he is not to be rewarded for being a victim. And providing compensation, the reasoning concludes, would only prompt the victim to instigate further crimes.

Another proposal (Schafer, 1968) suggests the "functional responsibility" of both the victim and the offender, and that the offender should compensate the victim when possible. Restitution to victims by offenders, it is suggested, would serve to rehabilitate the offender. Further, the victim is to prevent his own victimization and the offender is to account for his violation. This proposal, like the others, contains its own commonsense assumptions about the victim and his relation to the rest of the world. And the victim compensation programs (Geis, 1967) that have been instituted in various states and countries are based on these varying conceptions of the victim. Imagination has become policy.

Conclusion

The argument that I have been making throughout this paper is that "the victim" is a social construction. We all deal in a conventional wisdom that influences our perception of the world around us. This wisdom allows us to characterize the victims of crime. Moreover, it defines for us just who is the victim in any situation. What this also means is that alternative victims can be constructed. Why we conceive of some persons as victims and others not as victims is a consequence of our commonsense assumptions.

Our own character is indicated by the kinds of persons that we single out as being the victims of crime. Those who make proposals for victim compensation are writing as much about their own hearts and minds as they are about specific programs. When any person imagines a victim — and what should be done for or to him — he is displaying his own self. Similarly, whenever the criminologist confronts the victim, he is presenting his world view of reality.

Thus, it comes as no surprise that other contenders for the category of victim are usually excluded from criminological attention. It would take an alternative world view to conceive of alternative victims. And criminologists have tended to share a singular conception of reality.

With an alternative reality, we would certainly revise or at least expand our image of victimization. Breaking out of the theory of reality that had dominated criminological thought, we would begin to conceive of the victims of police force, the victims of war, the victims of the "correctional" system, the victims of state violence, the victims of oppression of any sort.

Because criminologists have tended to rely on a particular theory of reality, they have excluded these victims. This theory of reality, in its support of existing social order, has excluded those who might threaten that order and those who suffer because of that order. These persons are indeed victims in terms of a radical theory of reality.

In a deeper sense, then, what is at stake in any discussion of victimization is one's morality. Neither laws nor legal discussions can be devoid of morality. To eliminate morality from the law is to eliminate all laws. Morality is the very stuff of laws. Whether morality can be best served without law is another question, but one that I think is entirely possible. But to expect laws to be devoid of morality is to miss the point that someone's morality is embedded in every law.

To regard one class of persons as victims and another not as victims is thus an appeal to one's own morality. To argue, for example, that abortion is victimless is to exclude the living fetus as a victim. To regard the person who loses property as a victim is to value the sanctity of private property. To exclude the Vietnamese civilian suffering from criminal war operations is to accept national military policies. To conceive of the person who is assaulted as a victim is to hold a view of proper social conduct. And to regard prisoners as criminals rather than as victims of a system that places them there to begin with and that brutalizes them once they are there is to accept a particular notion of law and order. That we do not regard ourselves as victims of an oppressive—and often illegal—system says much about our own state of mind and our view of American society.

Perhaps it is time that we investigate our own minds—our own theories of reality. Without doing this, we run the risk of accepting the official reality. If we have any pretense of concern and independence of mind, it is our task to expose that which negates the liberation of us all (Quinney, 1972). To do this, I contend, we must develop a radical theory of reality. Only then can an alternative to our current existence be realized.

References

Biderman, A.D. and "On Exploring the 'Dark Figure' of Crime." *Annals of*
A.J. Reiss, Jr.   *Amer. Academy of Pol. and Social Sci.* 374 (November):
1967   1-15.

Childres, R. D.   "Compensation for Criminally Inflicted Personal Injury."
1964   *New York Univ. Law Rev.* 39 (May): 444-471.

Ennis, P. H.   "Crime, Victims, and the Police." *Trans-action* 4 (June):
1967   36-44.

Fry, M.   "Justice for Victims." *Observer* (July 7): 8.
1957

Geis, G.   "State Compensation to Victims of Violent Crime," pp.
1967   157-177, in President's Commission on Law Enforcement
                   and Administration of Justice, *Crime and Its Import–An
                   Assessment.* Washington, D.C.: Government Printing Office.

Hentig, H. von   *The Criminal and His Victim.* New Haven, Conn.: Yale
1948   Univ. Press.

Inbau, F. E.   "Compensation for Victims of Criminal Violence." *J. of Pub-
1959   lic Law* 8 (Spring): 201-203.

Miller, F. W.   "Compensation for Victims of Criminal Violence." *J. of Pub-
1959   lic Law* 8 (Spring): 203-209.

Mueller, G.O.W.   "Compensation for Victims of Crime: Thought before
1965   Action." *Minnesota Law Rev.* 50 (December): 213-221.

National Commission   *Crimes of Violence.* Washington, D.C.: Government
on the Causes and   Printing Office.
Prevention of Violence
1969

Northwestern University "Compensation to Victims of Violent Crimes."
Law Review   61 (March/April): 72-104.
1966

Perkins, R.M.   *Criminal Law.* Brooklyn: Foundation Press.
1957

President's Commission   *Crime and Its Impact–An Assessment.* Washington,
on Law Enforcement and   D.C.: Government Printing Office.
Administration of Justice
1967

Quinney, R.   "From Repression to Liberation: Social Theory in a Radical
1972   Age," in J. D. Douglas and R. A. Scott (eds.) *Theoretical
                  Perspectives on Deviance.* New York: Basic Books.

1970   *The Social Reality of Crime.* Boston: Little, Brown.

Schafer, S.   *The Victim and His Criminal.* New York: Random House.
1968

Schur, E. M.   *Crimes Without Victims.* Englewood Cliffs, N.J.: Prentice-Hall.
1965

Smigel, E. O.   "Public Attitudes Toward Stealing as Related to Size of Victim
1956   Organization." *Amer. Soc. Rev.* 1 (June): 320–327.

Smigel, E.O. and *Crimes Against Bureaucracy.* New York: Van Nostrand-
H.L. Ross (eds.) Reinhold.
1970

Starrs, J.E.   "A Modest Proposal to Insure Justice for Victims of Crime."
1965   *Minnesota Law Rev.* 50 (December): 285–310.

Weihofen, H.   "Compensation for Victims of Criminal Violence." *J. of Pub-
1959   lic Law* 8 (Spring): 209–218.

Wolfgang, M.E.   "Victim Compensation in Crimes of Personal Violence."
1965   *Minnesota Law Rev.* 50 (December): 223–241.

1958   *Patterns in Criminal Homicide.* Philadelphia: Univ. of Pennsyl-
                  vania Press.

Part II Bibliography

Abdel-Fattah, E. "Vers une Typologie Criminologique des Victimes," *Revue
                  Internationale de Police Criminelle* 1967, 22 (209): 162–169.

————.   *La Victime est-elle Coupable? Le Role de la Victime dans le
                  Meurtre en Vue de Vol.* Montreal: Presses Universitaires de
                  Montreal, 1971.

Amelunxen, C.   *Das Opfer der Straftat. Ein Beitrag zur Viktimologie* (The
                  Victim of the Criminal Act. A Contribution to Victimology).
                  Hamburg: Kriminalistik Verlag, 1970.

Amir, M.   "Victim-Precipitated Forcible Rape," *Journal of Criminal
                  Law, Criminology, and Police Science* 1967, 58 (4): 493–502.

————.   "Forcible Rape," *Federal Probation* 1967, 31 (March): 51–58.

————.   *Patterns of Forcible Rape.* Chicago: University of Chicago
                  Press, 1971.

Anderson, C. M.   "Molestation of Children," *Journal of the American Medical Women's Association* 1968, 23 (2): 204–206.

Antice, E.   "There Mustn't Be a Next Time," *World Medicine* (London) 1968, 4 (6): 50–51, 55–56, 59, 61.

Aromaa, K.   "Arkipäivän väkivaltaa suomessa" (Everyday Violence in Finland – A Survey). Helsinki: Institute of Criminology 1971, series M:11.

Bakan, D.   *Slaughter of the Innocents: A Study of the Battered Child Phenomen.* Lawrence, Mass.: Beacon Press, 1972.

Baker, S. P., L. S. Robertson, and W.U. Spitz   "Tattoos, Alcohol, and Violent Death," *Journal of Forensic Sciences* 1971, 16 (2): 219–225.

Bandini, T., and F. Filauro   "I Delitti contro la Persona dell' Omosessuale" (Crimes of Violence against Homosexuals), *Medicina Legale e delle Assicurazioni* 1964, 12 (4): 697–717.

Barocas, H. A.   "Children of Purgatory: Reflections on the Concentration Camp Survival Syndrome," *Correctional Psychiatry and Journal of Social Therapy* 1970, 16 (1,2,3,4): 51–58.

Bello, C.   "The Victim and the Crime of Swindle." Paper read at the American Society of Criminology Congress in Caracas (1972).

Bender, L.   "Offended and Offender Children," in R. Slovenko (ed.), *Sexual Behavior and the Law.* Springfield, Ill.: C. C. Thomas 1965, 687–703.

Blachly, P. H.   *Seduction: A Conceptual Model in the Drug Dependencies and Other Contagious Social Ills.* Springfield, Ill.: C. C. Thomas, 1970.

Blum, R. H.   *Deceivers and Deceived: Observations on Confidence Men and Their Victims.* Stanford, Calif.: Stanford University Press, 1972.

Boven, W.   "Delinquants Sexuels; Corrupteurs d'Enfants; Coupables et Victimes," *Schweizerische Archiv Für Neurologie Und Psychiatrie* 1943, 51: 14–25.

Brittain, R. P.   "The Sadistic Murderer," *Medicine, Science, and the Law* (London) 1970, (4): 198–207.

Calewaert, W.   "La Victimologie et l'Escroquerie," *Revue de Droit Pénal et de Criminologie* 1959, 39 (7): 602–616.

Canepa, G., and T. Bandini   "The Personality of Incest Victims," *International Criminal Police Review* (Paris) 1967, 22 (208): 140–145.

Capraro, V. J.   "Sexual Assault of Female Children," *Annals of the New York Academy of Sciences* 1967, 142 (3): 817–819.

Carroll, C. O.   *Crime is Your Business.* Seattle, King County Dept. of Public Safety.

Clinch, N. G. and C. Schurr   "Rape", *The Washingtonian Magazine* 1973, 8 (9): 86–91, 120–124.

Cohen, B.   "The Delinquency of Gangs and Spontaneous Groups," in *Delinquency Selected Studies.* New York: John Wiley and Sons, 1969, 61–111.

Coimbra, F.   "Ofensas Corporais" (Crimes against the Person), *Gazeta Medica Portuguesa* 1962, 15 (2): 216–222.

Colin, M., S. Buffard, and J. M. Botta   "Etude Clinique de Cinq Adolescents Meurtriers," *Annales de Médecine Légale* (Paris) 1967, 47 (6): 643–645.

Congress on Victims of Offenses   *Slachtoffers van Delicten.* (Victims of Offenses). Baarn: Uitgev. Bosch und Keuning, 1971.

Crespy, P.   "L'Aspect Sociologique du Viol Commis en Réunion," *Revue de Science Criminelle et de Droit Pénal Comparé* 1965, 20 (4): 837–866.
Criminal Homicides in Baltimore 1960–1964. Baltimore, Md.: Criminal Justice Commission, Inc.

De Francis, V.   "Protecting the Child Victim of Sex Crimes Committed by Adults," *Federal Probation* 1971, 35 (3): 15–20.

Erlich, C.   *Betrüger und ihre Opfer* (Impostors and Their Victims). Hamburg: Kriminalistik, 1967.

Ellenberger, H.   "Psychological Relationships between the Criminal and His Victim," *Archives of Criminal Psychodynamics* 1955, 2: 257–290. It appeared in French in *Revue Internationale de Criminologie et de Police Technique* 1954, 2: 103–121.

Gagnon, J. H.   "Female Child Victims of Sex Offenses," *Social Problems* 13: 176–192.

Gardon, V.   "Le Premier Génocide du XXe Siècle" (The First Genocide of the XXth Century), *Etudes Internationales de Psycho-Sociologie Criminelle* (Paris) 1968, 14 (15): 57–64.

Gasser, R. L.   "The Confidence Game," *Federal Probation* 1963, 27 (4): 47–54.

Geis, G. and   "Forcible Rape by Multiple Offenders," *Abstracts on*
D. Chappell   *Criminology and Penology* 1971, 11 (4, July-August): 431–436.

Goldner, H.S.   "Rape as a Heinous but Understudied Offense," *Journal of*
                   Criminal Law, Criminology, and Police Science 1972, 63 (3):
                   402–407.

Gratus, J.   *The Victims.* London: Hutchinson, 1969.

Gunn, A.D.G.   "Vulnerable Groups. 1. Lives of Loneliness: The Medical-
                   Social Problems of Divorce and Widowhood," *Nursing Times*
                   (London) 1968, 64 (12): 391–392.

Halleck, S.L.   "Emotional Effects of Victimization," in R. Slovenko (ed.),
                   Sexual Behavior and the Law. Springfield, Ill.: Charles C.
                   Thomas 1965, 673–686.

Hayman, C. R.,   "Sexual Assaults on Women and Children in the District of
W.F. Stewart,   Columbia," *Public Health Report* (Washington, D.C.) 1968,
and M. Grant   83 (12): 1021–1028.

Hemard, J.   "Le Consentement de la Victime dans le Délit de Coups et
                   Blessures," *Revue Critique de Législation et de Jurisprudence*
                   1939 (24): 293–319.

Henley, A.   "Muggers of the Mind," *Today's Health* 1971, 49 (February):
                   38–41.

Hepburn, J., and   "Patterns of Criminal Homicide: A Comparison of Chicago
H.L. Voss   and Philadelphia," *Criminology* 1970, 8 (1): 21–45.

Hogan, B.   "Victims as Parties to Crime," *Criminal Law Review* 1962:
                   683–695.

Holyst, B.   "Rola Ofiary W Genezie Zabojstwa" (The Victim's Role in
                   Homicide), *Lodz Panstwo i Prawo* (Warsaw) 1964, 19 (11):
                   746–755.

Hoppe, K.   "Psychosomatic Reactions and Disorders in Victims of Per-
                   secution," *Excerpta Medica Found* (Amsterdam) Intern.
                   Congr. Series no. 117, 1966 (233).

Hunt, M.   *The Mugging.* New York: Atheneum, 1972.

Illinois Legislative   *The Illegal Mexican Alien Problem.* 1971.
Investigating Commission.

John, A.W.   "Participation of the Victim in the Perpetration of Crime,"
                   Samaj-Seva (Poona) 1966, 17 (1): 11–14.

Johnson, E. H., and   "Self-Mutilations and Suicide," in E. Johnson, *Self-*
B. Benjamin   *Mutilations in Prisons.* Research Report, NIMH Grant MH-
                     12032, 1967.

Kainz, A.   "Kinder als Opfer Strafbarer Handlungen. Eine Untersuchung
                     für Österreich," (Children as Victims of Criminal Acts. A
                     Research in Austria), *Kriminalistik* 1967, 21 (11): 605–608.

Karoly, E., and   "The Victim of Crimes by Violence," *Hungarian National*
J. Vigh   *Report on Victimology.* VI International Congress on
                     Criminology, Madrid, 1970, 9–20.

Komiyama K.,   "Behaviorial Patterns of Forcible Rape. I. Situational Analysis
I. Matsumoto,   of Criminals. II. The Interpersonal Relationship of Offender
T. Doi, and   and Victim," *Rep. Nat. Res. Inst. Pol. Sci.* 1970, 11 (1): 50–
K. Saito   58, 59–72. (In Japanese).

Koudernik, C.   "Regression Psychotique Durable chez un Enfant de 4 Ans
                     Victime d'un Viol," *Annales Médico-Psychologiques* 1967,
                     2 (5): 809.

Lafon, R. et al.   "Victimologie et Criminologie des Attentats Sexuels sur les
                     Enfants et les Adolescents," *Annales de Médecine Légale et
                     de Criminologie* (Paris) 1961, 41 (1): 97–106.

Landesjugendamt   "A Study of Group Sex Offenses by Juveniles in Germany,"
Berlin   *International Bibliography on Crime and Delinquency* 1965,
                     3 (2): 158.

                     "Law Enforcement Officers Killed in the Line of Duty," *FBI
                     Law Enforcement Bulletin* 1972, 41 (3): 3–7.

Macdonald, J.M.   *The Murderer and His Victim.* Springfield, Ill.: C.C. Thomas,
                     1961.

————.   "Rape," *Police* 1969, 13 (4): 42–46.

————.   *Rape: Offenders and Their Victims.* Springfield, Ill.: C. C.
                     Thomas, 1971.

Macdonald, W.F.   "The Victim: A Socio-psychological Study." Berkeley, Calif.:
                     University of California at Berkeley, 1970. Unpublished
                     doctoral dissertation. Ann Arbor, Michigan: University Micro-
                     films 71–15693.

Maisch, H.   "Der Inzest und Seine Psychodynamische Entwicklung"
                     (Incest and its Psychodynamic Evolution), *Beiträge zur
                     Sexualforschung* 1965, 33:51–59.

Maurer, D.W.   "The Mark," in D. W. Maurer, *The Big Con.* Indianapolis, Ind.:
                     Bobbs-Merrill Co., 1940.

McCaghy, C.H.   "Child Molesting," *Sexual Behavior* 1971, 1 (5): 16–24.

McCaldon, R. J.   "Rape," *Canadian Journal of Corrections* 1967, 9 (1): 37–57.

Mitchell, R. S.   "The Homosexual as a Victim of Blackmail," in R. Mitchell, *The Homosexual and the Law*. New York: Arco, 1969, 63–65.

Morris, T.   *The Criminal Area: A Study in Social Ecology*. New York: Humanities Press, 1958.

Myers, S. A.   "The Child Slayer: A 25-Year Survey of Homicides involving Pre-Adolescent Victims," *Archives of General Psychiatry* (Chicago) 1967, 17 (2): 211–213.

Nahum, L. H.   "Reflections on Aggression in Man," *Connecticut Medicine* 1970, 34 (2): 80–81.

Nakata, O.   "Violent Crime in the Light of Victimology." Paper presented at the First Annual Meeting of the Japanese Association of Criminology, 1962.

———.   "Violent Crime in the Light of Victimology," *Abstracts on Criminology and Penology* 1964, 4 (4): 491. Abstract.

Nieves, H.   "The Need to Appraise the Behavior of the Victim." Paper read at the American Society of Criminology Congress in Caracas, Venezuela (1972).

Normandeau, A.   "Notes sur la Criminalité de Violence. Etude Comparative" *Annales Internationales de Criminologie* 1968, 7 (2): 393–402.

Oliver, B.J., Jr.   "The Sexual Law Violator," in B. Oliver, *Sexual Deviation in American Society*. New Haven: College and University Press, 1967.

Pečar, J.   "Vloga Žrtev Ubojih na Slovenskem" (The Role of Victim in Homicide in Slovenia), *Revija za Kriminalistiko in Kriminologijo* (Ljubljana) 1971, 22 (4): 258–265.

Plaisant, M. G.   "Personalità della Vittima del Reato" (Personality of the Victim of Crime). Thesis, Faculty of Law, University of Genova, 1958.

Pinatel, J.   "Les Aspects Interpersonnels de la Conduite Criminelle," *Revue de Science Criminelle et de Droit Pénal Comparé* (Paris) 1961: 392–399.

Raffalli, H. C.   "The Battered Child: An Overview of a Medical, Legal, and Social Problem," *Crime and Delinquency* 1970, 16 (7): 139–150.

Ranjeva, H.,   "La Notion de Victime Latente. Contribution Psychopath-
L. Gayral,   ologique à l'Etude de la Victimologie," *Annales Médico-*
P. Moron, and   *Psychologiques* (Paris) 1971, 2 (3): 349–366.
P. Fray

Rasch, W.   "Tötung des Intimpartners" (Killing of the Sex Partner),
                    Beiträge zur Sexualforschung 1964, 31.

Reiss, A.J., Jr.   "Offenses of Burglary, Robbery, and Shoplifting against Busi-
                    nesses or Organizations in Eight Police Precincts of Three
                    Cities." A Report to the President's Commission on Law
                    Enforcement and the Administration of Justice. Business and
                    Organizations Survey Report no. 2. October 8, 1966.

————.   "Field Survey." Appendix A of U. S. Congress, Senate Select
                    Committee on Small Business. *Crimes against Small Business.*
                    91st Cong. Washington D.C.: U.S. Government Printing Office,
                    1969.

————.   "Police Brutality: Answer to Key Questions" in M. Lipsky,
                    Police Encounters. Chicago: Aldine, 1970, 57–84.

Rimmerman, Y.   "Developmental Aspects in Juvenile Investigation," (Hebrew)
                    Delinquency and Society (Jerusalem) 1967, 2 (1): 18–33.

Robin, G. D.   "Justifiable Homicide by Police Officers," *Journal of Criminal
                    Law, Criminology, and Police Science* 1963, 54 (2): 225–231.

Rodenburg, M.   "Child Murder by Depressed Parents," *Canadian Psychiatric
                    Association Journal* (Ottawa) 1971, 16 (1): 41–48.

Royo-Villanova, R.   "El Agresor y la Victima," *Arch. Fac. Med. Madrid* 1965,
                    8 (3): 219–221.

Scarr, H.A. et alii   *Patterns of Burglary.* Washington, D.C.: U. S. Government
                    Printing Office, 1972 (esp. Ch. 3 and the bibliography).

Schafer, S.   *The Victim and His Criminal: A Study in Functional Respon-
                    sibility.* New York: Random House, 1968, ch. 1.

Schiff, A. F.   "Rape in Other Countries," *Medicine, Science and the Law*
                    (London) 1971, 11 (3): 139–143.

Schoenfelder, T.   "Die Initiative des Opfers" (The Initiative of the Victim),
                    Beiträge zur Sexualforschung 1965, 33: 109–115.

————.   "Die Rolle des Mädchens bei Sexualdelikten" (The Role of
                    the Girl in Sex Crimes), *Beiträge zur Sexualforschung* 1968,
                    42.

Schramm, E., and   "Der Homosexuelle Mann als Opfer von Kapitalverbrechen"
K. Kaiser   (The Homosexual as Victim of Capital Crimes), *Kriminalistik*
                    1962, 16 (6): 225–260.

Schultz, H.   "Kriminologische und Strafrechtliche Bemerkungen zur
                       Beziehung zwischen Täter und Opfer" (Criminological and
                       Penal Remarks on the Relationship between the Criminal and
                       the Victim), *Revue Pénale Suisse* 1958, 71: 171–192.

Schultz, Le R.G.   "The Victim-Offender Relationship," *Crime and Delinquency*
                       1968, 14 (2, April): 135–141.

Schwendinger, H.   "Delinquent Stereotypes of Probable Victims," in M. W.
and J.   Klein (ed.), *Juvenile Gangs in Context.* Englewood Cliffs, N.J.:
                       Prentice-Hall, 1967, 92–105.

Sempertegui, W.R.   "La Victima en la Estafa," *Estudios de Derecho Penal y
                       Criminologia,* I. Buenos Aires: Omeba 1961, 63–78.

Šeparovič, Z.   "Žrtva Krivičnog Djela" (The Victim of a Criminal Offense),
                       Zborn. Praun. Fak. Zagreb 1962, 12 (2): 111–123.

Short, J.F., Jr.   *Modern Criminals.* Chicago: Aldine, 1970.

Simon, J.   "Le Consentement de la Victime Justifie-t-il les Lésions
                       Corporelles?" *Revue de Droit Pénal et de Criminologie* 1933,
                       13 (5): 457–476.

Sttak, M.   "Tötungsdelikte aus Situationsbedingtem Affekt" (Cases of
                       Homicide Caused by an Affect Dependent on the Situation),
                       Beitr. Gerichtl. Med. 1970, 27: 144–146.

Sulimma, H. G.   "Zur Kriminologie der Sittlichkeits–delikte Minderjähriger"
                       (Crimes against Morality by Minors), *Die Neue Polizei* 1962,
                       16 (10): 232–235.

Sutherland, S.,   "Patterns of Response among Victims of Rape," *American
and D.J. Scherl   Journal of Orthopsychiatry* 1970, 40 (3): 503–511.

Svalastoga, K.   "Homicide and Social Contact in Denmark," *American
                       Journal of Sociology* 1956, 62: 37–41.

Syvrud, G.A.   "The Victim of Robbery." Ph.D. Dissertation, Washington
                       State University, Pullman, Wash. Dissertation Abstracts
                       International, vol. 28, no. 6. Ann Arbor, Mich.: University
                       Microfilms 67–15767.

Tahon, R..   "Le Consentement de la Victime," *Revue de Droit Pénal et de
                       Criminologie* 1952, 32: 323–342.

                       "The Tin Sin Kuk, Heavenly Swindle," *International Criminal
                       Police Review* 1963, 166: 81–83.

                       "The Police Officer: Primary Target of the Urban Guerrilla,"
                       FBI Law Enforcement Bulletin 1972, 41 (2): 21–23.

Thomas, J. E.   "Killed on Duty. An Analysis of Murders of English Prison
                     Service Staff since 1850," *Prison Service Journal* 1972 (7):
                     9–10.

Thornberry, T.P., and   "Victimization and Criminal Behavior in a Birth
R. N. Figlio   Cohort." Paper read at the American Society of Criminology
                     Congress in Caracas (1972).

Tormes, Y. M.   *Child Victims of Incest.* Washington, D.C.: U.S. Children's
                     Bureau, 1968.

Traini, R.   "You Are Never Too Old to Be Robbed," *Security Gazette*
                     1971, 13 (2): 81.

Trautman, E.C.   "Violence and Victims in Nazi Concentration Camps and the
                     Psychopathology of the Survivors," in H. Krystal, *Psychic
                     Traumatization.* Boston: Little, Brown, 1971, 115–133.

U.S. President's   "The Victims of Crime," in *The Challenge of Crime in a Free
Commission on Law   Society,* 1967, 38–43.
Enforcement and the
Administration of Justice

Unruh, C.   *Der Giftmord. Tat, Täter, Opfer* (Murder by Poisoning. The
                     Act, the Offender, the Victim). Berlin: H. Luchterhand
                     Verlag, 1965.

Van Ooijen, D.   "Rol van het Slachtoffer van Verkeersdelikten en Preventie"
                     (The Role of Victims of Traffic Offenses and Prevention),
                     Algemeen Politieblad (The Hague) 1971, 120 (22): 542–545.

Van Veen, C.J.F.   "Gezinsbehandeling en Delinkwentie," (Family Therapy and
                     Delinquency), *Delikt en Delinkwent* (Leiden) 1971, 1 (9):
                     457–67.

Ueno, S., and   "Ein Beitrag über die Analyse von Opfertypen. Die Statistische
I. Ishiyama   Analyse der 5340 Obduktionsfälle aus der Universität Tokyo"
                     (The Analysis of Types of Victims. Statistical Analysis of
                     5340 Autopsies from the University of Tokyo), *Deutsche
                     Zeitschrift für die Gesamte Gerichtliche Medizin* 1962, 53
                     (2): 55–71.

Versele, S. C.   "Appunti di Diritto e di Criminologia con Riguardo alle
                     'Vittime' dei Delitti" (Legal and Criminological Points in Rela-
                     tion to the 'Victims' of Crimes), *La Scuola Positiva* (Milano)
                     1962 (4): 593–620.

Voigt, J.   "Sexual Offenses in Copenhagen: A Medico-Legal Study,"
                     Forensic Science 1972, 1 (1): 67–76.

Von Baeyer, W.,   *Psychiatric der Verfolgten* (Psychiatry of the Persecuted).
H. Haefner, and   Berlin: Springer Verläg, 1964.
K. P. Kisker

Von Hentig, H.   *The Criminal and His Victim. Studies in the Socio-Biology of Crime.* New Haven: Yale University Press, 1948.

—————.   "Blutschandefaelle Mutter-Sohn" (Incest between Mother and Son) *Monatschrift für Kriminologie und Strafrechtsreform* 1962, 45 (1-2): 15–19.

—————.   "Das Mitopfer" (Second Victims), *Zeitschrift für die Gesamte Strafrechtwissenschaft* (Berlin) 1967, 78 (3): 407–419.

Voss, H.L., and   "Patterns in Criminal Homicide in Chicago," *Journal of Crimi-*
J. R. Hepburn   *nal Law, Criminology and Police Science* 1968, 59 (4): 499–508.

Weiner, I.B.   "On Incest: A Survey," *Abstracts on Criminology and Penology* 1964, 4: 137–155.

Whitlock, F.A.   *Death on the Road. A Study in Social Violence.* London: Tavistock Publications, 1971.

Wilkins, L.G.,   "Helpless under Attack: Hypnotic Abreaction in Hysterical
and P.B. Field   Loss of Vision," *American Journal of Clinical Hypnosis* 1968, 19 (4): 271–275.

Williams, G.   "Victims as Parties to Crimes: A Further Comment," *Criminal Law Review* (U.K.) 1964, 10: 686–691.

Willmer, A.P.   *Crime and Information Theory.* Edinburgh, Edinburgh University Press, 1970.

Wolfgang, M.E.   "The Victims of Crime," in M. E. Wolfgang, *Crime and Race:*
and B. Cohen   *Conceptions and Misconceptions.* New York: Institute of Human Relations Press, 1970, 40–56.

Woods, G. D.   "Some Aspects of Pack Rape in Sydney," *Australian and New Zealand Journal of Criminology* 1969, 2 (July): 105–119.

Yamaoka, K.   "Patterns of Criminal Behavior: Sexual Offenses," *Acta Criminologiae et Medicinae Legalis Japonica* (Tokyo) 1965, 31 (2): 73–74.

Yamaoka, K.   "Sexual Offenses in Urban Areas," *Acta Criminol. Med. Leg. Jap.* 1968, 34 (1): 32–33. (In Japanese).

Research investigators, clinicians, and the lay public seeking bibliographical information on the abused and battered child are referred to *Selected References on the Abused and Battered Child,* National Institute of Mental Health, DHEW Publication No. (HSM) 73–9034. Washington, D.C.: U.S. Government Printing Office, 1972. A supplemental list has been published in mimeographed form on June 1, 1973.

Introduction

The concept of victimization is generally limited to select types of interpersonal relationships, mostly involving drama, violence, and blood. More likely than not, most people would identify the notion of victim with a narrow range of crimes, like murder, assault, robbery, and rape. But it appears that this view of whom the victims are or can be is too limited. The current debate about consumer problems, the environment, poverty and malnutrition in the midst of affluence, the struggle of minorities and of women to gain recognition and economic power, the failures of the justice system, the scandals surrounding the treatment of old-aged people, mentally retarded, and mentally ill persons, require that an enlarged list of victims receive the attention of criminologists and other scholars. So do the recurring instances of genocide, displacement, and persecution of select groups at the hand of other, more powerful ones; the various forms of colonialism; the misuse of psychiatric labels and facilities to suppress dissent and stifle opposition; the acceptance and support of belief systems to justify oppression and discrimination, instead of examining the issues involved objectively and scientifically.

The victimological literature in this area is rather scarce. Apparently victimologists have accepted the most common, less controversial, more easily applicable definition of who the victims are. Fewer of them have ventured into that more perilous type of research and discourse which would make them vulnerable to accusations of social and political activism, lack of value-free and objective analysis, bleeding heart liberalism, and worse.

The article by Dadrian examines victimization through genocide as a function of intergroup conflict. In this light, victimization is viewed as a bilateral form of collective behavior in which perpetrator and victim act as interdependent units. Although the historical material used for this analysis refers to the extermination of the Armenians in Turkey, the analytical framework and the conclusions reached by Dadrian are applicable to similar instances elsewhere.

While illness, old age, being a woman are not usually thought of in deviation terms, Halleck shows how people in such conditions are actually victimized by society with the connivance, if not open cooperation, of the psychiatric profession. According to Halleck, the writings and teachings of psychiatry have helped to provide a rationale for negating change and justifying oppression.

121

In a similar vein, Dr. Ryan, the author of *Blaming the Victim,* believes that he has captured the essence of the ideology by which, mostly through subconcious processes, even those concerned with the plight of the impoverished and forgotten tend to further the existence of the causes that produce such plight instead of arresting or eliminating them. Scapegoating is nothing new, nor is there any reason to believe that wealth and power enable people to be honest and decent enough to control the mind's ever-ready capacity to fool itself and make use of others for all sorts of reasons. Ryan, a psychologist and a political activist, analyzes scapegoating as a social art by which society victimizes its less fortunate members.

11

The Structural-Functional Components of Genocide: A Victimological Approach to the Armenian Case

Vahakn N. Dadrian

A Methodogical Note

In order to somewhat circumscribe the discussion and to avoid terminological uncertainty, a tentative definition of genocide is offered here as a preliminary step.

> *Genocide* is the successful attempt by a dominant group, vested with formal authority and with preponderant access to the overall resources of power, to reduce by coercion or lethal violence the number of a minority group whose ultimate extermination is held desirable and useful and whose respective vulnerability is a major factor contributing to the decision of genocide.
>
> Genocide therefore requires at least two polar elements, i.e., a perpetrator and a victim whose patterned mutual relationships point to the *structural* dimensions[1] of the problem and whose conflict-oriented interactions signalize the dynamic character of a process of victimization through which a resolution of the conflict is sought. In this broader sense, genocide has a *functional* quality.

A principal argument of this definition is that victimization through genocide is a function of a special type of intergroup relation or more particularly, of intergroup conflict. In this sense, victimization is not viewed as a unilateral but rather a bilateral form of collective behavior in which perpetrator and victim are discerned as interdependent units. However, to the extent that such behavior is conflict-ridden and therefore is mainly bent on conflict resolution, it transcends the narrow limits of victimization as a problem-focus. Even though in conception, design and execution, genocide may be regarded as a phenomenon *sui generis,* in terms of underlying structural contingencies and projective goals, it is functional; it subserves the ultimate end of equilibrium of a system beset by disarray through acute group conflict. For the purpose of the present paper therefore, the following question will provide the framework of inquiry. Under what

Paper presented at the Interamerican Congress of Criminology, Caracas, Venezuela, November 1972. This slightly edited version is printed by permission of the author.

conditions does a social system yield certain types of group-relationships through which the bipolar elements of perpetrator and victim crystallize themselves? More importantly, what are the specific circumstances under which collective victimization does actually take place in such a system?

It is argued that certain social systems are inherently capable of generating patterns of intergroup conflict leading to the perpetrator-victim bipolarity, and as such are latent factors of genocide. By the same token, actual perpetrator and victim roles imply the attributes of potential perpetrator and potential victim, with potentiality being recognized as a factor that is residual in the social system. Departing from this premise, it is hypothesized that genocide is a special social process of interaction through which a potential perpetrator group and a potential victim group through a developing conflict are transformed into an actual perpetrator and an actual victim group. It goes without saying that such a hypothesis focusing on a process of transformation, having to deal with the interplay of certain existing and conflicting statuses and roles, refers only to a particular set of intergroup relations; it therefore precludes the idea of genocide occurring in *any* social setting with reference to *any* intergroup conflict.

Moreover, the interactional emphasis and the mutually attuned interpretations and symbolism implied by it, endows the above hypothesis with a perspective in which victim and perpetrator may be seen as dynamically intertwined subunits within a system in which and through which a genocide is enacted. Consequently, the overall purpose of the inquiry may better be served by the application of a broader context of analysis. Given the limitations of space, though, it must be emphasized that this entire discussion is, by necessity, a mere sketch of the ingredients of such an analysis.

The Historical Dimension of the Problem

Any discussion of a given social structure must by necessity by predicated upon some historical account. Structures are not mechanically supplied but they are developed over periods of time through a chain of interconnected events (Moore, 1958: 128). A pertinent analysis has therefore to reckon with the dual criteria of cumulativeness as well as interactiveness of the components of social structure, especially when developmental phases of intergroup relations are involved.

In considering the Armenian holocaust as a case of genocidal victimization, the historical advent of the Ottoman Empire and its social rudiments call for singling out. The advent is marked by the overthrow of the Byzantine Empire in the fifteenth century (1452) resulting in the capture of Constantinople. This success reflected the decisiveness of the preponderance of martial aptitudes and belligerence subsequently became a determinant in the career of the Ottoman Empire, particularly with reference to the nationalities and minorities thus falling under Ottoman rule. Such belligerence was best epitomized by the prevalent Turkish mott: *kilidjimin hakki ile,* i.e., "by the right of my sword," and it preempted the evolving social relations within the confines of the empire in terms of the two polar categories of victor and vanquished, or in terms of a categorical dominant group and subject minorities. A distinct feature of this development was the relative absoluteness and permanence of the social lines of demarcation which lasted almost five centuries — but not before its culmination in genocide that coincided with the demise of the empire. The fact of a historical military conquest was accented by a durable social structure reflecting that conquest.

In accounting for the durability of the Ottoman social system, or more specifically its social structure, one has to consider the concept and fact of theocracy. From its very inception, the Ottoman Empire has been animated by the religious laws of the Islam which, if regarded as an ideological axis, revolved around the two poles of (1) "peace" *(Dar-ul-Islam)* and (b) "war" *(Dar-ul-harb).* Whenever opportune, this duality constrained the theocratic system to wage holy war, *djihad,* against the infidels, i.e., non-Moslems, until such time as the entire society could be regarded as suffused with the conditions of Islam (Levy, 1962: 66).

On the other hand, however, in the Testament, one of the injunctions concerned the "protection" of non-Moslems — provided a price was exacted from them willingly or "under subjection, being humbled" (Koran 9, 29). Thus military conquest, theocracy, and a sense of economic utility combined to sustain the principle of subjugation on which the Ottoman social system became anchored.

The Potential Elements of Victimization —
The Structural Determinant of Power

Up until its historical disintegration, that is, 1918, the Ottoman Empire remained essentially theocratic and thereby it not only sanctioned conquest and belligerence as a *modus operandi* of its rulers, but it also reinforced the practice of sustained subjugation of non-Moslem nationalities and minorities. As a result, for nearly five centuries, political attitudes were fostered which formed a matrix of strain within the system. These attitudes were linked with certain stigmas which the Moslem dominant group attached to the existence of subject races, which were regarded as "flocks and herds" — to quote Toynbee (1957: 362). The label *raja* denoting the idea of cattle was an expression of this stigma. It was this "contempt" which prompted the Turk "to test the sharpness of his sword upon the neck of any Christian" (1918: 274, 280). The imposition of legal disabilities — Armenians could not bear arms (Toynbee, 1915): 20) in a society where martial spirit and lethal violence were established cultural patterns; their testimony in courts was of little value and they were precluded from military service —

helped institutionalize the principle of subjugation. Thus the Armenians were by and large left at the mercy of the members of the dominant group – both individually and as a group. This self-sustaining exposure to misuse and abuse in manifold forms not only helped embolden the dominant group, but it concomitantly emasculated the minority, rendering it helpless, meak, and a viable target for exploitation (heavy tax levies) and, in times of national crises, scapegoating. The leverages of power on the part of the dominant group were matched by the vulnerability on the part of the minority.

This disparate interdependence within the framework of Ottoman society found its reflection in certain types of social relationships which served to encourage victimization; the relationships were mainly capable of generating mutually attuned role patterns – coercion vs. submission – revolving around the bipolar axis of perpetrator and victim. The principle of potentiality stems from this condition. In brief, potentiality is seen here as a by-product of a power disparity issuing from unequal or disparate statuses and expressed in the twin concept of institutionalized superordination – subordination, and characterizing the perpetrator-victim relationship. The leverages of coercive power, attended by elements of strain in intergroup relations, point to the principle of potentiality as a structural determinant. The truism needs to be repeated that there are limits to which a powerless, subjugated minority can avert or even resist the schemes of a powerful, dominant group bent on its extermination. By the same token, given certain cultural traditions, an acute awareness of this fact by the dominant group – as well as by the minority itself – tends to amplify the condition of potentiality discussed above.

The Potential Elements of Victimization –
The Functions and Dysfunctions of Economic
Ascendancy of the Victim

By invoking the principle of "universalistic understanding of crime" as opposed to that of "formalistic-individualistic," Schafer depicts "the normative organization and value structure of the society in which the criminal and his victim live" as the proper perspective with which to study crime involving "complex interactions, group characteristics and social problems." He further perceives a "functional" nexus between perpetrator and victim whose "relationship to each other and the social values determine their correlate functional responsibilities." In this "unitary view of crime" the victim is discerned "as one injured by the crime and as a participant in it" (Schafer, 1968: 31-33).

The dominant Turks for centuries placed a high premium upon such occupations as the military, government and civil service, or land ownership, for example. This kind of criterion for high-status position was reinforced by a corresponding low esteem, bordering on contempt, for occupations involving commerce and industry. In line with such values, Armenians were excluded from the military, their government services were mostly incidental and *ex officio* and until the middle of the nineteenth century, a large segment of the Armenian population was pastoral and agricultural. The Turkish scorn for trade created a serious vacuum in the economy. Indeed, "to stoop to . . . trades and finances was degrading to a Turk" (Lengyel, 1941: 185. See also Mears, 1924: 398). Even though they represented a mere 12 percent of the total population of the Ottoman Empire – about 1.8 million altogether – the Armenians dominated the fields of banking and money lending. . . Moreover, by the second half of the nineteenth century clothing manufacturing, mining, shipping, and milling were mostly controlled by Armenians.

Status deficiencies and impediments served to generate adjustment processes on the part of the minority which in the long run helped establish a sort of equilibrium in the social system. In other words there developed and functioned what Shafer defines as "a nefarious symbiosis" (1968: 39). In his analysis of the Armenian case, Stryker in his turn confirms the operation of "symbiotic" relationships with the dominant group by virtue of which the subject Armenians "concentrated in occupations which were at the same time functionally important, financially remunerative, conspicuous, and socially despicable" (1959: 351). How firm or tenuous was this equilibrium, and what were the pitfalls under which it was liable to be disrupted and to give way to a state of disequilibrium? Such a transition or change is tantamount to a condition of functionalness alternating with, or being converted into, its opposite – dysfunctionalness.

In this sketchy utilization of the structural-functional approach, it may be necessary to touch on the incidence of this functional-dysfunctional dichotomy. First to consider in this respect is the process by which the Armenians in the Ottoman system emerged as a dominant group in commerce and industry. Notwithstanding prevailing notions suggesting that business acumen was "inborn" or was an inveterate national trait or characteristic of the Armenians, it was namely in large measure a question of available alternatives in the occupational hierarchy of the system, which prompted Armenians to gravitate to commerce – whether driven by ambition or by a sense of sheer survival. As Turkish attitudes of scorn persisted and consequently the field was almost totally degraded and neglected, large groups of Armenians, in spite of and perhaps even because of the handicaps, concentrated in commerce and industry.

In the absence of competition from members of the dominant group, the Armenian merchant class . . . attained a degree of prosperity which tended to defy its functional character and gradually assumed dysfunctional proportions, as far as the dominant group was concerned. (Two main noneconomic factors tended to contribute to this development: the rise of Turkish nationalism and a measure of Armenian ethnocentrism which resisted assimilation through conversion.) The burden of the entire argument is that Armenian economic ascendancy in terms of its extraeconomic impacts upon the system introduced psychic and political imbalances into that system. As a rule, the onset of imbalances in some parts of a system do find their reflection in or spill over other parts of the system. The onset may be (a) cumulative or (b) precipitate.

(a) The preceding discussion was intended to highlight the cumulative aspect of it; namely, the developmental affluence attained by the subject minority — a process which Toynbee suggested to be inevitable (1915: 20). When a minority group, suffering from a series of legal disabilities and from a denial of access to the resources of political power, achieves economic ascendancy, it acquires a leverage which is at once tenuous and dangerous. The danger lies in rendering itself a more attractive and a profitable target. It is tenuous because the powerful dominant group has the means to dispose of the accrued wealth — whenever and wherever opportune. The problem becomes compounded in relation to the degree to which the wealth of the minority is somehow commensurate to the lack of wealth of the dominant group — as perceived and defined by the latter. The social system becomes further strained with the encumbrance of status inconsistencies and role confusions which tend to upset the superordination-subordination principle.

An additional factor accenting this process of cumulative vulnerability of the Armenians was the crystallization of concrete negative images attending their commercial preponderance and economic prosperity. In drawing parallels between the Jews victimized in Germany and the Armenians, Stryker for instance mentions certain negative traits and characteristics attributed to the latter (1959: 346). Needless to say that the conditions of political oppression, legal handicaps, and memories of recurrent pogroms were germane to encouraging certain patterns of behavior in which resourcefulness, shrewdness, grasping, and opportunism became deviously intertwined, particularly with respect to the pursuit of business, which was so degraded by the dominant group. Whether viewed culturally or in terms of political realities, success was bound to be a dubious distinction and ultimately proved a liability — notwithstanding the fact that up until World War I, the bulk of the Armenian population in the Ottoman Empire were struggling peasants.

This is another instance of the argument recognizing the presence in a system of potential elements of victimization to which both perpetrator and victim are capable of contributing through differential and disparate statuses but interactive roles in that system.

(b) As mentioned above, the second type of imbalance refers to precipitate factors. The periodic and recurrent massacres preceding the genocide of World War I were the by-products of emergent crises besetting the rulers of the Ottoman Empire. Their culmination in the holocaust was mainly due to the exigencies, hardships, and setbacks ushered in by the episodes of World War I that produced mainfold and acute imbalances, particularly with respect to economics. They compounded the lesser but lingering imbalances resulting from the excesses of the monolithic Union and Program party of the Young Turks who acceeded to power in 1908, and specially resulting from the conflagrations of two Balkan wars preceding World War I (see Morgenthau, 1918: 279).

It is no accident that the two principal instances of genocide of this century coincided with the episodes of two global wars. As a cataclysmic agent of disequilibrium entailing manifold crises in the system, such wars tend to overshadow or displace regular social control mechanisms and open up new radical vistas of problem-solving behavior. Presently, one such radical vista was the definition of the sources of the conflict and the charting of an equally radical course of resolution of that conflict — in accord with one's relationship to the contestant. In other words, the quest of expediently locating and dealing with various agents of frustration became a cardinal preoccupation (Dadrian, 1971: 394-417). In this quest, great sensitivity was exercised toward the principle of vulnerability and availability of a subject to be victimized. Conflict issues were simplified and reduced (Dadrian, 1968: 115-122) and by recourse to a notion of economic exploitation attributed to the Armenians, the suitable and potential victims, the latter were converted into an actual victim (Higgins, 1963: 254); at the same time their victimization was "denied" through what Sykes and Matza call "techniques of neutralization" (1957: 668).

Interactive Nationalism and Ethnocentrism as Potential Factors of Victimization

To the extent that genocide is functional in both intent and consequence, its ultimate enactment is associated with the deliberate exercise of power which is more or less institutionalized and involves some form of political authority (Bierstedt, 15, no. 6:730-738). In the last resort, genocide must therefore be understood in a political context in which the interplay of rival resources, conflicting institutions and organizations, the pitting against each other of oppositional numbers and competing leadership strata emerge as the constitutive elements of the power syndrome. The disparate configuration of these elements has a structural character and their polar arrangement in the social system marks the line through which perpetrator and victim may be conceptually separated — conceptually but not empirically. For the thrust of this entire paper is to highlight the criminological principle of the dynamic and functional interdependence of perpetrator and victim through which "the contribution of the victim to the genesis of crime" is depicted as a factor in the conception, design, and implementation of the genocide under discussion.

In Ottoman society, the relationship between the Turks, the ruler, and the Armenians, the ruled, embodied the sociological principle of domination. In his cogent analysis of this phenomenon, Simmel aptly insisted that domination "is a case of interaction" and that "even in the most oppressive and cruel cases of subordination, there is still a considerable measure of personal freedom" for the oppressed, namely the will not to submit or to resist coercion. In the absence of such a will, interaction tends to sustain itself and becomes "mutually determined" (1957: 181-3).

With respect to the case at hand, these mutually determined interactions proved most consequential politically when they eventually crystallized themselves into movements involving the nationalism of the superordinate, on the one hand, and the ethnocentrism of the subordinate group, on the other. Naturally, depending on the conditions of a given social system, not only the forms of domination but also the forms of submission and response to domination may vary. In the theocratic and militant structure of Ottoman society, the forms of submission on the part of the Armenians were bound to be ethnocentric. The practice of social distance, religious absolutism, overall discrimination, and political disfranchising combined to foster a type of segregation in which ethnicity thrived. Whether on the level of community life in general, or in the sphere of religion and church activities, the Armenians were impelled to cultivate self-images in which a sense of separation and distinctness prevailed. This process was stimulated by an acute sense of antiquity marking the historical preeminence of the Armenians as the first nation to embrace Christianity about the turn of the fourth century. It was reinforced by the Ottoman regime which created and sanctioned the *millet* system by virtue of which, the Armenians like other non-Moslem minorities, were designated and treated as religious communities enjoying a corresponding autonomy. The formation of what Boettiger calls a "separate complex" involving attitudes of self-sufficiency and conservatism (1920: no. 14) was further accented by patriarchal familism and the character of the Armenian church which an eminent author called "a national church" (Ormanian, 1955: 189-92). Until mid-nineteenth century, the civil government of the Armenian community was controlled by the "autocratic rule of the Church" (Stryker, 1959: 347). Additional factors which helped ethnicity transform into an ethnocentric drive were the contagious advent of nationalism and national movements in Europe and the Bakans, the influx of Western ideas among the Armenian intellectuals (Etmekjian, 1964), the inroads made by protestant missionaries in Armenian communities and, most importantly, the rise of Armenian political parties bent on improving the minority status involved. While the bulk of the Armenians in Ottoman Turkey might be termed ethnocentric, the attitudes of the members of these parties — a very small fraction of the entire population — ranged from self-assertive to militant nationalism (Arpee, 1946).

It needs to be emphasized that all these activities and events transpired within the framework of Ottoman society and in constant interaction with the dominant group.

On the one hand beset by the processes of decay and disintegration of the empire, and on the other stirred by the pathos of sweeping nationalism (Nalbandian, 1963), the Ottoman Turks embarked upon a major campaign to change the social structure of the Ottoman society as an antidote to internal discord and conflict, and also as a means of recapturing imperial, Panturkic glory. By recourse to an admixture of religious and political ideologies, including Panturanism (Zarevand, 1971), they sought to *convert the society from its heterogenous makeup into a homogeneous unit. Here genocide became a means for the end of a radical structural change in the system.* Under the banner of a monolithic political party, i.e., Union and Progress, the Young Turks set out to eliminate what they considered to be a major obstacle in this respect — the Armenians. Their accession to power attended by organizational controls and purposive mobilization of resources was matched by the optimum emasculation of the Armenian community. In the key decision-making process and in the subsequent sensitizing and inciting of the masses against the selected target, seditious and conspiratorial designs and deeds were attributed to the Armenian population of the Empire when in fact the vast majority of that population was apolitical, let alone conspiratorial, in attitude (Bryce, 1916: 627, 629, 631, 633).

This particular aspect of intergroup conflict has a substantial bearing upon the mechanism of victimization in genocide, specially with respect to the two determinants of genocide, namely, (a) the leverages of power of the dominant group and (b) the vulnerabilities of the subject minority.

(a) When a segment of the leadership of the latter in interaction with the dominant group proves, or is defined to prove, provocative in terms of militancy involving some form of nationalism, the response of the dominant group is in large measure determined by the leverages of power it disposes. Naturally, culture, tradition, and precedents do also play a role. But the decisive factor in proceeding to condemn the entire group, instead of singling out the real or imaginary culprits, is the keen awareness of power and a willingness to mobilize the resources of that power for the act of total condemnation. Moreover, the resources of power do not need to be confined to the residues of formal authority. Indeed, in the present case, the scale and efficacy of the genocide was mainly due to the preponderance of the resources of informal power which the Union and Progress party of the Young Turks skillfully brought to bear upon the implementation phase of genocide; these resources exceeded and even overwhelmed the authority of the formal government of the Ottoman Empire.

(b) The problem of vulnerability of the potential victim is intimately and dynamically linked with the conditions of the power of the dominant group just discussed. A powerful potential perpetrator can easily afford to rationalize, distort, generalize, and simplify in defense of its schemes and acts of genocide. The absence of actual and effective deterrence and/or of fear of prospective retribution serve to embolden it, to the degree that the ire it generates is conveniently extended to the entire group. Thus, genocidal behavior is conditioned, if not invited, by the cardinal fact of the vulnerability of the potential victim and more importantly by an awareness and careful assessment of that fact by the perpetrator. What is implied here is the notion that a less vulnerable victim group, capable of resisting or of some measure of retaliation, may function to encumber the decision-making processes and to reduce the scope and intensity of victimization in genocide. In this sense, it may be observed that whereas conditions relative to designs of extermination may involve rational calculations, conditions of vulnerability, however, seem to invite irrational violence as a way of implementing the designs and as a by-product of these conditions of power.[2]

In brief, to the extent that the perpetrator avoids differentiating between specific sources of frustration and elects to discharge its anger against an entire group, marked by its availability and vulnerability, empirically the victim group becomes a contributor (Thomas, 1967: 42). As Shafer put it: "The victim's crime precipitation may range in intensity from making a person conscious of a criminal opportunity to simple passivity, a higher degree of irritation, incitement, instigation or provocation" (1968: 80).

The Opportunity Structure: The Ultimate Agent of Transforming a Potential Perpetrator-Victim Relationship into an Actual One

It was indicated earlier that the exigencies and deprivations of a war, particularly global war, tend to accentuate not only the frustration-aggression cycle affecting the perpetrator group, but they also optimize the vulnerability of the victim group. The dominant group is afforded all sorts of leeways and latitudes to marshall its resources to enact extreme measures bent on further impairing the victim group. Eventually, the latter is isolated, fragmented, and nearly totally emasculated through the control of channels of communication, wartime secrecy, the various sections of the wartime apparatus, police and secret service, and the constant invocation of the principle of national security. In the present case, the demographic factor of scattered Armenian communities, many of them having been situated in remote mountain areas and villages of the land, decisively aided the process of their isolation, fragmentation, and ultimate emasculation. In other words, the opportunity structure afforded by a war is but an extension of the category of vulnerability of the victim whose liability for victimization thus becomes more pronounced.

In other words, considering the risks of internal and external counteractions which are germane to any enactment of genocide, the emergency conditions of war serve to minimize these risks thereby maximizing the chances of success. Operationally as well as functionally, it is the principle of such success that is most crucial. Indeed, the anticipation of such success helps overcome scruples, hesitations, or inhibitions in the process of decision-making, serves to obviate fears of adverse consequences, emboldens the potential perpetrator, and given the impulses of the acute wartime nationalism of the perpetrator group, facilitates the investing of the entire genocidal enterprise with a sacrosanct purpose.

It is no accident that the two principal genocides of this century were consummated during the two World Wars of the century. The evidence of interconnection is provided by Hitler. During the Nuremberg trials, it was brought out and underscored that shortly before the Polish campaign, in a conference with high level German military commanders in charge of the campaign, Hitler outlined his genocidal designs. When confronted with expressions of dismay on the part of some of the military present, as a way of assuaging their anxieties, Hitler is known to have retorted: "Who after all speaks today of the annihilation of the Armenians? . . . The world believes in success alone."[3]

There are some points which call for depicting. First, the design for extermination is advanced in connection with military operations and within the framework of war and warfare. Second, to the onus which atrocities may momentarily bring forth, is counterposed the specter of mankind's obliviousness – in due course of time to follow with certainty. This point is substantiated with a specific reference to the Armenian holocaust. Finally, there is the enunciation of an ethos, a credo that in the last analysis it is not the horror of atrocities that will be consequential but rather the efficiency with which the atrocities may be carried out.

Whether in terms of decision-making processes, implementation, or overall leadership attitudes, in this posture a sense of wartime opportunity, of a concomitant optimum vulnerability of the potential victim, defiant boldness, and a measure of intoxication with the spell of anticipatory success are singularly intertwined.

About a quarter of a century earlier, Taleat, the Ottoman Minister of Internal Affairs, an ardent young Turk and a chief architect of the World War I genocide enunciated an almost identical credo. The wording of it is supplied by Halide Edib, herself a pillar of Turkish Panturanism, who tried to account for the Minister's "extermination of his kind," i.e., the Armenians, by labeling him as "an idealist." According to this authoress, Taleat formulated the main rationale for the genocide he engineered as follows: "I have the conviction that as long as a nation does the best for its interest and succeeds, the world admires it and thinks it moral."[4]

Once more, it should be stressed that the invocation of supreme national interests is not only common to all nations engaged in exacting warfare, but given certain cultural values and traditions, as well as structural determinants, it can become perilously critical for subject minorities, whose enhanced vulnerabilities for extermination via scapegoating, ideological designs, economic opportunism or homogenic nationalism on the part of the perpetrator group can, under opportune circumstances, stimulate the latter to become prepossessed with an elan for success in terms of its projective goals. Wartime conditions enable such a group to convert its genocidal propensities into genocidal proclivities. In this overall view, Taleat and Hitler emerge as supplying a connecting link between the two episodes of genocide and thereby also the social psychological mechanism of a common denominator for these episodes.

Notes

1. In exploring this theme, recognition is due to Smelser whose treatment of collective behavior in terms of its emphasis on structural determinants was a major source for the theoretical orientation of this paper. Smelser, *Theory of Collective Behavior,* New York: The Free Press of Glencoe (1963).
2. This massive lethal violence entailed more than one million victims. Precise figures are not available and understandably are hard to obtain. But the following adumbration of estimates and accounts may give an approximate picture of the number of Armenian casualties by death. Toynbee estimates that by midsummer 1916, i.e., in a period of about one year, 600,000 perished. He further points out that at this time there were 500,000 deported survivors in the desert regions of Der-er-Zor (Bryce, op. cit., p. 651), who eventually perished as a result of exposure, hunger and disease, as well as subsequent "three great massacres" on the spot. (*The Memoirs of Naim Bey,* AHRA publication, Philadelphia, 1964, p. XII)
3. Marjorie Housepian, "The Unremembered Genocide," *Commentary* 42, no. 3, September 1966.
4. *Memoirs of Halide Edib,* London, 1926, p. 387.

References

Aflalo, F.G.
1911 — *Regilding the Crescent,* Philadelphia: p. 195-96. (Also, L. Levonian, The Turkish Press: *Selections from the Turkish Press Showing Events and Opinions, 1925–1932.* Athens: 1932, p. 169–180.)

Arpee, Leon
1946 — *A Century of Armenian Protestantism.* New York: Armenian Missionary Association of America.

Bierstedt, Robert — "An Analysis of Social Power." *American Sociological Review* 15, no. 6: 730–738.

Boettiger, L.A.
1920 — *Armenian Legends and Festivals.* Minneapolis: Research Publications of the University of Minnesota, Studies in Social Sciences, no. 14,

Bryce, Viscount   *The Treatment of the Armenians in the Ottoman Empire.* Lon-
1916a   don: Sir J. Causton and Sons, p. 616.
1916b   *The Treatment of the Armenians in the Ottoman Empire.* Lon-
               don: Sir J. Causton and Sons, p. 627, 629, 631, 633. (In
               refuting this kind of charge Toynbee declared that it will not
               "bear examination . . . is easily rebutted [to conclude that]
               the war was merely an opportunity and not a cause." *Experi-
               ences,* Oxford, 1969. p. 341.)

Cahnmann, Werner   "Religion and Nationality," *Sociology and History.* Glencoe,
1964   Ill.: The Free Press, p. 275.

Dadrian, Vahakn   "Egocentric Factors in Ethnocentrism – The Structural Deter-
1968   minants of Modern Nationalism." *Sociologus* 18, no. 2: 115–
               122.
1971   "Factors of Anger and Aggression." *Journal of Human Rela-
               tions* 19, no. 3: 394–417.

Etmekjian, James   *The French Influence on the Western Armenian Renaissance.*
1964   New York: Twayne Publishers.

Glick, C.E.   "Social Roles and Types in Race Relations" in A. W. Lind
1955   (ed.), *Race Relations in World Perspective.* Honolulu: Univer-
               sity of Hawaii Press, p. 240.

Higgins, Trumbull   *Winston Churchill and the Dardanelles.* New York: Mac-
1963   millan, p. 254.

Lengyel, E.   *Turkey.* New York: Random House, p. 185
1941

Levy, Reubin   *The Social Structure of Islam.* Cambridge, England: Cambridge
1962   Univ. Press, p. 66.

Lieberson, Stanley   "A Societal Theory of Race and Ethnic Relations."
1961   *American Sociological Review* 26, no. 6 (December): 903.

Mears, E. G.   *Modern Turkey.* New York: Macmillan, p. 398.
1924

Moore, Barrington   *Political Power and Social Theory.* Cambridge, Massachu-
1958   setts: Harvard University Press, p. 128. (Also, Ralph Dahren-
               dorf, "Out of Utopia: Toward a Reorientation of Sociological
               Analysis," *American Journal of Sociology* 64:115.)

Morgenthau, Henry   *Ambassador Morgenthau's Story.* Garden City, New York:
1918   Doubleday and Page, p. 276–77.

Nalbandian, Louise   *The Armenian Revolutionary Movement.* Berkeley:
1963   University of California Press.

Naslian, Jean (Mgr.) *Les Memoirs.* Volumes I and II, Vienna: The Mechitarist
1955   Publishing House.

Ormanian, Malachia *The Church of Armenia, 2nd rev. ed. London:* Mowbray,
1955   Ch. 45: 189–192.

Shafer, Stephen *The Victim and His Criminal.* New York: Random House,
1968   p. 31–33.

Stryker, Sheldon "Social Structure and Prejudice." *Social Problems* 6: 346.
1959

Sykes, Gresham, and   "Techniques of Neutralization: A Theory of Delin-
Matza, David   quincy." *American Sociological Review* 22 (December):
1957   668.

Thomas, W. I.   *The Unadjusted Girl.* New York: Harper and Row, p. 42.
1967

Toynbee, Arnold   *A Study of History* (abridgement of vols. 7–10), New York:
1957   Oxford University Press, p. 362.
1915   *Armenian Atrocities – The Murder of a Nation.* London:
                Sir J. Causton and Sons, p. 20.

Williams, Talcott   *Turkey – A World Problem of Today.* New York: Double-
1921   day, p. 292.

Wolff, Kurt   *The Sociology of Georg Simmel.* Glencoe, Ill.: Free Press,
1957   p. 181–183.

Zarevand (V. N. Dadrian, translator)   *United and Independent Turania: Aims
1971   and Designs of the Turks.* Leiden: Brill Publishers.

12 The Uses of Abnormality

Seymour L. Halleck

The psychiatrist is granted more power than the ordinary man to influence the standards of conduct within his community. To begin with, he is allowed to certify the abnormality of certain people by making them become patients. As the one who decides who is to be a patient, the psychiatrist can comment liberally on what constitutes normal or abnormal behavior within his community. The psychiatrist's prestige as a doctor of medicine is such that the public is likely to take his pronouncements seriously.

The power to define standards of normality can be used either to change or stabilize the society. Some psychiatrists feel that community standards are overly restrictive; they are likely to encourage their patients and the public to believe that greater freedom in all areas of life is synonymous with mental health. Probably at least a few psychiatrists believe that community standards are not rigid enough; they will encourage their patients and the society to accept greater discipline and control. Most psychiatrists, however, define mental health, or normality, in terms of acceptable community standards. In their practice and in their public postures they tend to stabilize those institutions that are currently popular and acceptable to the majority of citizens.

By the very nature of his work the psychiatrist learns to equate deviation from community norms with abnormality or sickness. Sociologists and psychiatrists have long recognized that people who behave differently from their neighbors are more likely to become psychiatric patients than those who behave conventionally, but this relationship has never been satisfactorily explained.[1] Perhaps it exists because those who behave unconventionally are inherently unhappy people; perhaps they would be unhappy in any environment. Or, perhaps the socially deviant become patients because society imposes so many restrictions on them that they become unhappy. Or, conceivably, those who view the world a little differently from their neighbors are simply more accepting of the role of psychiatric patient. Whatever the reasons for the correlation, the psychiatrist regularly encounters and treats people who are both unhappy and different. Because he views his patient's unhappiness as a form of illness, he eventually learns to think of his patient's "difference" as a manifestation of illness.

The general impact of the psychiatrist's work with deviant individuals and his public pronouncements about them tends to be in the direction of negating the kinds of changes probably desired by those who are different. The patient role deprives one of power. To the extent that those who might initiate change in the society become patients, society is stabilized. Unfortunately, other repressive consequences also follow whenever the medical practitioner has the power to influence community morality. Some people suffer deeply as a result of being defined as abnormal by the psychiatrist. Even when he doesn't label people, his attitudes and public pronouncements may still contribute to keeping in a state of subjugation deviant individuals and groups who are already oppressed.

Again, the psychiatrists's political influence isn't restricted to his role in what Szasz calls "institutional psychiatry,"[2] since he can influence both voluntary and involuntary patients; for that matter his posture on moral issues can affect many who will never become his patients.

The Oppression of a Label

For the most part, the psychiatrist preaches the values of tolerance, permissiveness, and humane treatment in dealing with deviant individuals. However, he sometimes contributes to their oppression directly or indirectly. By virtue of his power to label deviant people as mentally ill, he can take away the freedom of those who are different by putting them in a hospital. The process of labeling also contributes to the oppression of deviant groups in a more subtle manner by strengthening the community's beliefs that those who are different are somehow dangerous or inferior. These issues have been discussed in detail by other psychiatrists such as Thomas Szasz,[3] Ronald Leifer,[4] and Karl Menninger,[5] but they are important enough to review briefly here.

In controlling people who are violent and whose violence seems irrational, the community may have good reason to treat them as if they were sick. But most deviant individuals, however irrational they may be judged, are not violent. Deviant behavior usually does not threaten the safety of others, but it may threaten the community by affronting standards of dignity or propriety or by appearing to reject the existing social order. When nonviolent deviant individuals are labeled as sick, however, the public tends to view them as if they were violent. The community is also likely to restrict them in the same harsh way as those who are violent.

When an individual is given a medical label, society is encouraged to believe that his behavior cannot be controlled; a nonmedical label, on the other hand, leads society to assume that an individual can control his behavior. Thus, a heavy drinker may be thought of as imprudent or obnoxious; however, once we call him an alcoholic, we assume that he cannot control his drinking. If a grown man becomes sexually intimate with a fourteen-year-old girl, we may think that he is gross, insensitive, or stupid. However, once we call him a pedophiliac, we fear that he cannot restrain himself from attacking small children. The movement from a moral to a medical or psychological evaluation of an individual's behavior has both positive and negative consequences. On the one hand, society treats the person who cannot seem to help himself with considerable solicitousness, but it also fears him because presumably he is unable to contain his impulses. Society views him as an inferior person who is dangerous because he lacks the autonomy and control that normal people have. Thus, the community feels justified in imposing restrictions upon him and in rejecting or ignoring whatever he might try to say.

There is, of course, considerable value to diagnosis in ordinary medical practice. Putting people into diagnostic categories makes it convenient for doctors to communicate with one another and enables research to be done. Frequently the diagnosis dictates treatment and enables the physician to prognosticate the patient's fate. In psychiatry, however, diagnostic categories such as schizophrenia, paranoia, psychopathy, or alcoholism are not sufficiently precise so that the doctor can have a clear idea of desirable treatment or prognosis. A schizophrenic may be treated in a variety of ways, all of which can be justified by some theoretical orientation; the diagnosis of schizophrenia tells the doctor little about how long or how severely the patient will suffer. Similar considerations apply to most psychiatric labels.

On the basis of a rather vague concept of what schizophrenia actually is, thousands of Americans are so labeled by psychiatric physicians. Once an individual is designated a schizophrenic he becomes a pariah: he is approached with a mixture of awe, distrust, and sometimes fear by both the doctor and the general public. Employment, particularly in sensitive or important jobs, may be denied to him. The patient's pride and self-confidence are often shattered; he may view himself as afflicted with a disease that makes him incapable of controlling his most undesirable impulses. The very word "schizophrenia" strikes fear in the hearts of many people. I have seen patients who are severely depressed, suicidal, and living in severe states of mental agony, but who seemed to find a perverse kind of reassurance when I told them that they were not schizophrenic.

The diagnostic term "paranoid" has taken on an almost totally pejorative meaning. The term is not restricted to those who behave strangely, are overly suspicious, or tend to blame their failings on others; professionals insensitively apply it to many people who take unusual or deviant positions on social issues, and even nonprofessionals bandy it about loosely. To accuse one's adversary of being paranoid has become a kind of trump card, a powerful weapon for negating the opponent's position.

Consider also the diagnosis of psychopathy. A number of chronically antisocial individuals are believed to be suffering from psychopathy or sociopathy. These individuals are assumed to have a personality defect, an organic defect, or some kind of psychological malfunction that produces their antisocial behavior. Psychiatrists have a great deal of difficulty defining the term "psychopath." Sometimes it is applied to only a few offenders, sometimes to the mass of offenders, and sometimes to any person whose behavior seems offensive. Although the term doesn't have a precise meaning, its social implications are profound; just the concept itself leads the public to believe that many of those who are antisocial are plagued with uncontrollable impulses and must, therefore, be harshly restrained in order to protect "normal" people.

In the area of drugs, a man who uses alcohol or other drugs to excess may be overwhelmed with all sorts of personal and social difficulties and still maintain a respectable role in society. However once he is labeled an alcoholic or addict, he is cast into an entirely different social role – he is viewed as a person who is diseased. Some people will pity him, but a sizable number will fear or scorn him. Under certain circumstances he could lose many of his rights, even though his use of drugs doesn't hurt anyone but himself.

We do not usually think of people who behave so peculiarly that they are labled "schizophrenic," "paranoid," "psychopathic," or "addicted" as would-be reformers of the social order. Yet, much of the behavior that psychiatrists consider symptomatic is at least partly an effort on the part of an individual to communicate with others in order to change something in his environment. The psychiatric label allows those whom the patient might wish to influence to ignore the content of his message and to focus instead on his dangerousness or defectiveness.

It is unlikely that psychiatry can advance scientifically unless its members continue to search for scientific means of classifying deviant behavior. Psychiatrists could help society immeasurably, however, if they would frankly admit that current diagnostic categories do not have much scientific meaning – that they are largely arbitrary. Then society might be able to confront rationally and humanely the moral questions raised by those who behave differently.

Even if the physician uses psychological rather than medical terms to describe his patients, his judgment of the normality of any given behavior has important social consequences. When used by a doctor, terms such as "emotionally disturbed," "conflicted," or "immature" have almost the same social impact as medical expressions. The repressive power of psychological – as opposed to medical – labeling is readily obvious in the area of sexual behavior. The Western world has long been dominated by the Judeo-Christian ethic which emphasizes the immorality of certain sexual practies. Masturbation, oral-genital relations, and other kinds of sexual gratification that do not lead to intercourse are often considered immoral. The same is true of any sexual relationships outside of marriage. The psychiatric profession has never labeled these practices as immoral, nor has it, in recent years at least, labeled them as evidence of illness. It has, however, repeatedly said that some of these behaviors indicate emotional disturbance or immaturity...[6]

It is hard to imagine how anyone could practice psychiatry without some idea of what behavior is good for people and what is not. There must be some standard of normality in order to decide whether a given person needs treatment, how he should be treated, and what should be the treament goals. This standard can be based on biological norms, social utility, or prevailing community mores. The problem here is that the psychiatrist is not required to, nor does he usually go to the trouble to, spell out his standards of normality. The community often believes that his definitions of normality are based on medical facts, while frequently he is only echoing the mores of the majority. Because they determine what is abnormal, psychiatrists can significantly affect the social order; therefore, they should critically reexamine their criteria for making such determinations. They should make these criteria known to their patients, and, when their public pronouncements touch on the question of normality, they should also reveal them to the public.

The Justification of Oppression

A number of social institutions in our country allow certain groups to hold power, while other groups are kept powerless. Many of these institutions came into existence at a time when they served some social or economic need. Laws and customs restricting nonreproductive sexual activity possibly helped to increase the labor force at some past time. The practice of slavery or the establishment of institutions to subjugate women or children may also have produced economic efficiency at some previous time. When social and economic conditions change, however, it becomes difficult to justify the oppression of selected groups on the basis of social utility. Yet, those who hold power are reluctant to give it up. One way in which they can retain power is to develop and perpetuate belief systems that reassure the oppressors (and sometimes convince the oppressed) that the subjugated are somehow dangerous or inferior. Such belief systems or, perhaps more correctly, myths serve to justify oppression.

The psychiatric profession has often loaned its talents to perpetuate unsubstantiated belief systems or myths. Through public pronouncements or attitudes toward patients, psychiatrists have attributed characteristics to oppressed groups that helped convince the rest of society that these people really were dangerous, inferior, or didn't mind being treated as inferior. Again, the psychiatrist has inadvertently used his position to deter society from confronting and dealing with inequities in the distribution of power.

The Homosexual

Acts of physical love with a member of the same sex sometimes bring harsh or brutal punishment. While other unconventional sexual behavior may engender attitudes of similar repressiveness, persecution of the homosexual has become quite common. The community, of course, will want to control the homosexual who attacks or molests children or who seeks his gratification in public. But most homosexuals are more discreet than heterosexuals and are far less predatory and violent. Persecution of the homosexual not only hurts those who have nonconventional sexual tastes, but indirectly helps to keep most males preoccupied with the need to appear virile and to engage in a somewhat aggressive form of heterosexuality.

When an increase in the population was economically desirable, there was probably some justification for imposing restrictions on those who sought sexual gratification through nonreproductive activities. With our present overpopulated world, however, such restrictions seem outmoded and detrimental. Oppression of the homosexual today is primarily maintained by the irrational fear that homosexuality threatens the stability of the society and by the irrational belief that tolerating homosexuality implies weakness.

While most psychiatrists have made repeated pleas for tolerance of homosexuality, their professional attitudes toward homosexual behavior have probably not helped the homosexual's plight. Psychiatrists insist that homosexuality should be treated as an illness,[7] yet there is no convincing evidence that the homosexual differs in any profound biological or psychological manner from the heterosexual. To assert that the homosexual is ill helps to convince both the individual and the public that he cannot control his behavior; this has a detrimental effect on both parties. The homosexual who believes that he is ill feels more driven and less responsible, and the public comes to assume that at any time he can be overwhelmed by a monstrous lust. Both parties are victims of a myth because the homosexual urge is no more powerful or irresistible than the heterosexual urge.

Describing the homosexual as sick has other repressive consequences. When placed in a medical category, the homosexual is usually diagnosed as a sexual deviate, the same category that applies to rapists, child molesters, and sadists. Since the public tends to view all sex deviates as violent, it assumes that the homosexual is potentially violent. Thus, the psychiatric diagnosis leads to restrictions being placed on the homosexual that may be as severe as those placed on the rapist or murderer.

Psychiatrists should frankly acknowledge that they have no way of knowing whether homosexual behavior has enough biological or genetic determinants to justify calling it a disease. Nor is there any justification, even in terms of social expediency, for thinking of consenting adult homosexuality as an illness. The homosexual who is not predatory, who does not bother children, and who is discreet should never be described as a sick person. He should only be thought of as a potential patient if he wants to be a patient.

Oppression of Women

Women generally have second-class status. There is no way of knowing if there is something in woman's psychological nature that makes her content to take a passive or submissive position vis-a-vis men, or if she has been forced into this role because of social needs or circumstances. At one time there was a rationale for confining women to a secondary position. When the ability to secure food and provide shelter were largely dependent upon physical strength, men could contribute more to the community than women. But in our modern technological society physical strength has become a relatively unimportant factor in survival, and there is no apparent rational purpose served by keeping women in a repressed condition.

The tendency of men to enjoy dominating women is quite understandable. So long as women are discouraged from establishing themselves in the business, academic, or political world, men are guaranteed an advantageous position from which to accumulate power and wealth. But men also have psychological reasons for fearing women as equals. If a man is to enjoy the sex act, he must have a sense of security that he is not being called upon to perform at a certain level and that he is not being judged as to his sexual abilities. Without this security he may have difficulty maintaining an erection. So long as women are viewed as second-class citizens, the male need not be too preoccupied with his potency. But if women are equal partners in sexual and other social relations, the male, particularly if he is insecure about his own status, is likely to feel on trial during the sex act. His fear of impotency is especially great at the present time because scientific research has shown that women are capable of enjoying sex as much as, and sometimes even more than, men. It is not too surprising, therefore, to find that even males who are committed to many other forms of human liberation are not too sympathetic toward women's attempts at liberation.

The writings and teachings of psychiatry have helped to provide a rationale for keeping women in a subservient position. The founders of psychoanalysis saw women as basically masochistic and passive — as needing a certain degree of masculine domination in order to feel comfortable and whole. Many outstanding psychiatrists still refer to women in terms of their needs for passivity, to be companions to men, or to be mothers,[8] little mention is made of their need to be active contributors to the larger society. A woman who enters psychotherapy will usually be exposed to a system of values that emphasizes the virtues of passivity; if she rejects these values her therapist may interpret her attitude as immature.

Sometimes the psychiatric view of the psychological needs of women seems to be suspiciously formulated on the assumption of male superiority.[9] For years most psychiatrists and psychoanalysts rigidly held to the doctrine that there was a major difference between clitoral and vaginal orgasms. It was assumed that a woman could not enjoy a vaginal orgasm until she was mature and that her maturity could only be evidenced by her willingness to be submissive and passive. Although the research of Masters and Johnson showed that there is no biological difference between a vaginal and a clitoral orgasm, the teachings of psychiatrists still significantly affect society.[10] Even today some women who experience powerful orgasms through clitoral manipulation but infrequent orgasms during intercourse worry that they may be defective or inadequate.

The repressive attitude of psychiatrists toward women is also apparent in their views on multiple orgasms. For many years psychiatrists doubted that women could have more than one orgasm during an ordinary period of love-making, but when Kinsey reported that some of his subjects frequently experienced multiple orgasms, they insisted that his subjects were either emotionally ill or lying.[11] Not until Masters and Johnson conclusively demonstrated that normal women commonly experience multiple orgasms did psychiatrists reluctantly concede that women (at least in their capacity to experience orgasm) were sexually more powerful than men.[12] Perhaps if male psychiatrists had listened to their patients (or their wives), they would have known better.

We do not really know if women are better off psychologically if they take a secondary role to man or if they have a role as an equal. Unfortunately, psychiatrists have not helped to clarify the situation; by accepting the prevailing belief systems of the community and by strengthening them with psychological interpretations, psychiatrists have deterred society from examining this issue objectively.[13] But if he does not wish to be an oppressor himself, the psychiatrist should be willing to allow his women patients a fair chance to experiment with more aggressive and, conceivably, more fulfilling patterns of behavior.

The Poor and the Black

Oppression of the poor and the black is one of the tragic realities of American life. At first glance the psychiatric profession's record in dealing with these groups looks good: with rare exceptions psychiatrists have emphasized that social discrimination and prejudice — rather than innate weakness or illness — are the main causes of the unhappiness of both groups. However, the profession has also taken an implied negative stand toward these people by ignoring their mental health needs. By failing to uncover, dramatize, or treat the problems of poverty-stricken or minority groups, the psychiatrist has made it easier for society to ignore their problems. Furthermore, even with a growing awareness of the susceptibility of oppressed groups to emotional disorders, psychiatrists still tend to assume that these people cannot be helped with the most highly valued varieties of psychiatric treatment. It is deplorable enough that psychiatrists do not offer the poor the same quality of treatment that they offer the affluent,[14] it is even worse when, in situations where ability to pay is not a crucial factor, psychiatrists tend to offer more prestigious (and perhaps more liberating) treatments, such as psychotherapy, to middle- or upper-class people and to use potentially repressive treatments, such as drug and other somatic therapy, to lower-class'people. This practice is reinforced by the psychiatrist's tendency to label lower-class people as schizophrenic — a diagnosis that reflects hopelessness, that implies the patient cannot communicate rationally, and that can be used to justify treatments that do not require much doctor-patient communication.

Psychiatrists who are well educated and have been raised in middle- or upper-class environments will obviously have some difficulty communicating with a relatively uneducated client. This probably accounts for much of their reluctance to treat the poor person with therapies that require verbal interaction and expansion of awareness. Many psychiatrists seem to have a subtle kind of prejudice toward lower-class persons, which increases the probability that they will treat such patients with nonverbal techniques. It is sometimes alleged that lower-class people are too impulsive, too eager for immediate gratification, or too simple-minded for psychotherapy; therefore, psychiatrists are more likely to talk *to* rather than *with* these people. There is an implied assumption of class superiority here. In dealing with the poor, the psychiatrist tends to assume the authoritarian role of the patrician or benefactor. . . .

The psychiatrist often has similar attitudes toward black patients; he rarely selects them for psychotherapy, and he is more likely to give them a diagnosis that will allow him to treat them with repressive therapies and keep them at a distance. Recently it has been fashionable to classify delinquent youth on the basis of whether sociological or psychological factors seem to be the main determinants of their antisocial behavior.[15] The so-called social delinquent is assumed to need education and a change in his value systems, whereas the neurotic delinquent is usually assumed to be under great psychological stress and to need some kind of psychotherapy. Implied in this classification is the belief that the neurotic delinquent is more unhappy and more fragile than the social delinquent. In my work in institutions for delinquent children I have noted an insidious tendency to view black children as social delinquents far more often than white children. In fact, in some institutions it is still extremely rare for a black child to be given psychotherapy, even though white children from the same socioeconomic background are more readily given such treatment. As in the case of the poor, much of this discrimination can be accounted for because of communication difficulties between blacks and whites. But in their attitudes and practices, psychiatrists seem to accept and perpetuate the myth that black children do not suffer as much as white children. . . .

The Elderly

Because of modern medicine and public health measures, the number of people who are living beyond their sixth decade has greatly increased. Millions of Americans who are now retired have few responsibilities except to keep themselves alive and entertained as they approach the certainties of illness and death. It would seem that our country would want to treat these people with special kindness, but this is not the case. There is no role for older people in our rapidly changing society, no work, no sense of usefulness, and little dignity.

Those who are both old and poor are among the most wretched: nearly isolated and bored, they are practically hidden in our ghettoes and rural communities. Even those with money face formidable stresses: many people who reach a certain age and can afford to do so go to live in a retirement community, which may be of great wealth or of limited comfort. In either case, it is an isolated community . . . . One sees thousands of old people with nothing to do and with no sense of purpose. Deprived of close contact with their families, they seem to wander through a series of aimless distractions as they await death.

The psychiatrist who interprets the misery of the elderly as an illness helps to perpetuate a vicious form of oppression. It is commonly assumed that people will naturally become more depressed as they grow older. Failing strength, illness, and the fear of death — all of which are associated with aging — are indeed formidable stresses, but there is absolutely no evidence that these stresses inevitably cause depression. If the elderly person has an important place in society, he can live with grace and dignity. To assume that aging is itself a major cause of depression may well be a social myth. But if the psychiatrist treats the unhappiness of the older person as an illness, he may help to justify society's unwillingness to treat that person decently.

The association of aging with illness has almost come to be taken for granted. A recent advertisement in a medical journal pictured a sad-faced elderly man and noted that he was about to go to a party to celebrate his retirement. The ad said that retirement was a great moment for this man, even though he would probably not sleep well that night and might frequently be depressed in the days to come, and it advised the physician of the importance of proper medication at such a crucial point in a patient's life. This advertisement illustrates the destructive manner in which medical treatment is used to justify oppression: the ad does not suggest that the psychiatrist or physician has any responsibility to help his patient find a more acceptable social role during his retirement, nor does it criticize or recognize the oppressiveness of a society that allows its elderly citizens to become useless and lonely.

Instead of merely treating the depression of elderly citizens, perhaps the psychiatrist should try to identify those factors that contribute to a decent and happy old age and those that help to make old age a nightmare. He should feel obligated not only to care for the victims of a brutal process, but to prevent this process from becoming worse.

Notes

1. Mechanic, D. *Mental Health and Social Policy.* Englewood Cliffs, N.J.: Prentice-Hall, 1969.
2. Szasz, T. *The Manufacture of Madness.* New York: Harper & Row, 1970.
3. Szasz, T. *Law, Liberty and Psychiatry.* New York: Macmillan, 1963.
4. Leifer, R. *In the Name of Mental Health.* New York: Science House, 1969.
5. Menninger, K. A. *The Vital Balance.* New York: Viking Press, 1967.
6. Freud, S. "Three Essays on the Theory of Sexuality." In the standard edition of the *Complete Psychological Works of Sigmund Freud,* edited by J. Strachey. London: Hogarth Press, 1953.
7. Socarides, C. *The Overt Homosexual.* New York: Grune & Stratton, 1968.
8. Fenichel, O. *Psychoanalytic Theory of the Neuroses.* New York: Norton, 1945.
9. Koedt, A. "The Myth of the Vaginal Orgasm." *The Radical Therapist* 1 (1970): 6-7.
10. Masters, W. H., and Johnson, V. E. *Human Sexual Response.* Boston: Little, Brown, 1966.
11. Kinsey, A. C.; Pomeroy, W. B.; Martin, C. E.; and Gebhard, P. H. *Sexual Behavior in the Human Female.* Philadelphia: Saunders, 1953.
12. Brecher, R., and Brecher, E. *An Analysis of Human Sexual Response.* Boston: Little, Brown, 1966.
13. Freud, S. *Some Psychological Consequences of the Anatomical Distinction Between the Sexes.* Collected Papers, vol. 5, edited by J. Strachey. London: Hogarth Press, 1950.
14. Hollingshead, A. B., and Redlich, F. C. *Social Class and Mental Illness.* New York: Wiley, 1958.
15. Jenkins, R. "Adaptive and Maladaptive Delinquency." *The Nervous Child* 11 (1955): 9-11.

13

The Art of Savage Discovery: How to Blame the Victim

William Ryan

Twenty years ago, Zero Mostel used to do a sketch in which he impersonated a Dixiecrat Senator conducting an investigation of the origins of World War II. At the climax of the sketch, the Senator boomed out, in an excruciating mixture of triumph and suspicion, "What was Pearl Harbor *doing* in the Pacific?" This is an extreme example of Blaming the Victim.

Twenty years ago, we could laugh at Zero Mostel's caricature. In recent years, however, the same process has been going on every day in the arena of social problems, public health, anti-poverty programs, and social welfare. A philosopher might analyze this process and prove that, technically, it is comic. But it is hardly ever funny.

Consider some victims. One is the miseducated child in the slum school. He is blamed for his own miseducation. He is said to contain within himself the causes of his inability to read and write well. The shorthand phrase is "cultural deprivation," which, to those in the know, conveys what they allege to be in-side information: that the poor child carries a scanty pack of cultural baggage as he enters school. He doesn't know about books and magazines and newspapers, they say. . . . They say that if he talks at all — an unlikely event since slum parents don't talk to their children — he certainly doesn't talk correctly. (Lower-class dialect spoken here or even God forbid! — Southern Negro). *(Ici on parle nigra)*. If you can manage to get him to sit in a chair, they say, he squirms and looks out the window. (Impulse-ridden, these kids, motoric rather than verbal.) In a word he is "disadvantaged" and "socially deprived," they say, and this, of course, accounts for his failure (*his* failure, they say) to learn much in school.

Note the similarity to the logic of Zero Mostel's Dixiecrat Senator. What is the culturally deprived child *doing* in the school? What is wrong with the victim? In pursuing this logic, no one remembers to ask questions about the collapsing buildings and torn textbooks, the frightened, insensitive teachers, the six additional desks in the room, the blustering, frightened principals, the relentless segregation, the callous administrator, the irrelevant curriculum, the bigoted or cowardly members of the school board, the insulting history book, the stingy

---

taxpayers, the fairy-tale readers, or the self-serving faculty of the local teachers' college. We are encouraged to confine our attention to the child and to dwell on all his alleged defects. Cultural deprivation becomes an omnibus explanation for the educational disaster area known as the inner-city school. This is Blaming the Victim.

Pointing to the supposedly deviant Negro family as the "fundamental weakness of the Negro community" is another way to blame the victim. Like "cultural deprivation," "Negro family" has become a shorthand phrase with sterotyped connotations of matriarchy, fatherlessness, and pervasive illegitimacy. Growing up in the "crumbling" Negro family is supposed to account for most of the racial evils in America. Is it any wonder the Negroes cannot achieve equality? From such families! And, against, by focusing our attention on the Negro family as the apparent *cause* of racial inequality, our eye is diverted. Racism, discrimination, segregation, and the powerlessness of the ghetto are subtly, but thoroughly, downgraded in importance.

The generic process of Blaming the Victim is applied to almost every American problem. The miserable health care of the poor is explained away on the grounds that the victim has poor motivation and lacks health information. The problems of slum housing are traced to the characteristics of tenants who are labeled as "Southern rural migrants" not yet "acculturated" to life in the big city. The "multiproblem" poor, it is claimed, suffer the psychological effects of impoverishment, the "culture of poverty," and the deviant value system of the lower classes; consequently, though unwittingly, they cause their own troubles. From such a viewpoint, the obvious fact that poverty is primarily an absence of money is easily overlooked or set aside.

The growing number of families receiving welfare are fallaciously linked together with the increased number of illegitimate children as twin results of promiscuity and sexual abandon among members of the lower orders. Every important social problem — crime, mental illness, civil disorder, unemployment — has been analyzed within the framework of the victim-blaming ideology. . . .

It would be possible for me to venture into other areas — one finds a perfect example in literature about the underdeveloped countries of the Third World, in which the lack of prosperity and technological progress is attributed to some aspect of the national character of the people, such as lack of "achievement motivation" — but I plan to stay within the confines of my own personal and professional experience, which is, generally, with racial injustice, social welfare, and human services in the city.

I have been listening to the victim-blamers and pondering their thought processes for a number of years. That process is often very subtle. Victim-blaming is cloaked in kindness and concern, and bears all the trappings and statistical furbelows of scientism; it is obscured by a perfumed haze of humanitarianism. In observing the process of Blaming the Victim, one tends to be confused and disoriented because those who practice this art display a deep concern for the victims that is quite genuine. In this way, the new ideology is very different from the open prejudice and reactionary tactics of the old days. Its adherents include sympathetic social scientists with social consciences in good working order, and liberal politicians with a genuine commitment to reform. They are very careful to dissociate themselves from vulgar Calvinism or crude racism; they indignantly condemn any notions of innate wickedness or genetic defect. "The Negro is *not born* inferior," they shout apoplectically. "Force of circumstances," they explain in reasonable tones, "has *made* him inferior." And they dismiss with self-righteous contempt any claims that the poor man in America is plainly unworthy or shiftless or enamored of idleness. No, they say, he is "caught in the cycle of poverty." . . . .

Blaming the Victim is, of course, quite different from old-fashioned conservative ideologies. The latter simply dismissed victims as inferior, genetically defective, or morally unfit; the emphasis is on the intrinsic, even hereditary, defect. The former shifts its emphasis to the environmental causation. The old-fashioned conservative could hold firmly to the belief that the oppressed and the victimized were born that way — "that way" being defective or inadequate in character or ability. The new ideology attributes defect and inadequacy to the malignant nature of poverty, injustice, slum life, and racial difficulties. The stigma that marks the victim and accounts for his victimization is an acquired stigma, a stigma of social, rather than genetic, origin. But the stigma, the defect, the fatal difference — though derived in the past from environmental forces — is still located *within* the victim, inside his skin. With such an elegant formulation, the humanitarian can have it both ways. He can, all at the same time, concentrate his charitable interest on the defects of the victim, condemn the vague social and environmental stresses that produced the defect (some time ago), and ignore the continuing effect of victimizing social forces (right now). It is a brilliant ideology for justifying a perverse form of social action designed to change, not society, as one might expect, but rather society's victim.

As a result, there is a terrifying sameness in the programs that arise from this kind of analysis. In education, we have programs of "compensatory education" to build up the skills and attitudes of the ghetto child, rather than structural changes in the schools. In race relations, we have social engineers who think up ways of "strengthening" the Negro family, rather than methods of eradicating racism. In health care, we develop new programs to provide health information (to correct the supposed ignorance of the poor) and to reach out and discover cases of untreated illness and disability (to compensate for their supposed unwillingness to seek treatment). Meanwhile, the gross inequities of our medical care delivery systems are left completely unchanged. As we might expect, the logical outcome of analyzing social problems in terms of the deficiencies of the victim is the development of programs aimed at correcting those deficiencies. The formula for action becomes extraordinarily simple: change the victim.

All of this happens so smoothly that it seems downright rational. First, identify a social problem. Second, study those affected by the problem and discover in what ways they are different from the rest of us as a consequence of deprivation and injustice. Third, define the differences as the cause of the social problem itself. Finally, of course, assign a government bureaucrat to invent a humanitarian action program to correct the differences.

Now no one in his right mind would quarrel with the assertion that social problems are present in abundance and are readily identifiable. God knows it is true that when hundreds of thousands of poor children drop out of school — or even graduate from school — they are barely literate. . . The fact of failure in their education is undisputed. And the racial situation in America is usually acknowledged to be a number one item on the nation's agenda. . . . . In addition, despite our assertions that Americans get the best health care in the world, the poor stubbornly remain unhealthy. They lose more work because of illness, have more carious teeth, lose more babies as a result of both miscarriage and infant death, and die considerably younger than the well-to-do.

The problems are there, and there in great quantities. They make us uneasy. Blaming the Victim is an ideal, almost painless, evasion.

The second step in applying this explanation is to look sympathetically at those who "have" the problem in question, to separate them out and define them in some way as a special group, a group that is *different* from the population in general. This is a crucial and essential step in the process, for that difference is in itself hampering and maladaptive. The Different Ones are seen as less competent, less skilled, less knowing — in short, less human. The ancient Greeks deduced from a single characteristic, a difference in language, that the barbarians — that is, the "babblers" who spoke a strange tongue — were wild, uncivilized, dangerous, rapacious, uneducated, lawless, and, indeed, scarcely more than animals. Automatically labeling strangers as savages, weird and inhuman creatures (thus explaining difference by exaggerating difference) not infrequently justifies mistreatment, enslavement, or even extermination of the Different Ones.

Blaming the Victim depends on a very similar process of identification (carried out, to be sure, in the most kindly, philanthropic, and intellectual manner) whereby the victim of social problems is identified as strange, different — in other words, as a barbarian, a savage. Discovering savages, then, is an essential component of, and prerequisite to, Blaming the Victim, and the art of Savage Discovery is a core skill that must be acquired by all aspiring Victim Blamers. They must learn how to demonstrate that the poor, the black, the ill, the jobless, the slum tenants, are different and strange. They must learn to conduct or interpret the research that shows how "these people" think in different forms, act in difference patterns, cling to different values, seek different goals, and learn different truths. Which is to say that they are strangers, barbarians, savages. This is how the distressed and disinherited are redefined in order to make it possible for us to look at society's problems and to attribute their causation to the individuals affected. . . .

Blaming the Victim can take its place in a long series of American ideologies that have rationalized cruelty and injustice.

Slavery, for example, was justified — even praised — on the basis of a complex ideology that showed quite conclusively how useful slavery was to society and how uplifting it was for the slaves.[1] Eminent physicians could be relied upon to provide the biological justification for slavery since after all, they said, the slaves were a separate species — as, for example, cattle are a separate species. No one in his right mind would dream of freeing the cows and fighting to abolish the ownership of cattle. In the view of the average American of 1825, it was important to preserve slavery, not simply because it was in accord with his own group interests (he was not fully aware of that), but because reason and logic showed clearly to the reasonable and intelligent man that slavery was good. In order to persuade a good and moral man to *do* evil, then, it is not necessary first to persuade him to *become* evil. It is only necessary to teach him that he is doing good.

In late-nineteenth-century America there flowered another ideology of injustice that seemed rational and just to the decent, progressive person. But Richard Hofstadter's analysis of the phenomenon of Social Darwinism[2] shows clearly its functional role in the preservation of the *status quo.* One can scarcely imagine a better fit than the one between this ideology and the purposes and actions of the robber barons, who descended like piranha fish on the America of this era and picked its bones clean. Their extraordinary unethical operations netted them not only hundreds of millions of dollars but also, perversely, the adoration of the nation. Behavior that would be, in many more rational land . . . more than enough to have landed them all in jail, was praised as the very model of a captain of modern industry. And the philosophy that justified their thievery was such that John D. Rockefeller would actually stand up and preach it in, . . . of all places, Sunday school:

> The growth of a large business is merely a survival of the fittest . . . .
> The American Beauty rose can be produced in the splendor and fragrance which bring cheer to its beholder only by sacrificing the early buds which grow up around it. This is not an evil tendency in business. It is merely the working-out of a law of nature and a law of God.[3]

This was the core of the gospel, adapted analogically from Darwin's writings on evolution. Herbert Spencer and, later, William Graham Sumner and other beginners in the social sciences considered Darwin's work to be directly applicable to social processes; ultimately as a guarantee that life was progressing toward perfection but, in the short run, as a justification for an absolutely uncontrolled laissez-faire economic system. The central concepts of "survival of the fittest," "natural selection," and "gradualism" were exalted in Rockefeller's preaching to the status of laws of God and Nature. Not only did this ideology justify the criminal rapacity of those who rose to the top of the industrial heap, defining them automatically as naturally superior, ... but at the same time it also required that those at the bottom of the heap be labeled as patently *unfit* — a label based solely on their position in society. According to the law of natural selection, they should be, in Spencer's judgment, eliminated. "The whole effort of nature is to get rid of such, to clear the world of them and make room for better."

For a generation, Social Darwinism was the orthodox doctrine in the social sciences, such as they were at that time. Opponents of this ideology were shut out of respectable intellectual life . . . .

If one is to think about ideologies in America in 1970, one must be prepared to consider the possibility that a body of ideas that might seem almost self-evident is, in fact, highly distorted and highly selective . . . It is important not to delude ourselves into thinking that ideological monstrosities were constructed by monsters. They were not; they are not. They are developed through a process that shows every sign of being valid scholarship, complete with tables of numbers, copious footnotes, and scientific terminology. Ideologies are quite often academically and socially respectable and in many instances hold positions of exclusive validity, so that disagreement is considered unrespectable or radical and risks being labeled as irresponsible, unenlightened, or trashy.

Blaming the Victim holds such a position. It is central in the mainstream of contemporary American social thought, and its ideas pervade our most crucial assumptions so thoroughly that they are hardly noticed. Moreover, the fruits of this ideology appear to be fraught with altruism and humanitarianism, so it is principally functioned to block social change. . . . .

We come finally to the question. Why? It is much easier to understand the process of Blaming the Victim as a way of thinking than it is to understand the motivation for it. Why do Victim Blamers, who are usually good people, blame the victim? The development and application of this ideology, and of all the mythologies associated with Savage Discovery, are readily exposed by careful analysis as hostile acts — one is almost tempted to say acts of war — directed against the disdavantaged, the distressed, the disinherited. It is class warfare in reverse. Yet those who are most fascinated and enchanted by this ideology tend to be progressive, humanitarian, and in the best sense of the word, charitable persons. They would usually define themselves as moderates or liberals. Why do they pursue this dreadful war against the poor and the oppressed?

Put briefly, the answer can be formulated best in psychological terms . . . The high-charged psychological problem confronting this hypothetical progressive, charitable person I am talking about is that of reconciling his own self-interest with the promptings of his humanitarian impulses. This psychological process of reconciliation is not worked out in a logical, rational, conscious way; it is a process that takes place far below the level of sharp consciousness, and the solution — Blaming the Victim — is arrived at subconsciously as a compromise that apparently satisfies both his self-interest and his charitable concerns. Let me elaborate.

First, the question of self-interest or, more accurately, class interest. The typical Victim Blamer is a middle-class person who is doing reasonably well in a material way; he has a good job, a good income, a good house, a good car. Basically, he likes the social system pretty much the way it is, at least in broad outline. . . . He heartily approves of the profit motive as the propelling engine of the economic system despite his awareness that there are abuses of that system, negative side effects, and substantial residual inequalities.

On the other hand, he is acutely aware of poverty, racial discrimination, exploitation, and deprivation, and, moreover, he wants to do something concrete to ameliorate the condtion of the poor, the black, and the disadvantaged. This is not an extraneous concern; it is central to his value system to insist on the worth of the individual, the equality of men, and the importance of justice.

What is to be done, then? What intellectual position can he take, and what line of action can he follow that will satisfy both of these important motivations? He quickly and self-consciously rejects two obvious alternatives, which he defines as "extremes." He cannot side with an openly reactionary, repressive position that accepts continued oppression and exploitation as the price of a privileged position for his own class. This is incompatible with his own morality and his basic political principles. He finds the extreme conservative position repugnant.

He is, if anything, more allergic to radicals, however, than he is to reactionaries. He rejects the "extreme" solution of radical social change, and this makes sense since such radical social change threatens his own well-being. A more equitable distribution of income might mean that he would have less . . . .

So our potential Victim Blamers are in a dilemma. In the words of an old Yiddish proverb, they are trying to dance at two weddings. They are old friends of both brides and fond of both kinds of dancing, and they want to accept both invitations. They cannot bring themselves to attack the system that has been so good to them, but they want so badly to be heplful to the victims of racism and economic injustice.

Their solution is a brilliant compromise. They turn their attention to the victim in his post-victimized state. They want to bind up wounds, inject penicillin, administer morphine, and evacuate the wounded for rehabilitation. They explain what's wrong with the victim in terms of social experiences *in the past,* experiences that have left wounds, defects, paralysis, and disability. And they take the cure of these wounds and the reduction of these disabilities as the first order of business. They want to make the victims less vulnerable, send them back into battle with better weapons, thicker armor, a higher level of morale.

In order to do so effectively, of course, they must analyze the victims carefully, dispassionately, objectively, scientifically, empathetically, mathematically, and hardheadedly, to see what made them so vulnerable in the first place.

What weapons, now, might they have lacked when they went into battle? Job skills? Education?

What armor was lacking that might have warded off their wounds? Better values? Habits of thrift and foresight?

And what might have ravaged their morale? Apathy? Ignorance? Deviant lower-class cultural patterns?

This is the solution of the dilemma, the solution of Blaming the Victim. And those who buy this solution with a sigh of relief are inevitably blinding themselves to the basic causes of the problems being addressed. They are, most crucially, rejecting the possibility of blaming, not the victims, but themselves. They are all unconsciously passing judgments on themselves and bringing in a unanimous verdict of Not Guilty.

If one comes to believe that the culture of poverty produces persons *fated* to be poor, who can find any fault with our corporation-dominated economy? And if the Negro family produces young men *incapable* of achieving equality, let's deal with that first before we go on to the task of changing the pervasive racism that informs and shapes and distorts our every social institution. And if unsatisfactory resolution of one's Oedipus complex accounts for all emotional distress and mental disorder, then by all means let us attend to that and postpone worrying about the pounding day-to-day stresses of life on the bottom rungs that drive so many to drink, dope, and madness.

That is the ideology of Blaming the Victim, the cunning Art of Savage Discovery. The tragic, frightening truth is that it is a mythology that is winning over the best people of our time, the very people who must resist this ideological temptation if we are to achieve nonviolent change in America.

Notes

1. For a good review of this general ideology, see I.A. Newby, *Jim Crow's Defense* (Baton Rouge, La.: Louisiana State University Press, 1965).
2. R. Hofstadter, *Social Darwinism in American Thought,* rev. ed., (Boston, Mass.: Beacon Press, 1955).
3. W.J. Ghent, *Our Benevolent Feudalism* (New York: The Macmillan Co., 1902), p. 29.

Part III Bibliography

Alexander, A., and   *Stealing.* New York: Cornerstone Library, 1969.
V. Moolman

Arsenian, J.   "The Escalation of Violence," *Psychiatric Opinion* 1968, 5
                    (3): 20–28.

Bacon, H. M.   "Psychiatric Aspects of Therapeutic Abortion," *Canada's*
                    Mental Health (Ottawa) 1969, 17 (1): 18–21.

Berkowitz, L.,   "The Stimulus Qualities of the Scapegoat," *Journal of Ab-*
and J.A. Green   *normal Social Psychology* 1962, 64 (4): 293–301.

Bernard, V.W.   "Why People Become Victims of Medical Quackery," *Ameri-*
                    can Journal of Public Health 1965, 55 (8): 1142–1147.

Blumberg, L.U.,   "The Skid Row Man and Skid Row Status Community: With
T.E. Shipley, Jr., Perspectives on their Future," *Quarterly Journal of Studies*
J.O. Moor, Jr.   *on Alcohol* 1971, 32 (4): 909–941.

Blumenthal, M.D.,   *Justifying Violence: Attitudes of American Men.* Ann Arbor,
R. L. Kahn,   Mich.: University of Michigan Institute for Social Research,
R. M. Andrews,   1972.
and K. B. Head

Bowers, W. J.   "Racial Discrimination in Capital Punishment: Characteristics
                    of the Condemned." Unpublished paper.

Brown, M. E.   "The Condemnation and Persecution of the Hippies," in E.Z.
                    Friedenberg (ed.), *The Anti-American Generation.* Chicago:
                    Aldine, 1971, 97–127.

Davis, A. J.   "Sexual Assaults in the Philadelphia Prison System," in J. H.
                    Gagnon and W. Simon, *The Sexual Scene.* Chicago: Aldine,
                    1970, 107–124.

Demaris, O.   *America the Violent.* Baltimore, Md.: Penguin Books, 1970.

Gil, D.G.   *Violence Against Children.* Cambridge, Mass.: Harvard Univer-
                    sity Press, 1972.

George, M.   "From 'Goodwife' to 'Mistress': The Transformation of the
                    Female in Bourgeois Culture," *Science and Society* 1973, 37
                    (2): 152–177.

Greer, G.   "Seduction is a Four-letter Word," *Playboy* 1973, 20 (1):
                    80–82, 164, 178, 224–228.

Harkins, A.M.   "Alienation and Related Concepts," *Kansas Journal of*
                    Sociology 1965, 1 (2): 78–89.

Hendin, H.   "A Psychoanalyst Looks at Student Revolutionaries," *New York Times Magazine* 1971, January 17, 16–30.

Hollister, L.E.   "Criminal Laws and the Control of Drugs of Abuse: An Historical View of the Law (Or It's the Lawyer's Fault)," *Journal of Clinical Pharmacology* 1969, 9 (6): 345–348.

Kittrie, N.   "The Psychopaths: A Medical and Scientific Critique" in *The Right to Be Different: Deviance and Enforced Therapy.* Baltimore, Md.: John Hopkins Press, 1971, 193–199.

Margolis, C.   "Some Psychological and Ideological Perspectives on the Black Community," in K. Wolff, *Social and Cultural Factors in Mental Health and Mental Illness.* Springfield, Ill.: Charles C. Thomas, 1971.

Mayorca, O., and   "The Victims of Television." Papers presented at the Ameri-
R. Zuazua   can Society of Criminology Congress in Caracas (1972).

Menninger, K.   *The Crime of Punishment.* New York: Viking Press, 1966 (esp. chs. 6 and 7).

Millett, K.   "Theory of Sexual Politics," in *Sexual Politics.* Garden City, N.Y.: Doubleday, 1970, 39–46.

Mueller-Hegemann, D.,   "Reihenuntersuchungen bei Verfolgten des Nazire-
and G. Spitzner   gimes, mit besonderer Berücksichtigung von Einzelhaftfolgen" (Series of Investigations of Victims of the Nazi Regime, with special Reference to the Consequences of Solitary Confinement), *Deutsche Gesundheitswesen* (Leipzig) 1963, 18 (3): 107–116.

Nagel, S.S.   "The Tipped Scales of American Justice," in A.S. Blumberg (ed.), *The Scale of Justice.* Chicago: Aldine, 1970, 31–49.

Niederland, W.G.   "Psychiatric Disorders among Persecution Victims. A Contribution to the Understanding of Concentration Camp Pathology and its After-effects," *Journal of Nervous and Mental Disease* 1964, 139 (5): 458–474.

Parker, G.E.   "Bill C-150: Abortion Reform," *Criminal Law Quarterly* 1969, 11 (30): 267–274.

Pinderhughes, C.A.   "Televised Violence and Social Behavior," *Psychiatric Opinion* 1972, 9 (2): 28–36.

Rainwater, L.   "Crucible of Identity: The Negro Lower Class Family," in T. Parsons and K.B. Clark (eds.), *The Negro American.* Boston: Beacon Press, 1966, 160–204.

Rector, M.G. "Heroin Maintenance: A Rational Approach," *Crime and Delinquency* 1972, 18 (3): 241–242.

Reiss, A.J., Jr. "Police Brutality: Answer to Key Questions," in *Trans-Action* 1968, 5 (8): 10–19.

Rodell, F. "Our Unlovable Sex Laws," in J.H. Gagnon and W. Simon (eds.), *The Sexual Scene*. Chicago: Aldine, 1970, 81–89.

Rosenthal, A.M. *Thirty-Eight Witnesses*. New York: McGraw-Hill, 1964.

Rossi, A.L. "Abortion Laws and Their Victims," in J.H. Gagnon and W. Simon (eds.), *The Sexual Scene*. Chicago: Aldine, 1970.

Samuels, F.G. "The Negro Tavern: A Microcosm of Slum Life." Ph.D. dissertation, University of Illinois, Urbana-Champaign, Ill. Ann Arbor, Michigan, Univ. Microfilms 71–5224.

Schafer, S. "The Responsibility of Economic Conditions," in S. Schafer, *Theories in Criminology*. New York: Random House, 1969, 255–290.

Schur, E.M. *Our Criminal Society*. Englewood Cliffs, N.J.: Prentice-Hall, 1969.

Strauss, A.L. "Medical Ghettoes," in A.L. Strauss (eds.), *Where Medicine Fails,* Chicago: Aldine, 1970, 9–26.

Stryker, S. "Social Structure and Prejudice," *Social Problems* 1959, 6: 340–354.

Svalastoga, K. "Rape and Social Structure," *Pacific Sociological Review* 1962, 5: 48–53.

Szasz, T. "There Is No Such Thing as Mental Illness," *Medical World News* 1970, 11 (12).

The National Commission of the Causes and Prevention of Violence *The History of Violence in America*. New York: Bantam Books, 1969 (esp. chs. 13, 14, 15, 21).

The National Commission of the Causes and Prevention of Violence. *Law and Order Reconsidered* (Staff Report). New York: Bantam Books, 1970 (esp. ch. 23).

Thomas, A., and S. Sillen *Racism and Psychiatry*. New York: Bruhner–Mazel, 1972.

Toch, H. *Violent Men: An Inquiry into the Psychology of Violence*. Chicago: Aldine, 1969.

Wald, P. M.   "Poverty and Criminal Justice," Task Force Report, *The Courts,* 1967, Appendix C, 139–151.

Wiseman, J. P.   *Stations of the Lost: The Treatment of Skid Row Alcoholics.* Englewood Cliffs, N.J.: Prentice-Hall, 1970.

Wolfahrt, S.   "The Actual Situation of the Victims of Concentration Camps," *Svenska Läkartidningen* (Stockholm) 1964, 61 (52): 4107–4124.

Wolfgang, M. E.   "Violence, U.S.A. Riots and Crime," *Crime and Delinquency* 1968, 14 (4): 289–305.

Part IV
The Victim and the
Administration of Justice

Introduction

Statistical criminology has its roots in what was once called "Moral Statistics." The subject which has most preoccupied the field of criminal statistics since its beginning is the search for the key moral statistic: a measure of the criminality present among a given population. However, anyone who tries to uncover facts and figures about crime and criminals learns quickly that there are many figures but few facts.

Moreover, "there is simply no way or provision for any real auditing of the methods used by local agencies in counting offenses to insure that measurement of crime, as is now reported, will produce accurate or satisfactory facts on which a high degree of dependence can be placed."[1]

In any event, seldom does the classification used in law and in criminal statistics bear any relationship to the seriousness of the offense. No data about the circumstances surrounding the commission of crimes are currently published, except insofar as the geographic area of the arrest.

To determine the extent of unreported crime, the President's Commission on Law Enforcement and the Administration of Justice introduced a new methodology, the victimization survey.[2] The product of the first national survey of crime victimization ever made in the United States were important substantive findings. The paper by Hood and Sparks — two British criminologists — comments on the use of the survey method to study the incidence of victimization among the general population, on the findings, on the methodological problems which must be taken into account when interpreting the results of the surveys, and on the reasons why crime is unreported or unrecorded.

Crosby and Snyder present results based on the summer 1969 *Black Buyer Survey*, a continuing study of the urban black heads of households. It is an important paper for those having an interest and a desire to find out the extent and effects of crime in urban black America.

Moving on to consider the reaction of the administration of justice system to victimization, the article by Sebba examines the controversial requirement of corroboration for rape and sexual assault cases. For example, in the United States, fifteen States have some form of such requirement. In those jurisdictions the state's attorney must prove "beyond reasonable doubt" three points on behalf of the victim: the identity of the rapist; corroborative evidence of the rape itself (proof of physical injury, like bruises, torn clothing, lacerations,

161

and/or medical proof of live sperm in her vagina); and proof that she did not "consent" by word or action, thus affirming that force, or threat of force, was used. Corroboration has come increasingly under fire in recent times as the law's most inequitable requirement. With few exceptions, rape is a secret, lonely crime. It generally occurs indoors, and thus rarely has witnesses. While originally corroboration was required to protect men against women who might bring false charges of rape, today many consider it a clear expression of negative social attitudes toward women: "ladies lie."

The paper by Landy and Aronson deals with the relationship between the personal characteristics of the victim of a crime and the desire or tendency of individuals to punish the person accused of committing that crime. The authors describe two experiments they conducted to research such question, and present the results.

Maurice Goldsmith in his article discusses basic problems of business ethics, and of moral and scientific responsibility resulting from the manner in which we now manipulate our physiological processes through chemical products. He is referring, in particular, to the thalidomide tragedy.

Notes

1. California Criminal Statistics Bureau, *Crime and Delinquency in California,* 1967, Sacramento, California, 1968:20.
2. U.S. President's Commission on Law Enforcement and the Administration of Justice, *Criminal Victimization in the United States: A Report of a National Survey.* National Opinion Research Center, prepared by Phillip H. Ennis. Washington, D.C.: U.S. Government Printing Office, 1967. Also, *Report of a Pilot Study in the District of Columbia on Victimization and Attitudes Toward Law Enforcement.* Bureau of Social Science Inc., prepared by Albert D. Biderman and others. Washington, D.C.: U.S. Government Printing Office, 1967.

14

Citizens' Attitudes and Police Practice in Reporting Offenses

Roger Hood and Richard Sparks

The use of the survey method to study the incidence of victimisation among the general population is an entirely new approach to estimating the dark figure. The only work so far published is contained in three reports prepared in the United States for the President's Commission in 1967. One report deals with the amount of crime committed against members of a representative sample of 10,000 United States households, another with pilot studies in four precincts of the District of Columbia (Washington), and the third with high and low crime-rate areas in Boston and Chicago.[1]

Major Findings of Victim Studies

The Commission's representative national survey found that one in five households in the United States had been a victim of a serious crime in 1966. About twice as many major crimes were committed as were known to the police, as reported in the Uniform Crime Reports by the Federal Bureau of Investigation (FBI). Uniform Crime Reports are made in the United States for all major crimes. The offences are divided into two parts. Part I offences are the most serious, some of these are called Index offences as they are used for Crime Index purposes. Part II offences are generally less serious or are less likely to be reported to the police and so are less reliable for Index purposes. For example, larceny of $50 and over is a part I offence. Under $50 it is a part II offence. These distinctions will be seen clearly in some of the following tables and charts.

Figure 14-1 shows that of the more serious offences, the most frequently unknown were burglaries, rapes, aggravated assaults, and larceny of over $50. Only a third of burglaries were known, and 75 per cent of rapes were not reported. While there was twice as much minor crime as serious offences, the dark figure was apparently much smaller (see table 14-1). It seems from the Washington study, however, that interviewees find the greatest difficulty in remembering any but the most recent serious offences committed against them. The figures for minor offences are therefore probably considerable underestimates.

The Washington enquiry was much smaller and covered only 511 households (plus a further validation study); it was mainly concerned, in fact, with methodological problems. Thirty-eight per cent of the surveyed population were victims of a serious crime within a year, compared with an estimate of ten per cent based on police statistics. For every type of serious crime the dark figure was substantially larger in Washington than in the USA as a whole. This reflected the finding in the national survey taht the rate of victimisation was very much higher in the metropolitan centres than in small cities and rural areas. In addition, there are good reasons for believing the methodology of the Washington study was better adapted for gaining reports of victimisation. Figure 14-2 shows overall 5.3 times more serious crime than was known to the police. For serious larceny ($50 and over) the proportion is fifteen times: only about seven per cent is known!

The Boston-Chicago respondents were asked about crimes committed against them in a period of a year from July 1965-6. Table 14-2 compares the number of Index offences found by the survey with those known to the police. In the two Boston precincts there were five and three times as much crime. The figures for Fillmore in Chicago are probably only so different because the survey ran simultaneously with a riot!

Methodological Problems of Victim Studies

Because these studies are new there are a number of major methodological problems which must be taken into account in interpreting the results of all three surveys. We shall spell these out in some detail since this kind of research is of great potential value and likely to be used by other investigators in the future.

It should be first borne in mind that only one of the studies purports to collect a sample representative of the United States as a whole: both the Washington and Boston-Chicago enquiries were limited to specific precincts of these cities, chosen for other than representative reasons, and therefore it is dangerous to generalise from their results. Furthermore, over a quarter of those approached refused to be interviewed and this may be an additional biasing factor.

Figure 14-1. Rates of Serious Crime in the United States, 1965: Comparison of Official Statistics and Survey Estimates.

Note: The figures for homicides and vehicle theft in the survey are *fewer* than reported to the police. Of course one cannot interview the victim of a homicide, and this crime may break up households. The figures for vehicle theft are not easy to explain, except on the assumption that all thefts are reported to the police for insurance reasons, but some householders fail to report the offence to the survey interviewer.

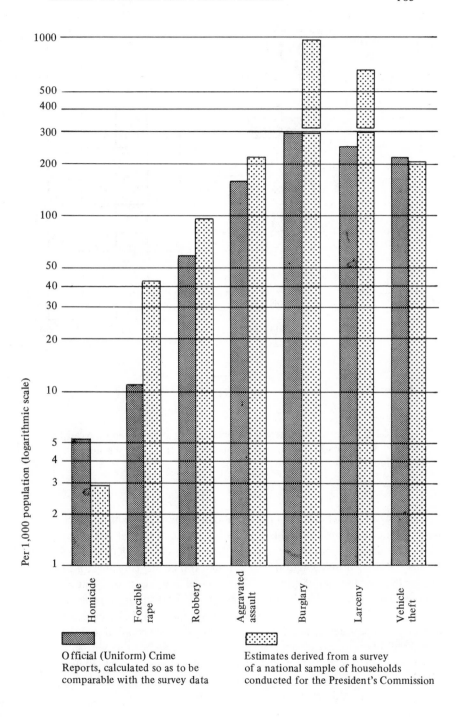

Per 1,000 population (logarithmic scale)

Homicide

Forcible rape

Robbery

Aggravated assault

Burglary

Larceny

Vehicle theft

Official (Uniform) Crime
Reports, calculated so as to be
comparable with the survey data

Estimates derived from a survey
of a national sample of households
conducted for the President's Commission

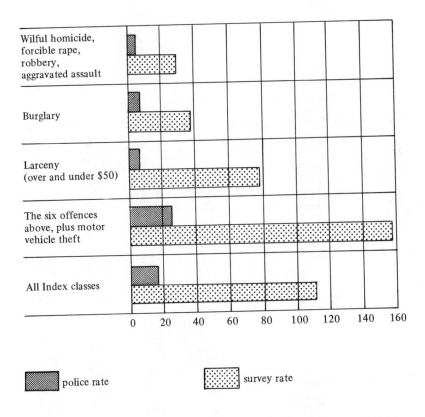

Figure 14-2. Estimated Rates of Offences, per 1,000 Residents Aged 18 or Over: Comparison of Police and Survey Data for Three Washington, D. C. Precincts

A survey of households can only ask about a limited range of offences: those specifically against individuals or the household in general. No information can be gleaned about offences where there is no specific victim, such as vagrancy or being drunk and disorderly. It may also be difficult to get information, by this method, about crimes of a consensual or conspiratorial nature—for example those connected with drug use, gambling, prostitution and abortion. In these, the 'victim' (if we can speak of one) is involved in the offence, and would have to be asked to admit to offences for which he could himself be prosecuted. The national survey concluded that it would be quite wrong 'for the survey method to be used as an instrument of confession'. Nevertheless, such an approach has been successfully used in self-report studies, although admittedly not in a doorstep-to-doorstep setting.

Although these are household surveys, it is doubtful whether they reveal all the crimes committed against *all* household members. The national survey questioned any adult (over 18) in the household and asked about offences committed against him or her personally and then about those committed against others in the household. This method produced an over-representation of older persons and women in the sample (as they are more likely to be at home). The two other surveys therefore chose at random the adult to be interviewed so as to get a more representative sample of the household. But whichever method is used there is still the problem of estimating the accuracy of the information given by the respondent about other members of his household. In all three studies there was a suspiciously large difference between the number of incidents reported by the respondent about himself and those concerning others. In the national sample it was estimated that the amount of crime committed against Negro families uncovered by the survey was only half of the actual amount of victimisation. It was especially felt that reports about offences committed against young members of the family would be less well known by respondents and therefore in the two city surveys all acts which had been committed against those under 18 years were not taken into consideration.

In comparing the survey-derived data with police records of crime reported over the same period, it was necessary to take into account the limited range of offences covered, the age range of the respondents, and other factors such as excluding from police data crimes committed against respondents outside the police jurisdiction. These problems could not be solved precisely and therefore the comparisons between the survey findings and police statistics are estimates, with an uncertain margin of error.

For the future, however, the most important questions centre around the validity and reliability of the information given by respondents: the extent to which they were willing or able to tell the truth. The validity of answers is

Table 14-1
Official Rates of Minor Crimes in a Metropolitan Area Compared with Survey Estimates from Metropolitan Areas in the United States, 1965, (per 100,000 population).

Minor Crimes	Survey Sample	Official Crime Rate
Simple assault	569	528
Petty larceny	1,532	1,462

Table 14-2
A Comparison between the Numbers of Index Offences (and
Rate per Person) Reported by Victims in a Survey of Four
Precincts of Boston and Chicago, and Official Statistics of
Crimes Known to the Police, 1965.

	Boston		Chicago	
	Dorchester	Roxbury	Fillmore	Town Hall
1 Gross estimate of number of Index offences from survey data	9,605	12,612	9,328	17,356
2 Gross estimate of *rate* Index offences (i.e., proportion per person), from survey data	.16	.24	.11	.13
3 Index offences known to the police, for the same age group	1,881	3,651	6,732	4,372
4 *Rate* of Index offences known to the police	.03	.07	.08	.03
5 Proportion of offences in the survey known to the police (per cent)	18.7	29.2	72.7	23.1

most difficult to check, but in general there was little evidence of fabrication of
events. Two kinds of problems emerged: first whether there was concealment
or exaggeration of serious offences; secondly whether respondents reported incidents which were not crimes. All three surveys found that the relative
frequency of serious crimes reported by respondents mirrored their frequency
in the official Uniform Crime Reports, thus supporting the view that respondents
did not exaggerate the incidence of lurid crimes. On the other hand, a much
higher proportion of all crimes than would have been expected was in the
'serious' category. As the Boston-Chicago report comments 'if anything, the
survey procedure is biased against securing the trivial incident and recall tends
to take only the more "salient" serious experiences'. There is, apparently,
no over-reporting of serious crime, but a considerable under-representation of
petty offences in the findings of these enquiries.

In the national and Boston-Chicago surveys special procedures were built in to check the testimony of respondents to ensure that only 'real crimes' were recorded for comparison with police data. The major criteria used were: Was the respondent credible? Was the event a crime? Was it serious enough to warrant action, or was it committed by a minor? Was there sufficient evidence? Was it committed within the area and time period included in the survey? The national study used two research assistants to evaluate whether a crime had been committed. They agreed that about one quarter of all reports were not crimes, and excluded these and doubtful cases (nine per cent) from the total number of crimes to be compared with police data. But the assistants themselves may not have been entirely accurate in their assessments: a sample of their work was checked by lawyers and policemen who reached the conclusion that only about two-thirds of the events recorded as crime by the assistants were in fact crimes. Similarly, 21 per cent of the reports in Boston-Chicago were excluded—but only 12 of 502 reported incidents were excluded as noncredible. In the Washington enquiry no special procedures were used and a low 'unfounding rate' of 4.4 per cent—the rate of reports the police normally assume not to be real crimes—was deducted from the total number of offences reported. The Washington estimates are therefore probably too high.

The truthfulness of the accounts given by respondents does not seem to be a major problem, but the reliability of their answers is. Respondents were asked to account for all criminal incidents of which they had been a victim within the past year. One problem affecting the reliability of answers has already been discussed—the respondents' ability to report for other household members—but there are three others: the time the respondents were prepared to give the interviewer; the 'telescoping forward' into the survey year of events which occurred in a previous year; and the forgetting of incidents that had happened within the survey year. The first and last of these errors would tend to lead to underestimates of the amount of victimisation, whereas telescoping-forward would lead to an exaggeration.

Part of the Washington study used an interview method in which the respondent was asked for details about each event as he mentioned it. It seems that this led to a considerable under-reporting of incidents. In a survey of an additional precinct in Washington a new method was used: the respondent was asked to say whether he had been the victim of any crime on a list, and only after the whole list had been checked was he asked for details of each offence. In this precinct the number of victimisation incidents per respondent was 2.0 compared with 0.8 for the other Washington precincts with a similar official crime rate. Commenting on the method, the Boston-Chicago report states, 'it soon became clear that a respondent controls the number of experiences he or she had on the basis of what they consider a sufficient amount of time they had given the interviewer'. There was certainly a suspiciously high number of people who were only victims of one crime, as against two, three or four! Thus, again, the surveys probably *underestimate* the amount of victimisation.

By far the most important problem, however, is forgetfulness. Figure 14-3 compares the seasonal incidence of offences that would be expected if there were no telescoping and forgetfulness. They show clearly that although there is apparently some telescoping (about 10 per cent telescoped), the preponderance of reported events is in the recent past: 'most respondents seemed to find it difficult to remember incidents of victimisation other than recent cases'. To check the amount of under-reporting, a separate survey was designed in Boston and Chicago. A note was taken over a period of all incidents in which citizens called the police, and several months later a sample of these citizens was interviewed. Over a fifth of the respondents failed to mention the experience which had been recorded by the investigators!

In summary, it seems that the most satisfactory victimisation study would be one in which a very large sample of the population was asked about incidents which occurred in a period of not more than three months before the interview date. Obviously this would be an extremely expensive method.

All the methodological limitations mentioned above indicate that the estimates derived from these victim surveys *under*-represent the real amount of crime committed within a specified time and area. If respondents had perfect recall, were willing to give an unlimited amount of their time to an interview, and had perfect knowledge of the victim-experiences of their fellow household members, the disparities between survey estimates of crime and police figures shown above would certainly have been considerably larger.

Why Is Crime Unreported or Unrecorded?

Although there are substantial differences in the estimates obtained from the self-report and victimisation studies, they nevertheless all show that even crimes generally considered to be the most serious (robbery, aggravated violence and burglary) are under-represented in criminal statistics to a substantial degree. Why is this? Criminological literature abounds with commonsense assumptions about the factors inhibiting the reporting of crime. To begin with, behaviour may not be perceived as 'crime' by the victim or other witnesses. Where lies the difference between unsolicited sexual familiarity and indecent assault? When is a 'lost' wallet assumed to be stolen? Is a stock shrinkage of fifty hair combs due to theft, and if so to fifty thefts or one? Secondly, the victim may know that a crime has been committed, but still not report it. He may have sympathy with the offender—a relative for example; he may dislike or distrust the police and the courts; he may live in a community where it would be deviant to report a crime—where, for example, if one is hurt in a fight the consequence must be suffered in silence; he may fear reprisals or regard the harm done as too

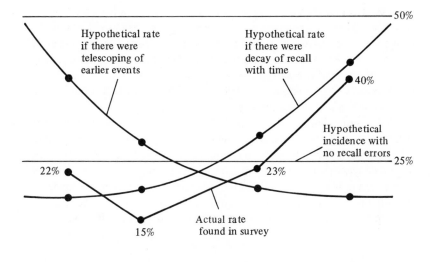

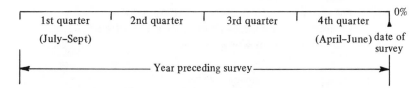

Figure 14-3. Effects of Telescoping and Forgetfulness on Victim's Report of Crime: The Proportions of Offences Reported in Each Quarter of a Preceding Year

trivial in relation to the consequences for the offender of a conviction; he may fear that his own deviant activity will be exposed (this, for example, is assumed to apply to the victims of theft by prostitutes and their pimps); and there are numerous other possible reasons. Behaviour regarded as criminal by the police may not be so regarded by those involved. This is especially thought to be true of offences such as violence committed in working-class areas and taking small amounts of material from work: this activity may be defined as 'perks' rather than theft. As an example of the latter J. P. Martin found, in a study of business in Reading, England, that they drew a line between 'reasonable pilfering' and theft. Half the firms stated that theft only began when the goods were worth £5 or more. [2]

The social tolerance of crime is not only high in areas where it is prevalent. It may also be rife in middle-class areas where misbehaviour by the young can be defined as 'part of growing up' or 'youthful pranks'. Such behaviour may not be reported if it is to lead to the stigma of a conviction. The action of the victim is, of course, not the only variable. The extent of police activity is especially important where there is no specific victim—as in the cases of drunkenness—or where one cannot properly speak of a victim—as in drug and abortion cases. From year to year, therefore, there may be dramatic changes in the proportion of these offences included in the statistics: the figures for abortions known to the police in England and Wales for the three years 1961-3 were 245, 406 and 239 respectively.[3]

Victimisation studies shed a good deal of light on the reasons for not re-porting crime and on the disparities between reported acts and those recorded by the police. In each of the three studies referred to above, those interviewed were asked whether the offence committed against them had been reported to the police, and if not, why? In the national sample an attempt was made to trace what happened after the victim had called the police: whether they came, considered the incident a crime, traced the offender, charged him, etc.

Table 14-3
A Comparison of Crimes Survey Respondents
Claimed Were Reported to the Police and Official
Police Statistics of Known Crimes.

Crime	Survey sample	Police statistics 1965	Percentage difference
Homicide	3·0	5·1	− 42
Forcible rape	30·3	11·6	+ 187
Robbery	60·6	61·4	− 1
Aggravated assault	136·4	106·8	+ 28
Burglary	545·8	296·6	+ 83
Larceny ($50)	360·8	267·4	+ 35
Vehicle theft	175·8	226·0	− 22
Total	1,312·7	974·7	+ 35

These figures refer to the United States National Sample.

In general the results are remarkably similar. As expected, the more serious the offence the more likely the victim was to report it. In Washington, of 121 index crimes committed 32 were not reported to the police, whereas for non-index crimes 83 of 132 were not reported. Even so, as table 14-3 shows about a third of the most serious crimes which victims claimed to have reported were unrecorded by the police. There is, however, considerable variation from of-fence to offence. Leaving aside homicide, car theft is the only offence both studies show to be invariably recorded: presumably because of the possibilities of claiming from an insurance company. But here the figures are difficult to interpret as more crime seemed to be recorded than was reported! In comparison, in the Washington study 64 per cent of the minor crimes were not reported to the police.

Why did the victims not report crimes to the police? The reasons varied between persons in different income brackets and more especially between whites and Negroes, as well as for different types of offence, but over half the respondents felt that nothing would be achieved by involving the police, and over a third felt that it was nothing to do with the police or expressed other negative attitudes. Only two per cent gave fear of reprisals from the offender as their reason. But of course, these findings may not be relevant to societies where there is a tradition of personal retaliation.

After those crimes which were not reported by victims were taken into account there still remained, in all three surveys, substantial discrepancies between the crimes supposedly reported and the police statistics of crimes known.

Notes

1. These reports are published as *Field Surveys I, Field Surveys II, Field Surveys III*, vol. 1.
2. J. P. Martin, *Offenders as Employees,* London: Macmillan, (1962), 114-19. There have been a number of German unpublished dissertations on the organisational containment of crimes committed by workers and public servants. See, for example, Dieter Goos, *Die Kriminalität in Betrieben der Elektroindustrie in den Jahren 1955-1960* (Diss. Bonn), (1963). Quoted in F. H. McClintock, *Criminological and Penological Aspects of the Dark Figure of Crime and Criminality*, (1969), Sixth European Conference of Directors of Criminological Research Institutes. Council of Europe, Strasbourg. For a general essay on social toleration, see T. Morris, The social toleration of crime. In H. J. Klare, ed., *Changing Concepts of Crime and Its Treatment*, London: Pergamon Press, (1966).
3. B. M. Dickens, *Abortion and the Law*, London: Macgibbon and Kee, (1966).

15 Crime Victimization in the Black Community. Results of the Black Buyer Survey

Robert Crosby and David Snyder

Introduction

The problems of crime are in the forefront of national interest.[1] The rate of crime is continuing to increase in the cities of the United States. Every day, people read in the newspapers about acts of violence, theft, rapes, and other serious offenses committed against the person. Consequently, a fear of crime throughout the urban centers of the nation has eroded the basic quality of life among many Americans. In addition, more people are victimized by crime than is shown in crime statistics; many crimes are not reported; and relations between the community and police are often strained.

It is impossible to determine the nature and extent of the problems crime causes by merely reviewing the latest crime statistics. Contact must be established and maintained with the victims of crime.[2] RMC and Roy Littlejohn Associates, in an effort to bridge the gap between crime statistics and society's opinions towards crime, evaluated the attitudes of black Americans about the crime problem in the cities. Several questions were asked on victimization, propensity to report crime, and satisfaction with police protection. This document summarizes the responses to these and other questions and interprets certain key points.

Admittedly, this is not a research paper that purports to draw conclusions of unequivocal significance; it is meant instead to be a convenient summary of the survey results, along with some cautious interpretive comments. Those who have an interest and a desire to find out the extent and effects of crime in urban black America are urged to study these results and develop their own conclusions.

Overview of the Findings

The black community generally believes that crime occurs more often than reported by officials, indicating the existence of an information gap in the black

Research Document RD-026, Resource Management Corporation, Bethesda, Maryland, 1969. Reprinted by permission of Resource Management Corporation.

175

urban centers throughout the nation. The survey showed that one out of every three respondents believed that crime occurs more often than reported by official figures. Feelings of distrust of the police may be a contributing cause of this gap.

Nearly one out of five urban blacks (19 percent) has been victimized by crime at some point in his life. The Uniform Crime Reports of 1968 found that approximately 1 percent of the general population is victimized by crime in one year; the average crime rate for individuals over the past 30 years is approximately 0.6 percent per year. It is interesting to note that using a standard probability formula, the victimization percent over time using UCR data is 22 percent, a figure comparable with our findings.[3]

Seventeen percent of those who had been victimized by crime indicated they had not reported it to the police. This contrasts with a survey of 10,000 households conducted in 1965 and 1966 for the President's Commission on Law Enforcement and Administration of Justice, which indicated that approximately 50 percent of all crimes committed in the general population had not been reported or had not entered the statistical system.[4] Thus, either the black urbanite reports crime more readily than the general population or there are serious deficiencies in the present statistical system for gathering crime statistics.

One out of three blacks who reported a crime indicated that police response had not met their expectations, while 41 percent of the crime victims themselves were not satisfied with the police response. For those victims who had not reported the crime, a surprisingly high percentage could or would not give a reason for not reporting the offense. The most prevalent reason for not reporting among those willing to say was the belief that nothing could be done.

The *Report of the National Advisory Commission on Civil Disorders* (March 1968) cited "deep hostility between police and ghetto communities as a primary cause of disorders surveyed by the Commission. . . . Abrasive relationships between police and Negroes and other minority groups have been a major source of grievance, tension, and, ultimately, disorder." Although our statistics do not reflect this hostility, they do picture a black urbanite who distrusts the police and is not satisfied with the services police provide. Table 15-1 presents a general summary of our findings. The following sections discuss these findings in detail.

Table 15-1
Summary of Findings

Information Gap	33 percent feel crime occurs more often than reported.
Victimization	19 percent had been victims of crime.
Reporting Crime	17 percent had not reported crime to police.
Expectation	31 percent felt police response was less than what they would expect.
Satisfaction with Police	41 percent felt police response was unsatisfactory.
Failure to Report Crime	61 percent of victims not reporting crime could or would not give a reason.

Information Gap

Overall, one of every three respondents believed that crime occurs more often than what is reported by officials. More blacks between 15 and 34 years old indicated crime occurs more often than reported (as opposed to the over 34 age group), reflecting either a distrustful attitude of the young or more exposure to crime. By sex, 37 percent of the males as opposed to 30 percent of females believed more crime occurred than was reported. Forty-two percent of the college-educated blacks felt that more crime occurred than was reported, as compared with only 31 percent of the noncollege-educated. Forty percent of the white-collar professional workers and blue-collar foremen, as compared with about 30 percent of the laborers, clerical, and nonprofessional occupations, believed that crime statistics understated reality, which verified that a distinction could be made by occupation. This distinction became clear when correlating these answers to household income. As income increases, people felt that crime occurs more often than reported. Figure 15-1 highlights this point; this trend has been tested and found statistically significant.

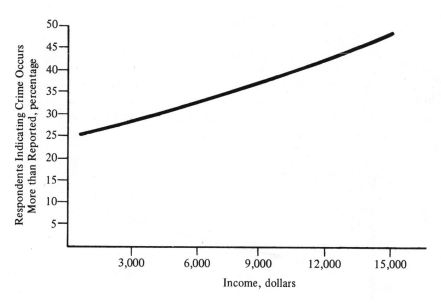

Figure 15-1.

Table 15-2
Crime Occurs More Often Than Reported by Officials

Overall	33 percent of all respondents
Age	35 percent of those younger than 34; 31 percent of those older than 34
Sex	37 percent of males; 30 percent of females
Education	42 percent of college-educated; 31 percent of noncollege-educated
Profession	40 percent of professionals; 30 percent of nonprofessionals
Income	50 percent of high-income group, decreasing with decreasing income

Victimization

Approximately 19 percent of the respondents had been victims of crime. Of these, more blacks under 35 had been victims than those over 35. Approximately one and one-half times more males are victimized than females. The victimization survey conducted by the President's Crime Commission indicated that the ratio between male and female victimization approaches 3.0 in the general population; i.e., three times as many males are victimized as females. In the white community, the white woman is victimized significantly less than the man, according to the Commission. In the black community, on the other hand, the female is a victim almost as often as the male.

The college graduates are victimized almost twice as often as noncollege graduates. As expected, a similar difference in victimization is found when occupation is considered. A higher percentage of professional workers are victimized. The percentage of an income group that is victimized appears to increase with the higher income categories, as shown in Figure 15-2. This trend has also been tested to be statistically significant.

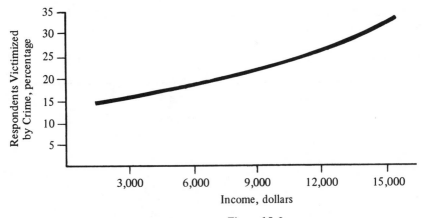

Figure 15-2

Table 15-3
Victims of Crime

Overall	19 percent of all respondents
Age	22 percent of the under-35 age group; 17 percent of the over-35 group
Sex	24 percent of males; 15 percent of females
Education	30 percent of college graduates; 17 percent of nongraduates
Income	33 percent of high-income group, decreasing with decreasing income

Reporting Crime

Seventeen percent of the victimized respondents had not reported the crime. Most of the 65-and-over victims reported crimes to the police, while one out of every four victims in the 15-to-24 age group had not reported the crime, which indicates that young blacks do not feel as compelled to report crimes as their elders.

Male victims refused to report crime considerably more often than the females. Level of education did not seem to be a deciding factor on a person's propensity to report crime to police. However, the victims engaged in labor occupations indicated a relatively high failure-to-report percentage; more than one of every four in these categories had not reported the crime. A higher percentage of respondents in the low-income groups (less than $6,000 annual income) had not reported the crime as compared with the higher income groups (more than $6,000 annually), indicating that income probably has an effect on a person's propensity to report crime.

Table 15-4 presents these data.

Table 15-4
Crime Not Reported to Police

Overall	17 percent of all respondents
Age	25 percent of the 15-to-24 age group; 14 percent of the older group
Sex	20 percent of males; 10 percent of females
Occupation	25 percent of the laborers; 14 percent of other occupations
Income	20 percent of low-income group; 14 percent of high-income group

Expectation of Police Response

Of all crime victims who reported to police, 31 percent received less police response than they expected. Almost two out of every five respondents in the youngest (15 to 24) and the oldest (over 55) age groups received less response than anticipated. More males than females indicated that police response had not met their expectations. A large portion of the college graduates, who may be more critical due to their educational attainment, indicated that police response to the reported crimes was less than expected. Occupation and income were not determining factors on this percentage.

Table 15-5 presents these statistics.

Table 15-5
Police Response Less Than Expected

Overall	31 percent of all respondents
Age	36 percent of the youngest and oldest age groups; 26 percent of the middle age group
Sex	36 percent of males; 26 percent of females
Education	43 percent of college graduates; 29 percent of nongraduates

Satisfaction with Police

A high degree of respondents who had a direct experience with the police felt that police response was unsatisfactory. Almost one out of every two respondents less than 35 years old were not satisfied with the police response, indicating that this age group is either not receiving adequate service or is highly critical of the police. Forty-five percent of the males as opposed to 37 percent of the females said that police response was unsatisfactory. Nearly 52 percent of the college graduates were not satisfied with police response, indicating that the college-educated may be more demanding of police. The highest degree of dissatisfaction was experienced with the black people engaged in a professional or technical occupation, with 53 percent of this group indicating unsatisfactory police response. No trend could be established with income.

Table 15-6 presents the results of this phase of the survey.

Table 15-6
Police Response Unsatisfactory

Overall	41 percent of all respondents
Age	46 percent of age group less than 35; 38 percent of group older than 35
Sex	45 percent of males; 37 percent of females
Education	52 percent of college-educated; 39 percent of noncollege-educated
Occupation	53 percent of professional and technical; 39 percent of other occupations

These statistics are alarming. The policeman's main function is to enforce the law and maintain order in the community he serves. How well he is performing this job is usually assessed by crime statistics. However, the opinions of people that are served must also be considered. Four of ten people in the black community are not satisfied with the response of the police. This is an extremely high degree of dissatisfaction and may be an important cause in the breakdown of relations and communications between police and the community.

Failure to Report Crime

Of those who did not report the crime, a very high percentage did not give a reason why they had not reported it to police. Almost 61 percent of the respondents could or would not state a reason. At this time we cannot directly assess the cause for such a high percentage of respondents not being able to state a reason, but RMC plans to investigate this further in a forthcoming survey. For those who gave a reason, a majority indicated that they did not think anything could be done, supporting the finding of the President's Crime Commission. Only 3 percent of the respondents to this question cited a reason relating to the effectiveness or relationship with the police, such as police are uninterested, police brutality, or no results from police. Due to the small base in the *Black Buyer* Survey, no analysis could be made of the age, sex, education, occupation, or income factors.

Table 15-7
Reasons for Not Reporting Crime

Overall	61 percent could give no reason.
Most Frequent	They gave personal reasons not relating to police.
Police	Only 3 percent indicated a reason related to police.

Notes

1. The research results presented here are based on the summer 1969 *Black Buyer* Survey, a continuing study of the urban Negro heads of households, conducted by Resource Management Corporation in cooperation with Roy Littlejohn and Associates.
2. In 1967, the President's Crime Commission conducted the first national survey survey of crime victimization.
3. $V = 1 - (1 - r)^n$ where r is the percentage of the average yearly crime rate, n is the average age of respondents to our survey (42 years old), and V is the

victimization percentage over time.
4. President's Commission on Law Enforcement and Administration of Justice, *The Challenge of Crime in a Free Society* (Washington, 1967).

16 The Requirement of Corroboration in Sex Offences

Leslie Sebba

Introduction

Under Israel law a person cannot be convicted for a sexual offence unless there is corroborative evidence. This means that if the accused denies that he has committed the offence, he cannot be convicted solely on the basis of the complainant's evidence.

Under English law the requirement is somewhat less rigorous: the judge must merely warn the jury of the danger of convicting without corroboration in such cases. The jury may convict in the absence of corroboration provided such a warning is given. There are, however, even in England, certain statutory offences[1] where the more exacting requirement found in the Israel law is applied (i.e., that corroborative evidence be actually submitted).

It has been suggested[2] that the English warning rule is inadequate, and that the stricter form of the rule should apply to *all* sexual offences. On the other hand, the view has been expressed in Israel[3] that (a) it is illogical that the rule here should be stricter than in England, and that (b) the existence of any form of restrictive rule of this nature is unnecessary. There are thus basically three possibilities:

(i) a strict rule requiring actual corroboration;

(ii) a rule requiring merely a warning;

(iii) no special rule at all.[4]

The importance which we must attach to making the right selection from these three possibilities depends partly on how frequently the problem of corroboration arises in jurisdictions which maintain some form of rule, in other words, whether the rule has an effect on the course of criminal proceedings resulting from complaints of sexual offences. At the request of the Israel Ministry of Justice, a survey was conducted for the purpose of ascertaining the part played by the corroboration rule in Israel. The survey was undertaken by the

Reprinted by permission of the Editorial Board of the *Israel Law Review*, Copyright ©1968, 3 (1): 67-87. Also, by permission of the author.

This is an edited version of the original article. A detailed description and discussion of the historical development of the law of corroboration in Israel has been omitted here.

Institute of Criminology of the Law Faculty of the Hebrew University of Jerusalem, and executed by L. Sebba of the Institute and A. Wagman of the Tel-Aviv District Attorney's office.

The survey was designed to provide information on various aspects of the problem: to discover the outcomes of the complaints of serious sexual offences made to the police in terms of the proceedings which followed, i.e., the closure of the file or the instigation of a prosecution, and in the latter case the conviction or acquittal of the accused; to note in particular any direct effect of the requirement of corroboration on the various stages of the proceedings; and to examine the type of corroboration which was in issue in the different cases, i.e., what aspect of the complaint lacked corroboration.

Information was also elicited, in so far as it was available from the records, as to the character of the complaints, in particular social information regarding the suspect and the victim, the relationship between them and the circumstances of the offence; and to establish possible relationships between them and the circumstances of the offence; and to establish possible relationships between the character of the complaints and their outcome. This aspect of the study is less immediately connected with the problem of corroboration and will not be dealt with here.

The survey itself was descriptive. It did not attempt to evaluate the effects of the rule, and the results were submitted to the Ministry of Justice without any specific recommendation.

Sample and Method

The investigation was confined to complaints of sexual offences of a serious nature, viz., rape, attempted rape, and indecent assault.[5] All complaints of these three offences which reached the police between April 1st, 1961,[6] and March 31st, 1963, were examined on the basis of the files of the police, district attorneys and courts. The number of such complaints was 155. Some complaints involved more than one suspect; the number of suspects was 195.

Details of the act complained of, the persons involved and the circumstances of the complaint were derived primarily from the police files. The results of each complaint were obtained by reference to the proceedings which followed. Most complaints were referred to one of the district attorneys.[7] The district attorney's evaluation of the case was then examined, in particular the decision whether or not to prosecute and its connection if any with the problem of corroboration. Where a prosecution followed, the investigation was pursued to the court proceedings, and the judgment of the trial court (and, where appropriate, of the appeal court) was examined.

Results of the Complaints

The outcome of the 155 complaints was as follows:

Files closed by the police:	20
Files closed by the district attorney:	63
Cases brought before the magistrates' courts:	21
Cases brought before the district courts:	51
Total:	155

Thus, of 155 offences initially classified as felonies over half did not reach the courts at all, while fewer than one-third reached the district courts, which have exclusive jurisdiction for the trial of felonies.

Files Closed by the Prosecution

The prosecution authorities have a discretionary power to close the file, i.e., to refrain from initiating a prosecution, where, for example, they see no possibility of securing a conviction or where they consider that the public interest does not require that proceedings be taken. The grounds on which 83 files in this sample were closed are given in Table 16-1.

Table 16-1

	Not in public interest to proceed	*No corroboration*	*Complainant disbelieved*	*No corroboration & complainant disbelieved*	*Others*	*Total*
Files closed by police	1	10	4	5	0	20
Files closed by district attorney	8	16	5	25	9	63
Total	9	26	9	30	9	83

Thus, while lack of corroboration was the sole declared reason for closing the file in only 26 out of 83 cases (31%), it played a part in the closing of 56 (67%).

Court Prosecutions

Of the 72 files which were proceeded with, most prosecutions were for the offence originally alleged, but in some cases the charge was modified by the prosecuting authority.

Table 16-2

	Charged with offense originally alleged	Charge modified	Total
District Court	47	4	51
Magistrates' Court	7	11	18
Total[8]	54	15	69

In nearly half of the cases in which the charge was modified, the modification took place because of lack of corroboration for the offence originally suspected.

Table 16-3

	Charge Modified		
	For lack of corroboration	For other reasons	Total
District Court	2	2	4
Magistrates' Court	5	6	11
Total	7	8	15

Results of Court Proceedings

The possible outcomes of court proceedings were (a) conviction for the offence for which the prosecution was brought (the "main offence") or (b) conviction for a lesser offence or (c) acquittal. The results of the 72 cases proceeded with are shown in Table 16-4.

Table 16-4

	Conviction			Acquittal	Result unknown	Total
	Main offense	Lesser offense	Total			
District Court	27	8	35	15	1	51
Magistrates' Court	12	2	14	4	3	21
Total	39	10	49	19	4	72

Thus 72% of cases proceeded with (where the outcome is known) resulted in a conviction, but only 57% in conviction for the "main offence". Moreover, not more than 28 out of 155 (18%) complaints resulted in conviction in the district court for the felony originally complained of, and not more than 53 complaints (34%) resulted in a conviction of any kind.

The cases which resulted in conviction for lesser offences owing to lack of corroboration were as follows:

Table 16-5

	Convicted of Lesser Offense		
	For lack of corroboration	For other reasons	Total
District Court	3	5	8
Magistrates' Court	1	1	2
Total	4	6	10

The cases which resulted in acquittal for lack of corroboration are as follows:

Table 16-6

	Acquittals		
	For lack of corroboration	For other reasons	Total
District Court	9	6	15
Magistrates' Court	0	4	4
Total	9	10	19

The total number of proceedings affected by the requirement of corroboration (taking together Tables 16-3, 16-5, and 16-6) were as follows:

Table 16-7

	Lack of Corroboration Resulting In:			
	Modification of charge by prosecuting authority	Conviction for lesser offence	Acquittal	Total
District Court	2	3	9	14
Magistrates' Court	5	1	0	6
Total	7	4	9	20

Type of Corroboration

To support a conviction for a sexual assault, corroboration is required of all the material facts. There are in practice three elements which must be proved:
  (a) the identity of the offender;
  (b) the commission of the alleged act;

(c) lack of consent on the part of the victim.

The absence of corroboration of any one of these may result in:

(i) the closing of the file by the prosecuting authority (i.e., the district attorney or the police) or

(ii) modification of the charge by the prosecuting authority (i.e., its alteration to a charge which does not require corroboration, or to which the accused will plead guilty) or

(iii) the acquittal of the accused by the court or

(iv) modification by the court of the offence for which it convicts the accused.

The respective frequencies of the three elements for which corroboration may be lacking at the different stages of the criminal process are shown in the Table 16-8.

Table 16-8
Type of Corroboration Absent by Stage of Proceedings

	Unspe-cified	Iden-tity of sus-pect	Com-mission of act	Lack of con-sent	Total
File closed by prosecuting authority for absence of corroboration alone	0	2	20	4	26
File closed by prosecuting authority for absence of corroboration and lack of belief in complaint	6	1	7	16	30
Prosecutor's charge modified	2	0	5	0	7
Conviction modified	4	0	0	0	4
Acquittal	0	1	4	4	9
Total	12	4	36	24	76

Note: For the logical order in which corroboration is sought, the table must be read from left to right. Thus, where the absence of corroboration for the commission of the act is specified, this implies that there *was* corroboration of the identity of the suspect. Similarly, where the absence of corroboration for the lack of consent on the part of the victim is specified, this implies that there was corroboration of the identity of the suspect and the commission of the act.

Thus, in the cases in which the absence of corroboration played a part and details were specified, it was the commission of the physical act which most often lacked corroboration. The absence of corroboration for the lack of consent on the part of the victim was less common, while lack of corroboration for the identity of the suspect was comparatively rare. If only the cases where the lack of corroboration was *decisive* are taken (i.e., excluding the second row in Table 16-8) the "commission of the act" category was even more preponderant; in cases where *consent* was an issue the complainant tended in any case to be disbelieved (i.e., was considered by the prosecution authorities to be insufficiently convincing to support a court prosecution).

Discussion

The Survey confirmed the importance of the rule requiring corroboration in sexual cases inasmuch as it was frequently cited by the prosecuting authorities as the reason for closing a file or modifying a charge, and by courts as necessitating an acquittal. The significance of this is not, of course, unequivocal: one cannot be certain that these cases would be decided otherwise if the rule (in Israel) were abolished, since (a) it may be that the prosecution authorities might anyway consider that many uncorroborated complaints lacked sufficient evidence to put before a court, or (b) it may be that even in the absence of the rule the court would be unlikely to consider the charge proved beyond reasonable doubt in such cases.

Thus the survey could not and did not attempt to answer the vital question: in which cases had the offence actually been committed? In particular, are the cases in which conviction is apparently prevented by the requirements of corroboration actually the cases in which the alleged attacker had not in fact committed the offence, or are guilty persons saved by the rule? Conversely, would wrongful convictions take place if the rule were relaxed in Israel, and do they in fact occur in England? In other words, from the point of view of the substantive law, is justice done? The desirability of retaining the rule in Israel, or of extending its application in England, must depend upon the answers to these questions.

The Strict Rule, the Warning, or No Rule?

We now return to the question of which rule leads to greater approximation to justice in the trial of sexual offences: the absolute requirement of actual corroboration, or the requirement of a mere warning? Or would it be preferable to have no special requirement whatsoever in these cases?

In *Ben Hamo's* case Cohn J. invoked *Wigmore* in support of his argument that any special requirement is indefensible and merely serves as an obstacle in

the path of justice.[9] This was a somewhat misleading invocation since *Wigmore*
did not simply propose to abolish any restraint on the court's power to convict on the sole testimony of the complainant, thereby leaving the assessment
of the complainant's veracity entirely to the court's evaluative skill. He in fact
proposed the replacement of the requirement of corroboration by a more
scientific assessment of the complainant's veracity which will be discussed below.[10]

An unqualified objection to restrictive rules on corroboration appears in
Wigmore's discussion on the evidence of accomplices.[11] We have seen that the
courts tend to take a similar approach to the two distinct problems of the reliability of the evidence of complainants in sex offences and the reliability of
the evidence of accomplices. In England, the same requirement of a warning
to the jury applies in both cases. In Palestine there was a deliberate attempt to
impose the stricter rule in a case concerned with accomplices and the same
practice seems to have been followed automatically with regard to sex offences.
. . . Since the root of the problem so far as sexual offences are concerned
lies in the reliability or otherwise of complainants, the need for any special
requirement of corroboration would be reduced, perhaps even eliminated (and
this is in essence *Wigmore's* argument) if provision were made for a psychological
assessment of the complainant which could provide a clear indication of her
veracity.

Prevailing court rules and procedure do not enable such an assessment of
the complainant to be made. "A plausible tale by an attractive, innocent-
looking girl may lead to a life sentence for the accused, because the rules of
Evidence (and the judge's unacquaintance with modern psychiatry) permit no
probing of the witness' veracity."[12] The complainant may be questioned as
to her chastity, but her answers will be final since they are relevant not to the
issue but "merely" to her credibility—unless the questions relate to her chastity with the *accused*, in which case rebutting evidence may be adduced by
the defence. Evidence is also admissible of "general reputation" for veracity
or reliability—but not for specific instances of it. Finally, the House of Lords
has held in a recent decision[13] that evidence of mental abnormality on the
part of a witness is admissible. While the decision is welcome, its helpfulness
in the present context will depend upon (a) the flexibility with which the term
"mental abnormality" is interpreted and (b) the availability of such evidence
in appropriate cases.

A Committee of the American Bar Association[14] has recommended that
"in all charges for sex offences, the complaining witness be required to be
examined before trial by competent psychiatrists for the purpose of ascertaining her probable credibility, the report to be presented in evidence." This is
the type of scheme which *Wigmore* himself favours, to be facilitated by the
relaxation of the rules of evidence to allow in particular opinion evidence (of

professional experts) as to moral character. Dr. Williams considered that a psychiatric examination would involve administering a "truth drug" and commented:

> To subject a female complainant to examination and investigation in this way would be a serious indignity, and would tend to hinder charges from being brought even when they were clearly well founded. The development in the United States of 'lie-detector' (polygraph) techniques offers much better promise of detecting falsehood by simple means, and a requirement that a prosecutrix should take a lie-detector test would not be open to the objections raised against a similar proposal with regard to defendants.[15]

He nevertheless foresaw practical difficulties in the way of immediate implementation of this method and meanwhile recommended, as mentioned above, that the corroboration warning be maintained or preferably that the statutory rule be extended.

Conclusion

The weight of opinion seems to be that the weakness of a rule requiring corroboration in all cases lies in its artificiality as a test of the veracity of the complainant. Such a rule will probably have the effect of preventing the conviction of an innocent accused, but will also quite possibly prevent the conviction of many guilty ones. It is wrong, however, to describe the rule as "an anomaly . . . because it requires the judge to supplement the 100 per cent certainty he has already derived from the main evidence.[16] The principle behind the rule lies in the recognition that the judge *cannot* be certain whether the complaint is genuine on the sole basis of his own assessment of the complainant and her story, for such certainty cannot be acquired by traditional court procedure. *Within the framework of this procedure no safeguard seems to be adequate short of requiring actual corroboration.* Thus the conclusion of Dr. Williams, that unless and until a new method is introduced of assessing the veracity of complainants (or of defendants) the strict (Israel) version of the rule is preferable, appears to be irrefutable.

The high proportion of complaints in the sample studied (more than 65 per cent) which did not result in convictions, however, calls out for further investigation of these cases on the lines suggested by *Wigmore*. An alternative to the introduction of a general requirement of a full psychological examination in all cases would be to conduct such an examination of a *sample* of complainants. The information thus provided, especially that derived from cases in which no corroborative evidence was available, might indicate the extent to which guilty persons evaded conviction when the strict rule applied.

Notes

1. The procuration of women for the purposes of prostitution and the use of unlawful means, such as drugs, to obtain sexual intercourse: see sec. 2-4 of the Sexual Offences Act, 1956. In the U.S., the rule is also found (in some states for certain offences) in the form of a statutory requirement: see Wigmore, *Evidence* (3rd ed.) Vol. VII, secs. 2044 & 2061.
2. G. L. Willaims, "Corroboration—Sexual Cases" (1962) Criminal L.R. 662.
3. Cohn J. in *Ben Hamo* v. *A. G.* (1963) 17 *P.D.* 2857, 2866.
4. Various modifications of these alternatives are also possible. A rule of types (i) and (ii) could be required only for certain offences; or a warning of type (ii) could be at the judge's discretion.
5. Offences under secs. 152, 154 and 157 respectively, of the Criminal Code Ordinance, 1936; all these offences are felonies under Israel law, i.e., punishable by more than three years' imprisonment.
6. In 1961 Police Headquarters opened a central register of sex offenders, to which all sex offences are reported by the police in the locality in which they occur. The complaints in the sample were traced through this register.
7. Complaints of felonies must be dealt with by the district attorney; the police may recommend closure of a file but cannot close it themselves.
8. Three cases are omitted here: one was brought in a juvenile court; one was transferred to a Military Court; and in the third case the accused was confined to a mental institution.
9. It does not follow that the new charge did not require corroboration; it may be that the accused was charged with a lesser (sexual) offence which he admitted.

   The question of which charges require corroboration has proved a controversial one in Israel and has arisen in a number of Supreme Court judgments, culminating in *Ben Hamo's case* (op. cit.). If X is suspected of burglary and rape, and of an indecent assault, but in neither case is there corroborative evidence of the complainant's story, may X be charged—and convicted—of burglary with intent to commit a felony, and Y of assault with intent to commit a felony? Or may Y simply be convicted of common assault? The majority opinion in *Ben Hamo's* case was that a conviction for burglary with intent was possible (i.e., in X's case) since (a) the offence itself is non-sexual and (b) the facts constituting the burglary can be distinguished from the sexual element. It was not permissible, however, (e.g., in the case of the assault) to convict of a non-sexual offence based on the same set of facts which would constitute a sexual offence, i.e. merely by altering the name of the offence.

   The minority held that corroboration is required for sexual *offences* and not for sexual *acts*, so that the court may—indeed it must—convict of a non-sexual offence in all these cases, if it believes the complainant and if the elements of a non-sexual offence are proved. The practical importance of this question is indicated by the following observation of Cohn J. in his minority opinion, at p. 2866: "There is hardly ever a sexual offence committed which does not involve also the commission of a non-sexual offence". A ruthless application of this view could thus denude the corroboration rule of its effect.

10. Wigmore's first objection to rules requiring corroboration in sexual offences (see vol. VII, sec. 2061) was that while there was some danger of false testimony in these cases, the consequences of letting these offences go unpunished were serious.

11. "The facts is that, in the light of modern psychology, this technical rule of corroboration seems but a crude and childish measure, if it be relied upon as an adequate means for determining the credibility of the complaining witness in such charges. The problem of estimating the veracity of feminine testimony in complaints against masculine offenders is baffling enough to the experienced psychologist. This statutory rule is unfortunate in that it tends to produce reliance upon a rule of thumb. *Better to inculcate the resort to an expert scientific analysis of the particular witness' mentality as the true measure of enlightenment.*" (My italics.) *Ibid*.

12. *Op. cit.* sec. 2057.

13. Wigmore, *op. cit.* Vol. III, sec. 924a. p. 459. N.B: The corroboration rule has also been applied when the victim is male: See *Burgess'* case, 40 Cr. App. Rep. 144.

14. *Tookey* v. *Metropolitan Police Commissioner* [1965] 1 All E.R. 506, overruling the decisions of the Court of Criminal Appeal in that case and *Gunewardene's* case. [1951] 2 All E.R. 290.

15. Report of the Committee on the Improvement of the Law of Evidence, 63 A.B.A. Rep. 570: cited in *Wigmore*, vol. III, sec. 942a. p. 466.

16. [1962] Crim. L.R. at p. 664.

17. Silberg J. in *Shvili* v. *A.G.* (1964) 18 *P.D.* 438, 445; cited by Berinson J. in *Pick* v. *A.G.* (1951) 5 *P.D.* 662, 667.

17

The Influence of the Character of the Criminal and His Victim on the Decisions of Simulated Jurors

David Landy and Elliot Aronson

Several writers have commented on the irrational tendency of people to exaggerate a person's causal responsibility for an event while underestimating the role of other causal factors which are logically involved in the occurrence of that event (Heider, 1944, 1958; Jones and Davis, 1965). This tendency to perceive persons as causal origins often influences the manner in which we evaluate or judge other individuals. That is, we often judge a person in terms of the consequences or effects of which we perceive him to be the causal origin. This occurs even in situations where there are many factors beyond the person's control which, from a logical point of view, are responsible for the specific effects.

For example, an experiment by Walster (1966) demonstrated that the more serious the consequences of an accident, the greater was the tendency for subjects to assign responsibility for the accident to someone who could *possibly* be held responsible for it . . . It is likely that people somehow view a crime as being more serious if the victim of the crime is a good, attractive person. If this is the case, one might ask whether individuals have a tendency to judge a criminal defendant more harshly when the *victim* of the crime is an attractive individual than when the victim is an unattractive individual. While "the law" makes no such distinction (i.e., a criminal is not held to be more responsible, guilty, or deserving of punishment the more sympathetic and attractive his victim), it is quite possible that the decision of a jury will be affected by the character of the victim in a criminal case.

This possibility apparently has not escaped the attention of criminals' counsel. Percy Foreman, a noted criminal defense lawyer, has claimed that "The best defense in a murder case is the fact that the deceased should have been killed regardless of how it happened" (Smith, 1966). In one case in which Foreman represented a woman who had confessed to shooting her husband, Foreman so effectively vilified the victim that he felt "The jury was ready to dig up the deceased and shoot him all over again" (Smith, 1966). The jury did acquit his client.

Reprinted from the *Journal of Experimental Social Psychology*, 1969, 5(2): 141-152, by permission of the Publisher, Academic Press, Inc. Also, by permission of the authors.

The present research deals with the relationship between the personal characteristics of the victim of a crime and the desire or tendency of individuals to punish the person accused of committing that crime. In Experiment I the personal characteristics of the victim of a criminal offense are varied. We have predicted that when the victim of a criminal offense is presented as having positive characteristics, subjects will be more severe in their "sentencing" of the defendant than when the victim of the identical offense is presented as having negative characteristics.

While the present research is not directly concerned with the law or legal system *per se*, it does have obvious implications for both. The juridical analog seems to provide the most logical means of testing our hypothesis. For obvious reasons, however, we were unable to utilize real juries in actual criminal trials. The investigator of legal processes and judicial decision is confronted with numerous social, economic, and methodological difficulties (Kalven and Zeisal, 1966; Zeisal, 1962; Strodtbeck, 1962; James and Strodbeck, 1957; Redmount, 1961). An attempt to manipulate variables within the context of an actual trial would be impossible. In addition, since there are a multiplicity of factors entering into a determination of guilt, we wanted to employ a situation in which there was little or no doubt in the minds of our subjects about the guilt of the defendant, i.e., a situation in which it would be clear that he had actually perpetrated the offense. We could then ask our subjects to sentence the defendant to what they felt was an appropriate number of years of imprisonment. This would provide us with a continuous variable, indicating severity of punishment, for our major dependent variable. Furthermore, we wanted to be able to control the circumstances of the crime so that it would not only be identical for all subjects but also be completely independent of the characteristics of the victim.

Experiment I

Method

Subjects were 261 male and female sophomores at the University of Texas who had agreed to participate in a study dealing with "Juridical Judgment" in order to fulfill a requirement in their introductory psychology course. Twelve experimental sessions were scheduled on 4 consecutive days with from 20 to 30 subjects participating in each session.

The experimental sessions were all held in a university classroom. At the start of each session the experimenter greeted the subjects and then made the following comments:

"We are interested in studying the manner in which people judge various criminal offenses. I am going to give each of you a booklet

which contains a brief account of a criminal offense. When you
have finished reading the case account, you will be asked to give
your personal opinion concerning the case. That is, we want you
to sentence the defendant described in the case account to a
specific number of years of imprisonment. Take as much time as
you want in reading and contemplating the case before you finally
sentence the defendant. Remember that we are interested in your
personal opinion, so please give your own personal judgment and
not how you feel others might react to the case or how you feel
you should react to it. One other thing—in making your sentence,
consider the question of parole as being beyond your jurisdiction.
That is, sentence the defendant irrespective of whether or not
you feel he should have opportunity for parole after a certain
number of years in prison.

The experimenter then passed out copies of a case account of a negligent
automobile homocide. These were identical for all subjects except in one
respect: In approximately one-half of the case accounts the victim of the negligent homicide was presented as an unattractive individual, while in the other half
of the case accounts the victim was presented as an attractive individual. The
assignment of subjects to either the Attractive or Unattractive Victim condition
was, of course, random. There were 129 subjects in the Attractive Victim condition and 132 subjects in the Unattractive Victim condition.

The description of the crime as presented in the case account is presented
below:

John Sander was driving home from an annual Christmas office party
on the evening of December 24 when his automobile struck and killed a
pedestrian by the name of Martin Lowe. The circumstances leading to
this event were as follows: The employees of the insurance office where
Sander worked began to party at around 2:00 p.m. on the afternoon of
the 24th. By 5:00 p.m. some people were already leaving for home, although many continued to drink and socialize. Sander, who by this
time had had several drinks, was offered a lift home by a friend who did
not drink and who suggested that Sander leave his car at the office and
pick it up when he was in 'better shape.' Sander declined the offer,
claiming he was 'stone sober' and would manage fine. By the time
Sander had finished another drink, the party was beginning to break
up. Sander left the office building and walked to the garage where he
had parked his car, a four-door 1965 Chevrolet. It had just started to
snow. He wished the garage attendant a Merry Christmas and pulled out
into the street. Traffic was very heavy at the time. Sander was six blocks
from the garage when he was stopped by a policeman for reckless driv-

ing. It was quite apparent to the officer that Sander had been drinking, but rather than give him a ticket on Christmas Eve, he said that he would let Sander off if he would promise to leave his car and take a taxi. Sander agreed. The officer hailed a taxi and Sander go into it. The minute the taxi had turned a corner, however, Sander told the driver to pull over to the curb and let him out. Sander paid the driver and started back to where he had parked his own car. Upon reaching his car he proceeded to start it up and drove off. He had driven four blocks from the street where the police officer had stopped him when he ran a red light and struck Lowe, who was crossing the street. Sander immediately stopped the car. Lowe died a few minutes later on the way to the hospital. It was later ascertained that internal hemorrhaging was the cause of death. Sander was apprehended and charged with negligent homicide. The police medical examiner's report indicated that Sander's estimated blood alcohol concentration was between 2.5 and 3.0% at the time of the accident."

Manipulation of the Description of the Victim. The next paragraph in the case account contained a description of the victim, which differed for subjects in each of the two experimental conditions.

Attractive Victim. "The victim, 48-year-old Martin Lowe, was a senior partner of a successful stock brokerage firm and an active member of the community welfare board. He was a widower and is survived by his son and daughter-in-law, Mr. and Mrs. Thomas Lowe. At the time of the accident the victim was on his way to the Lincoln Orphanage, of which he was a founding member, with Christmas gifts."

Unattractive Victim. "The victim, 48-year-old Martin Lowe, was a notorious hoodlum and ex-convict who had been convicted of assault and extortion. He was a henchman for a crime syndicate which had been under police investigation for some time. A loaded 32-caliber pistol was found on his body."

The final paragraph of the case account contained a description of the defendant, which was the same for all subjects. The defendant was described as a 37-year-old insurance adjustor and divorcee. While he had no previous criminal record, he did have several serious violations on his traffic record.

The last page of the case account booklet contained instructions to the subjects to judge and sentence the defendant. In these, the subjects were requested to consider the crime as being punishable for from 1 to 60 years of imprisonment, and to sentence the defendant to a specific number of years of imprisonment according to their own personal judgment. They were told to take as much time as they wanted in making their decision.

When all of the subjects had completed sentencing the defendant, the experimenter collected the booklets. He then explained the nature of the experiment to the subjects.

Results

Each subject sentenced the defendent in the automobile homicide case to a
specific number of years of imprisonment. We predicted that those subjects to
whom the victim of the crime had been described as possessing positive
characteristics would sentence the defendant to a greater number of years of
imprisonment than those subjects to whom the victim had been presented
as possessing negative characteristics. The results of the study lend support
to this prediction. The mean sentence of subjects in the Attractive Victim
condition was 15.77 years, while the mean sentence of subjects in the
Unattractive Victim condition was 12.90 years. However, this difference did
not reach the conventional level of significance (F = 3.18, 1 and 257 $df, p < .08$).

Experiment II

Because of the marginal nature of the above results, we repeated the experiment with some slight modifications designed to make the manipulation more
powerful. In addition, we manipulated the character of the defendant in order
to assess the effect of this variable on the judgment of the subjects.

It is a common belief that jurors in a criminal trial are often influenced by
the personal characteristics of the *defendant*. That is, they have a tendency
to be more lenient in their decision when the defendant possesses certain
positive characteristics and more severe when he possesses certain negative
characteristics, even when these are apparently unrelated to the offense or
circumstances in which it took place.

There is, in fact, some empirical evidence which indicates that sentiments
about the defendant—his court appearance, family, occupation, etc.—may
actually influence the decision of a jury. In a large-scale study of the decisions
of judges and juries, Kalven and Zeisal (1966) asked judges to report by mail
questionnaire on criminal cases which were tried before them with juries.
The judges reported the actual verdict handed down by the jury, what their
own verdict would have been had the case been tried before them without a
jury, and the reasons which they thought accounted for disagreements when
the two verdicts differed. In a sample of 962 cases in which the judge and jury
disagreed about the verdict, the judges attributed 11% of the disagreements
to factors related to the impression created by the defendant. In another
sample of 293 disagreement cases in which judges were asked to indicate
on the questionnaire whether they felt the impression made by the defendant
was sympathetic, average, or unattractive, 14% of the disagreements were
attributed to sentiments about the defendant.

These results seem to indicate that an attractive defendant can move the
jury to be more lenient than the judge would have been, i.e., acquit rather

than convict. Still, the investigators note that the defendant factor rarely accounted for judge-jury disagreements in and of itself, but rather, acted in conjunction with other variables such as (a) disparity in the quality of the prosecution and defense counsel and (b) the ambiguity of the evidence presented during the trial. There is, of course, no information presented with regard to the extent which the judge himself is motivated in his decision by feelings about the defendant. However, the assumption is that the judge is less influenced than the jury by such sentiments . . .

In Experiment II the characteristics of both the defendant and the victim are varied. We have predicted that the more unattractive the presentation of the defendant, the more severe will be the sentence he receives. The prediction concerning the relationship between severity of sentence and the nature of the victim is, of course, the same as that in Experiment I—the more attractive the victim, the more severe the sentence.

Method

Subjects were 116 male and female students in two sections of an introductory government course at the University of Texas . . .

The basic case account of the automobile homicide offense presented to the subjects was nearly identical to that presented in Experiment I. In the present experiment, however, both the nature of the defendant and the nature of the victim were systematically varied in a 2 X 3 design with two levels of victim character: Attractive and unattractive; and three levels of defendant character: Attractive, unattractive, and neutral. In addition, the descriptions of the defendant and victim were interpolated throughout the case account instead of appearing complete at the end of the account . . .

Below are the aggregate descriptions of the defendant and the victim. . . . The descriptions were based, in part, on the comments made by the judges in Kalven and Zeisal's (1966) study concerning the characteristics of individual defendants which appeared to influence jury sentiments.

Attractive Victim. "Lowe is a noted architect and prominent member of the community. He had designed many well-known buildings throughout the state . . . was an active member of the community welfare board. At the time of the incident, Lowe was on his way to the Lincoln Orphanage, of which he was a founding member, with Christmas gifts. He is survived by his wife and two children, ages 11 and 15."

Unattractive Victim. "Lowe is a notorious gangster and syndicate boss who had been vying for power in the syndicate controlling the state's underworld activities. He was best known for his alleged responsibility in the River-

view massacre of five men. At the time of the incident, Lowe was carrying
a loaded 32-caliber pistol which was found on his body. He had been out of
jail on bond, awaiting trial on a double indictment of mail fraud and income
tax evasion."

Attractive Defendant. "Sander is a sixty-four-year-old insurance adjustor
who has been employed by the same insurance firm for 42 years. Sander
was friendly with everyone and was known as a good worker. Sander is a
widower, his wife having died of cancer the previous year, and he is, consequently, spending Christmas Eve with his son and daughter-in-law. When the
incident occurred, Sander's leg banged the steering column, reaggravating
a gun wound which had been the source of a slight limp and much pain.
Sander's traffic record shows he has received three tickets in the past five
years, two of which were moving violations."

Unattractive Defendant. "Sander is a thirty-three-year-old janitor. In the
building where Sander has been working as a janitor for the past two months, he
was not known by many of the firm employees, but was nevertheless invited to
join the party. Sander is a two-time divorcee, with three children by his first wife,
who has since remarried. He was going to spend Christmas Eve with his girlfriend
in her apartment. The effect of the incident on Sander was negligible; he was
slightly shaken up by the impact, but suffered no major injuries. Sander has two
misdemeanors on his criminal record in the past five years — breaking and entering and a drug violation. His traffic record shows three tickets in the same space
of time."

Neutral Defendant.   "Sander is employed in the area. He went to the
office party in the insurance firm headquarters shortly after the party had
begun. After the party Sander was heading in the direction of home. When the
incident occurred, Sander was slightly shaken up by the impact, but suffered
no major injuries. His traffic record shows he has received three traffic tickets
in the past five years, two of which were moving violations."
The case accounts ended as follows: "Sander, who had stopped his car
at the scene of the accident, was apprehended and charged with negligent
automobile homicide, a crime which in the State is punishable by imprisonment
of one to twenty-five years."
Following the description of the offense was a page of instructions request-
ing the subjects to judge and sentence the defendant. The subjects were requested to consider the crime of negligent automobile homicide as punishable
for from 1 to 25 years imprisonment, and to sentence the defendant to a
specific number of years of imprisonment, according to their *own personal
judgment.*

The last page of the case account booklets contained several additional questions pertaining to the subject's feeling about the guilt of the defendant, and his impressions of the defendant and the victim. Each of these questions was answered on a 9-point scale appropriately labeled at the end points.

Results and Discussion

In order to assess the effectiveness of the character descriptions of the defendant and the victim, we asked the subjects to indicate their impressions of the defendant and the victim on a 9-point scale on which "9" meant "extremely negative (unfavorable)" and "1" meant "extremely positive (favorable)." The mean impression rating of the victim for the subjects in the Attractive Victim (AV) conditions was 2.52, while the mean impression rating of the victim for subjects in the Unattractive Victim (UV) conditions was 7.64. This difference was significant at beyond the .001 level of probability ($F = 354.21$, 1 and 111 df). The mean impression ratings of the defendant were as follows: For subjects in the Attractive Defendant (AD) conditions, 5.53; for subjects in the Neutral Defendant (ND) conditions, 6.04; and for subjects in the Unattractive Defendant (UD) conditions, 7.08. An analysis of variance performed on these data yielded $F = 8.11$ (2 and 111 df, $p < .001$). It is thus apparent that the character descriptions of the defendant and the victim had their intended effect.

The subjects were also requested to rate how guilty they felt the defendant was. We, of course, expected that there would be no differences in the subjects' guilt ratings of the defendant across experimental conditions and that the defendant would be perceived as having been definitely guilty of the crime. On a scale where "9" meant "definitely guilty of the crime," the subjects' guilt ratings of the defendant ranged from a mean of 8.00 (for subjects in the ND-UV condition) to a mean of 8.67 (for subjects in the AD-UV condition). The difference between these two extremes did not reach the conventional level of significance ($t = 1.47$, 39 df). The null hypothesis, of course, cannot be proved; nevertheless, the guilt rating data does afford some support regarding the subjects' uniform perception of the defendant's guilt.

With regard to the effect of the character description of the victim on the severity of sentence passed on the defendant, the results of Experiment II parallel those of Experiment I. Table 17-1 presents the means and standard deviations of the sentences made by the subjects in each of the experimental conditions.

An examination of this table indicates that, as predicted, the average sentence made by subjects in the AV conditions, 10.55 years imprisonment, was greater than the average sentence made by the subjects in the UV conditions, 8.48 years imprisonment. While the data in both Experiments I and II lend directional support to the hypothesis concerning the relationship between the character of the victim and the severity of sentencing, in neither experiment does the magnitude of the obtained differences between the AV and UV conditions reach the conventional level of significance.

Table 17-1
Means and Standard Deviations of the Sentences
(Expressed as Years of Imprisonment) Made by
Subjects in Each of the Experimental Conditions
of Experiment II

		Victim		
		Attractive	*Unattractive*	*Total*
Defendant				
Attractive	M	8.72	8.44	8.58
	σ	4.18	6.60	
	N	18.	18.	36.
Neutral	M	9.05	7.39	8.22
	σ	9.01	7.63	
	N	21.	23.	44.
Unattractive	M	13.89	9.61	11.75
	σ	5.76	5.98	
	N	18.	18.	36.
Total	M	10.55	8.48	
	N	57.	59.	

Taken as a whole, our results suggest that both the character of the defendant and the character of the victim are important variables in the severity of the sentence imposed. While the results of these laboratory experiments may have important implications for actual jury trials, a direct and literal extrapolation would be imprudent. . . . At the same time, we are encouraged by the fact that in the absence of extraneous stimuli, our results paralleled some of the findings of Kalven and Zeisal (1966) in their examination of actual cases.

References

Gaudet, F. J.   "Individual Differences in the Sentencing Tendencies of Judges."
1938   *Archives of Psychology* 32, no. 230.

Heider, F.   Social perception and phenomenal casualty. *Psychological*
1944   *Review* 51: 358–374.

Heider, F.   *The Psychology of Interpersonal Relations.* New York: Wiley.
       1958

James, R.M., and   "An Attempted Replication of a Jury Experiment by Use
Strodtbeck, F.L.   of Radio and Newspaper." *Public Opinion Quarterly* 21:
       1957   313–318.

Jones, E.E., and   "From Acts to Dispositions: The Attribution Process in
Davis, K.E.   Person Perception." In L. Berkowitz (ed.), *Advances in*
       1965   *Experimental Social Psychology* vol. 2. New York: Academic
                    Press, pp. 219–266.

Kalven, H., Jr.   *The American Jury.* Boston: Little, Brown.
and Zeisal, H.
       1966

Redmount, R.S.   "Psychology and the Law." In H. Toch (ed.), *Legal and*
       1961   *Criminal Psychology.* New York: Holt, pp. 22–50.

Smith, M.   "Percy Foreman: Top Trial Lawyer." *Life,* 60: 92–101.
       1966

Strodtbeck, F.   "Social Process, the Law, and Jury Functioning." In W. M.
       1962   Evan (ed.), *Law and Sociology.* New York: Free Press of
                    Glencoe, pp. 144–164.

Walster, E.   "Assignment of Responsibility for an Accident." *Journal of*
       1966   *Personality and Social Psychology* 3: 73–79.

Zeisal, H.   "Social Research and the Law: The Ideal and the Practical."
       1962   In W. M. Evan (ed.), *Law and Sociology.* New York: Free
                    Press of Glencoe, pp. 124–143.

18 The Thalidomide Affair

Maurice Goldsmith

It will ease our conscience if the thalidomide children, hauntingly, cause us to develop social mechanisms for ensuring that their tragedy is unlikely to occur again. This will not be easy for we are dealing with great unknowns resulting from the manner in which we now manipulate our physiological processes. And this poses basic problems of business ethics, and moral and scientific responsibility which, at the moment, we are not competent to define and, therefore, to solve.

What lessons can we draw from the thalidomide tragedy?

In 1958, the Distillers Company, one of the largest in Britain with some 200,000 shareholders and a stock market value of more than £600 million, began to market thalidomide under the trade name of Distavel, declaring it "can be given with complete safety to pregnant women." This marketing went on for three years, despite reports of adverse neurological effects of the drug in adults that appeared in the weekly *British Medical Journal* in December 1960, and on eight separate occasions in the following year.

However, doctors believed the drug to be outstandingly safe, and assured of its relative innocuousness some put pressure on reluctant parents to make use of it.

Then, in December 1961, Distillers announced withdrawal of the drug because of reports "from two overseas sources possibly associating thalidomide with harmful effects on the foetus." In fact, in Britain the use of the drug resulted in the birth of 432 malformed and deformed babies.

But it is only in the last few months that a 10-year campaign to let the public know the real nature of the tragedy has begun to be successful. We are now aware that these children are approaching adolescence without arms or legs and, in some cases, without organs.

What kind of adolescence will a 10-year-old boy look forward to when he has no arms, no legs, one eye, no pelvic girdle, and is only two feet tall, the height of two whisky bottles placed one on top of the other?

Reprinted by permission of *Science and Public Affairs* 1973, 29 (3): 40-41, the Bulletin of the Atomic Scientists. Copyright ©1973 by the Educational Foundation for Nuclear Science.

How can an 11-year-old girl look forward to laughing and loving when
she has no hand to be held and no legs to dance on?

I quote from a most moving speech given by the deaf Labour MP, Jack
Ashley, when on Nov. 30, 1972 he initiated a debate in the House of Commons
on the thalidomide children. Thanks to his efforts the voices of the thalidomide
families have been heard throughout the land, and some government action has
been taken. Thanks are due also to the weekly newspaper, *The Sunday Times,*
without whose determined voice the problem might have remained in legal
limbo for ever. Harold Evans, its editor, has been threatened with jail, and some
articles he wished to print are under legal embargo.

Indeed, the efforts of Mary, Lady Hoare, and her Trust for Thalidomide
and Other Disabled Children, to spread the facts were blocked also because of
the prolonged litigation which has led to the muzzling of the mass media. As
the matter is still *sub judice* freedom to comment is limited, and only the
privileged voice of MPs in the House of Commons may be presented.

The debate as reported had a great impact. It demonstrated the need to
ensure public awareness of social problems, and the overwhelming value of
a free Press. By coincidence, Distillers, who denied any legal liability, made
improved financial offers to settle outstanding thalidomide claims immediately
before and just after the debate. It is clear that Britain will join West Germany
and Sweden in arriving at a general settlement, for in the early days of January
the Company increased its compensation offer to nearly £ 22 million. If this
is accepted by the High Court and the parents, and this is likely, the Company
would pay £ 2 million a year for 10 years into a charitable trust fund to give a
sizable income to the victims, and each set of parents would receive £ 5,000 in
cash, costing about £ 2 million. The legal aspects, however, are most complicated. The British government does not propose to follow the example of the
other two countries in providing special legislation governing taxation on the
resulting fund.

What has puzzled many people is why it is taking so long to arrive at a
general financial settlement. Can any major business continue to operate without incorporating into its ethic an acceptance of liability for the effect of its
products? The answer now seems to be, No. The new Distillers offer followed
a unique mounting pressure, unknown previously in the City of London, in
which the small shareholders were joined by major financial institutions with
large holdings. Once these major bodies had decided that action from a moral
and social standpoint was being imposed on them, a meeting behind closed
doors was inevitable—and the last offer emerged just over 24 hours later.

In Britain, we shall need to reconsider the procedures for assessing "the
value" of a victim of the kind represented by the Thalidomide child. The procedure has been for him to be examined professionally and then the court,
without actuarial provision, assessed his minimum likely needs. This was

turned into a financial sum, as would be done for a child involved in, say, a
car accident. The child would then get 40 per cent of the minimum of what
the court decided was absolutely essential for his future. Dr. Gerard Vaughan
described this, in the House of Commons debate, as "a manifest social injustice. In a recent case, a girl who was blinded at school—a very tragic
thing—got a very large sum. Here, because of our legal procedures, somebody
else who has been accidentally damaged is likely to get a pittance, a token
of what he actually needs."

The majority of the thalidomide children are of normal intelligence, and
some are highly intelligent. In Britain, 90 percent of them have been kept at
home, whereas in Germany most have gone into institutions. Thus, parents
are under great stress. Dr. Vaughan said that he had examined medically 60
cases which had been before the courts. Every one of the mothers of that
group had been ill with nervous conditions almost continuously since the
children were born, and were taking tranquilizers. Some families had broken
up, although some had drawn together.

The children were highly critical, particularly of the artificial limbs they
had been presented to use. "One sees a small child coming into a room looking like a deep-sea diver dressed up in a mechanical abortion; and at the first
opportunity he throws the whole lot off because he says it is intolerable to
him." Dr. Vaughan went on, "Those who have feet have developed the most
outstanding ability to feed themselves, to write, to unlock doors and to
undertake a great range of activities to show how clever they are. All this is
very disturbing to the parents who have to look after them."

Much research is needed into the provision of equipment for them, and
into the social and educational services they and their parents need.

Social Responsibility

What of social responsibility? The lesson is not all that clear, but the behaviour
does set a precedent: social responsibility has been written into corporate behaviour. It will be some time before "social responsibility" appears together
with "financial responsibility" as an item in the annual accounts of corporations. But it is a beginning, and a victory for the "quality of life" protagonists.
It would be stupid not to see that immediately the Distillers' offer resulted
from the wish of the major institutions to protect the long-term value of their
investment. In fact, when City opinion was convinced an acceptable settlement was on the way, Distillers shares, which had been tumbling, began to
recover. But if we assumed that industrialists, businessmen and scientists are
concerned in their different ways with not seeking deliberately to do harm to
the consumer, then what is lacking is a method to secure this.

First, we should seek to promote a climate of opinion in which "profit" is seen to include a social element in addition to the essential financial one. Second, we must recognise that we need to include in the research program statements on the second and third-order effects of the new technology— (drugs, devices, processes) we are seeking to introduce. It is no longer sufficient to consider only the primary, desired effect, which is all the research project is concerned with.

This kind of necessary opportunism is dangerous. For example, early last year (1972), the British Airport Authority issued special instructions for ground men working near Boeing 747 jumbo jets, because of breathing problems noticed by workers near the jets in other parts of the world. The statement declared, "A very large airflow passes through the 747 engines which can cause a reduced oxygen content in the areas behind the aircraft, especially in calm or light winds, or when the aircraft is aligned with the wind direction." Ground personnel were asked to ensure that no other aircraft was on the taxi-way behind the 747 before giving clearance to the captain of the jumbo to start engines.

The affair of the thalidomide children has served to demonstrate that although we are in the late 20th century technologically, in terms of social machinery we are still in the Middle Ages. Science policy . . . is concerned with bringing the latter into line with the former.

Part IV Bibliography

Abdel-Fattah, E.   "Quelques Problèmes Posés à la Justice Pénale par la Victimologie" *Annales Internationales de Criminologie* 1966, 355–361.

Acchiappati, G.   "Sull' Obbligo Giuridico del Conducente di Soccorrere l'Investito" (The Motorist's Legal Obligation to Assist the Road Victim), *Minerva Medicolegale* 1962, 82 (6): 377–381.

Banay, R. S.   "Police Dilemma with Sexual Crimes," *Medical Aspects of Human Sexuality* 1971, 5 (9): 208–209, 214-216.

California Dept. of   *Robberies of Banks and Savings and Loan Associations in*
Justice, Division of   *California.* Sacramento, California: Calif. Dept. of Justice,
Law Enforcement,   1967.
Bur. of Criminal
Statistics

Clark, R.   *Remarks to the National Commission on Causes and Prevention of Violence.* Washington, D.C., 1968.

Elders, J.L.M.   "De Plaats van het Slachtoffer in het Strafrecht" (The Position of the Victim in Criminal Law), *1823* (Nederlands Genootschap tot Reclassering) 1969, 7: 110–112.

English, P.   "What did Section 3 do to the Law of Provocation?" *Criminal Law Review* 1970, May: 249–267.

Ennis, P.H.　　　"Crime, Victims, and the Police," *Trans-Action* 1967, 4 (7): 36–44.

Fishbein, M.,　　"Attribution of Responsibility: A Theoretical Note," *Journal*
and I. Ajzen　　*of Experimental Social Psychology* 1973, 9:148–153.

Green, E.　　　*Judicial Attitudes in Sentencing. A Study of the Factors under-lying the Sentencing Practice of the Criminal Court of Philadelphia.* London: MacMillan, 1961.

Hummelen, P.　　"Schadevergoeding als Middel ter Vermindering van de Recidive van de Misdaad" (Restitution as a Means for Reducing Recidivism), *Nederlands Tijdschrift voor Criminologie* 1963, 5 (6): 186–197.

Institute for Local　*Criminal Victimization in Maricopa County.* Berkeley:
Self Government　Institute for Local Self Government, 1969.

Jimenez Huerta, M.　"El Ministerio Publico y la Proteccion a la Victima del Delito," *Criminalia* (Mexico) 1963, 29 (9): 629–138.

Kalthoff, A.J.　　"De Benadeelde in het Strafproces" (The Injured Party in Criminal Proceedings), *1823* (Nederlands Genootschap tot Reclassering) 1969, 7: 108–109, 112.

Kat'kalo, S.I.　　"K Voprosu o Ponjatii Poterpevšego V Sovetskom Ugolovnom Processe" (The Concept of the Victim in Soviet Criminal Procedure), *Vestn. Leningr. Univ., Ser. Ekon. Filos. i Prava* 1964, 11: 113–122.

Kiester, E., Jr.　　*Crimes with No Victims: How Legislating Morality Defeats the Cause of Justice.* New York: Alliance for Safer New York, 1972.

Knudten, R.D.　　"The Prevalence and Distribution of Crime," in R. Knudten, *Crime in a Complex Society.* Homewood, Ill.: Dorsey Press, 1970, 58–86.

Kočev, K.　　　"The Victim Concept in Criminal Proceedings," *Pravna Misal* 1968, 12 (2): 34–36. (In Bulgarian).

Koh, K.L.　　　"Consent and Responsibility in Sexual Offenses," *Criminal Law Review* 1968, 2 (2): 81–91, and (3): 150–162.

Lambert, J.R.　　*Crime, Police, and Race Relations.* New York: Oxford University Press, 1970.

Maharashtra State　"Remand Homes in Maharashtra: Their Unique Position,"
Probation and　*Samaj Seva* (Poona, India) 1969, 19 (10): 1–3.
After-Care
Association.

Mathias, W.J.   "Perceptions of Police Relationships," *Police Chief,* 1971,
                    38: 78–85.

Mendelsohn, B.   "Le Rapport entre la Victimologie et le Problème du
                    Génocide. Pour un Code de Prévention du Génocide," *Etudes
                    Internationales de Psycho-Sociologie Criminelle* (Paris) 1968,
                    14 (15): 47–53.

Mueller, G.O.W.   "Seduction and the Law," *Medical Aspects of Human
                    Sexuality* 1972, 6 (1): 14–15, 20, 23, 27.

Mulvihill, D.J.,   *Crimes of Violence.* Washington, D.C.: U.S. Government
M.M. Tumin,   Printing Office, 1969.
and L.A. Curtis

Ostrovskiy D., and   "Nekotoryye Voprosy Zashchity Po Delam Ob
I. Ostrovskiy   Iznasilovanii" (Some Problems of Defense in Rape
                     Cases), *Sovetskaya Yustitsiya* (Moscow) 1969, 9: 17–18.

President's Commission   "The Victims of Crime," in B. Cohen, *Crime in
on Law Enforcement   America*. Itasca, Ill.: F.E. Peacock, 1970, 441–449.
and the Administration
of Justice.

Richette, L.A.   *The Throaway Children.* Philadelphia and New York:
                    J.B. Lippincott, 1969.

Savickij, V.M., and   "Poterpevsij V Sovetskom Ugolovnom Processe" (The
I.I. Poteruzu   Victim in Soviet Criminal Trials), *Gosjurisdat* (Moskva)
                      1963.

Schraven, E.   "Betekenis van het Slachtoffer," (Significance of the Victim),
                    Maanblad voor Berechting en Reclassering (Nederlands) 1964,
                    43 (1): 18–21.

Schultz, L.G.   "Interviewing the Sex Offender's Victim," *Journal of Criminal
                    Law, Criminology, and Police Science* 1960, 50 (5): 448–452.

————   "The Pre-Sentence Investigation and Victimology," *U.M.K.C.
                    Law Review* 1968, 35 (2): 247–260.

Schumacher, M.   *Violent Offending: A Report on Recent Trends in Violent
                    Offending and Some Characteristics of the Violent Offender.*
                    Wellington, New Zealand: A.R. Shearer, 1971.

Sornarajah, M.   "The Doctrine of Continuing Provocation," *Journal of Ceylon
                    Law* 1971, 2 (1): 101–117.

Stanciu, V.V.   *La Prophylaxie du Génocide II.* Paris: Etudes Internationales
                    de Psycho-Sociologie Criminelle, 1968.

Stokes, R.E.   "A Research Approach to Sexual Offenses involving Children,"
                    Canadian Journal of Corrections 1964, 6 (1): 87–94.

Stutte, H., and   "Das Problem der Prävention von Gewaltverbrechen an
M. L. Stutte   Kindern" (The Problem of Preventing Crimes of Violence on
                       Children), *Münchener Medizinische Wochenschrift* 1965, 107
                       (4): 168–170.

Szpunar, A.   "Damages for Pain and Suffering in the Civil Code" (In Polish),
                       Panstwo i Prawo (Lodz) 1965, 20 (3): 359–372.

Task Force on   "Public Attitudes toward Crime and Law Enforce-
Assessment of the   ment," in P. Lerman, *Delinquency and Social Policy*.
President's Committee   New York: Praeger, 358–377.
on Law Enforcement
and the Administration
of Justice.

Todd, A.C.   "Standing to Sue by the Victim of Racial Discrimination,"
                       Southwestern Law Journal 1970, 24 (3): 557–563.

Walster, E.   "Assignment of Responsibility for an Accident." *Journal of
                       Personality and Social Psychology* (Washington, D.C.) 1966,
                       3 (1): 73–79.

Wilson, F.W.   "The Law and the Urban Age," *FBI Law Enforcement
                       Bulletin* 1970, 39 (2): 3–6, 16–17.

Winslow, R.   *Crime in a Free Society*. Belmont, Calif.: Dickinson Publishing,
                       1968, 1–33.

Younger, A.   "The Requirement of Corroboration in Prosecution for Sex
                       Offenses," 40 *Fordham Law Review* 263 (1971).

                       "The Rape Corroboration Requirement: Repeal, not Reform,"
                       Yale Law Journal 1972, 81 (7): 1365–1391.

                       "Corroborating Charges of Rape," 67 *Columbia Law Review*,
                       (1967) 1137.

                       "Whipping as a Penal Sanction: Its consideration in a Recent
                       Case," *Australian and New Zealand Journal of Criminology*
                       1968, 1 (1): 10–25.

Part V
The Social Reaction to Victimization

Introduction

Restitution and punishment are ancient institutions with an established position in the history of law and the administration of justice. If one accepts the fundamental premise that all legal relations are between persons, then one realizes the preeminence of private revenge and blood feud as tools of social control when individuals were alone or attached to small groups in the struggle for existence. As Schafer has stated: "the blood feud served an unromantic and vital interest. The tribe, clan, or family could continue living and functioning only if its strength and power remained intact and efficient enough to repulse dangerous attacks. Thus, blood-revenge was aimed essentially at the restoration of the balance of power in the world of primitive societies. . . . Such punishment was . . . an expression of social defense."[1]

While the blood feud remained the common means of compensation and punishment in simpler societies, an interesting evolution took place among the economically more advanced ones: physical or mental damage was equated with material goods. Thus the concept and the practice of compensation was introduced. For example, Tacitus, the Roman historian, tells us that the Germanic murderer of the first century after Christ, when convicted, paid a fine. Among the Yuroks of northern California every person, except bastards and slaves, had a full set of demand rights, privilege rights, powers and immunities which he could use for litigation purposes on the slightest provocation. In fixing damages, the Yuroks were guided by well-established principles of value. Except for bastards and slaves, every person possessed a fixed and immutable wergild, every material object its fixed worth, every intangible property right its customarily recognized valuation. Injury to the person was scaled in accordance with the seriousness of the trespass and the wergild evaluation of the aggrieved.[2] This was also the practice in Germanic common law. The amount of compensation was determined by taking into account the nature and consequences of the offense, and the age, rank, sex, and prestige of the victim. Obviously, this legal mechanism presupposed a stratified society anxious to insure stability and tranquillity, as conditions conducive to prosperity, by eliminating disruptive vendettas. If the offender was unable to pay the amount demanded, he would be ostracized from his community. Stripped of his legal rights and of the group's protection, he was in serious danger of being enslaved or even murdered by anybody with immunity.[3]

With the rise of the state power, the importance of restitution and the strength of the individual victim's claim against the wrongdoer declined. The state was attempting to gain more control over the lives and the behavior of its subjects. The evolution of law occurred in the direction of mounting state intervention and share in litigation cases, and of increasing separation of the individual—both as plaintiff and as offender—from his family, clan or tribe. In other words, the focus of legal consideration was shifted from collective to individual responsibility. This theoretical and legal shift was sealed in the newly introduced distinction between crime and tort: *crime* is an offense against the state, while *tort* is an offense against individual rights only. Since then, modern law has sharply distinguished between criminal and civil proceedings. The criminal is thought to owe a debt to society, which must be paid in the context of a criminal prosecution, whose purpose is to secure the safety of the people by the punishment of offenders. In these public proceedings, the victim himself is supposed to be a disinterested witness, whose personal remedy is to be found in private action in tort. Dissatisfaction with the results of this modern dichotomy in recent years began with the writings of the late Margery Fry, an English penal reformer, and finally led to the establishment of crime compensation tribunals.

The articles by B. R. Jacobs, M. Fooner, D. E. J. Mac Namara and J. J. Sullivan, discuss at length issues related to victim compensation. F. Watman, in her paper on Sex Offenses against Children and Minors, calls for a reexamination of stereotypes commonly held about the sexual offender and the victims of sexual assaults, and for changes in the law which might better effectuate the policy for which it was created. Finally, the recommendations of the Task Force to Study the Treatment of Victims of Sexual Assaults, Prince George's County, Maryland, condemn many current practices and procedures, while calling for significant reforms.

Notes

1. S. Schafer, *The Victim and His Criminal.* New York: Random House, 1968: 10-11.
2. E. A. Hoebel, *The Law of Primitive Man.* New York: Atheneum, 1970: 52-53.
3. F. Pollock and F.W. Maitland, *The History of English Law,* 2nd ed., Cambridge, 1898, 2: 451.

19

Reparation or Restitution by the Criminal Offender to His Victim: Applicability of an Ancient Concept in the Modern Correctional Process

Bruce R. Jacob

A. Brief Historical Background of the Concept of Reparation or Restitution

In primitive cultures the victim of crime punished the offender through personal retaliation or revenge. He inflicted physical injury or damage and took what he wanted from the offender as reparation for the commission of the crime. In a case involving an act committed against a family, clan or one of its members by a person outside the group, the group joined in the process of retaliation, or the "blood revenge" or "blood feud," as it has been called.

As primitive groups settled, reached higher levels of economic development, and began to possess a richer inventory of economic goods, the goods themselves came to be equated with physical or mental injury; and unregulated revenge was gradually replaced by a system of negotiation between offender and victim and indemnification to the victim through payment of goods or money. The process of negotiation and the payment to the victim has become known as the process of "composition."

In England, under this system, the offender could "buy back the peace he had broken" by paying "bot" to the victim or his kin according to a schedule of injury tariffs. The "Dooms of Alfred," laws in effect during the time of King Alfred, for example, provided that if a man knocked out the front teeth of another man, he was to pay him eight shillings; if it was an eye tooth, four shillings; and if a molar, fifteen shillings. By Alfred's time, about 870 A.D., private revenge by the victim was sanctioned by society only after a demand for composition had been made by the victim and his demand had been refused by the offender. An offender who failed to provide composition to his victim was stigmatized as an "outlaw," and this allowed any member of the community to kill him with impunity.

Reprinted by special permission of the *Journal of Criminal Law, Criminology, and Police Science*, 61 (2): 154-157, Copyright © 1970 by Northwestern University Law School.

The transition or evolution from private revenge to composition has apparently occurred in many primitive cultures or societies as they have settled down and become economically stable. As a striking example of this, in primitive areas of Arabia about one hundred years ago it was noted that blood vengeance was practiced among the nomadic tribes outside the towns, while those living in the towns utilized the composition process as the means of redressing criminal wrongs in order to avoid the socially disintegrating effects of retaliation. Composition was used as a means of punishing crime and obtaining indemnification for the victim among the ancient Babylonians (under the Code of Hammurabi); the Hebrews (under Mosaic law); the ancient Greeks, the Romans; and the ancient Germans. It is clear that the origins of modern systems of criminal law are found in the victim's right to reparation for the wrong done to him.

In England, the king and his lords or barons required that the offender pay not only "bot" to the victim but a sum called "wite" to the lord or king as a commission for assistance in bringing about a reconciliation between the offender and victim, and for protection against further retaliation by the victim. In the Twelfth Century the victim's share began to decrease greatly. The "wite" was increased until finally the king or overlord took the entire payment. The victim's right to reparation, at this point, was replaced by what has become known as a fine, assessed by a tribunal against the offender. The disappearance of the concept of reparation to the victim and the complete shift to the state of control over the criminal law was apparently the result of a number of factors, including desire on the part of the king and his lords to exercise stronger control over the populace and greed on the part of feudal lords who sought to gain the victim's share of composition.

B. The Reparation or Restitution Concept in the Modern Criminal Process

The ancient concept of composition or reparation to the victim has in more modern times become incorporated into the civil law of torts. Nevertheless, vestiges of the reparation concept are present in modern systems of criminal justice.

In the German legal system there is a process termed the "adhesive" procedure in which a civil claim for compensation by the victim of a crime can be dealt with in the criminal proceeding against the offender, in the discretion of the court. This procedure is apparently utilized in about half of the German states.

In pre-Castro Cuba compensation to the victim was awarded during the criminal proceeding against the offender, and the government established a fund, containing the earnings of prisoners, fines and other contributions, from which the victim was paid. The fund did not possess sufficient amounts to provide full compensation to all victims, and compensation was often paid on a partial basis. The government was subrogated to the right of the victim to sue the offender.

At the beginning of the nineteenth century in the United States several states had laws providing that a person convicted of larceny, in addition to his punishment, could be required to return to the owner an amount of money twice or three times the value of the stolen goods or, in the case of insolvency, to perform labor for the victim for a certain period of time. In England there are presently statutes which empower magistrates' courts to order a person convicted of felony to pay compensation to the victim for the loss of property resulting from the crime and to order a person convicted of committing malicious damage to property to pay compensation for the damage.

Reparation by the offender to the victim is required by criminal courts today chiefly in cases involving property crimes and principally in connection with the use of the suspended sentence or probation. Restitution is often imposed as a condition of probation,[2] and it is not uncommon for a large probation agency to supervise the collection of millions of dollars in restitution for crime victims each year.[3] The victim's civil remedy remains unaffected by the existence of the probation condition. If the victim obtains a judgment against the offender, payments made under the probation order can apparently be used to offset the civil damages awarded; also, a finding for the defendant in the civil action will not necessarily terminate his obligation to make payments as a condition of probation.[4]

In addition to formal procedures providing for restitution to the crime victim, informal methods have evolved which achieve the same end. For example, one of the prevalent methods used by professional thieves when they are arrested is to suggest to the victim that the stolen property will be restored if the victim refuses to prosecute. Other types of prosecutions, as well, are terminated (or never initiated) as a consequence of an informal arrangement under which the criminal has agreed to make restitution. Embezzlement cases are a typical example of this.

C. Reparation or Restitution as a Means of Rehabilitating the Offender

Stephen Schafer, the author of several works on restitution or reparation by the offender to his victim,[5] conducted a research study among inmates in the Florida correctional system several years ago to determine their attitudes on the subject. He surveyed inmates who had committed three types of offenses—criminal homicide, aggravated assault, and theft with violence. His study indicated that the overwhelming majority of those who had committed some form of criminal homicide wished that they could make some reparation. The author could detect no attitude, positive or negative, in most of the offenders in the other two categories. Schafer believes that the high percentage among criminal homicide offenders is at least partially due to the fact that many of those surveyed were soon to be executed for their crimes, and that their desire to make reparation might have been attributable to their proximity to death . . . It is Schafer's position that the offender should be made to recognize his responsibility to the injured victim and that this can be accomplished through the process of reparation.

Albert Eglash, a psychologist interested in corrections, has suggested that restitution, if properly used as a correctional technique, can be an effective rehabilitative device.[6] Since restitution requires effort by the inmate, it may be especially effective as a means of rehabilitating the passive-compliant inmate who adapts well to institutional routine without becoming trained for freedom and initiative or responsibility. Restitution as a constructive activity may contribute to an offender's self-esteem. Since restitution is offense-related, it may redirect in a constructive manner those same conscious or unconscious thoughts, emotions, or conflicts which motivated the offense. Further he believes that restitution can alleviate guilt and axiety, which can otherwise precipitate further offenses. Eglash was of the view that, although a prison inmate can be encouraged to participate in a restitutional program, the inmate himself should decide to engage in the program if it is to have rehabilitative value.

D. Reparation as a Philosophical Aim of Penology

The concept of reparation by the offender to the victim, which for many centuries had an established position in the punishment of crime, is largely disregarded in modern criminal law. The emphasis in current criminal law theory is on the reformative or rehabilitative aspects of punishment while the victim's plight is ignored. As Schafer has said, "It is rather absurd that the state undertakes to protect the public against crime and then, when a loss occurs, takes the entire payment and offers no effective remedy to the individual victim."[7]

What is needed is a fundamental rethinking of our philosophy concerning the purposes of the criminal law, penology and punishment, with a view toward developing a new formulation or synthesis of these aims. Generally speaking, the aims of penology in recent years have been rehabilitation, protection of society through neutralization or removal of the dangerous offender from the community, deterrence and retribution. The concept of reparation could be added to this list as a separate aim or as a corollary of one or more of the other four. As has already been pointed out, reparation, if properly utilized in the correctional process, might contribute significantly to the rehabilitation of offenders. Reparation as an element of the correctional process would provide the victim with the satisfaction or retribution which he seeks, both in the spiritual and in the material sense.

In 1959 a White Paper entitled *Penal Practice in a Changing Society* was presented to the British Parliament and was one of the factors which led the British government to adopt a victim compensation plan. The paper stated:

> The basis of early law was personal reparation by the offender to the victim, a concept of which modern criminal law has almost completely lost sight. The assumption that the claims of the victim are sufficiently satisfied if the offender is punished by society becomes less persuasive as society in its dealings with offenders increasingly emphasizes the reformative aspects of punishment. Indeed in the public mind the interests of the offender may not infrequently seem to be placed before those of the victim.
>
> This is certainly not the correct emphasis. It may well be that our penal system would not only provide a more effective deterrent to crime, but would also find a greater moral value, if the concept of personal reparation to the victim were added to the concepts of deterrence by punishment and of reformation by training. It is also possible to hold that the redemptive value of punishment to the individual offender would be greater if it were made to include a realisation of the injury he had done to his victim as well as to the order of society, and the need to make personal reparation for that injury.[8]

It seems clear that the concept of reparation or restitution to the victim should be incorporated as a major aim of modern correctional theory and practice. However, the committee which produced the above document emphasized that the concept of reparation could be successfully incorporated into modern correctional programs only if the convicted offender's earnings can be raised. The problem of achieving wages for prison inmates commensurate with those prevailing in the outside world will not be resolved, they indicated, "until society as a whole accepts that prisons do not work in an economic vacuum, and that prisoners are members of the working community, temporarily segregated, and not economic outcasts."[9] Furthermore, no solution will be reached, "until the general level of productivity and efficiency of prison industry approximates much more closely . . . that of outside industry."[10]

Notes

1. Much of the material summarized here is derived from the works of S. Schafer and M. Wolfgang. See this section's bibliography for references. (Note of the Editors).
2. See, e.g. 18 U.S.C.A. § 3651 (1969) and N.Y. Code Cr. Pro. § 932(j) (McKinney 1958), which allow restitution to be required as a condition of probation.

3. President's Commission on Law Enforcement and Administration of Justice, *Task Force Report: Correction* (1967): p. 35.

4. Comment, *Judicial Review of Probation Conditions,* 67 Columbia Law Review (1967), pp. 181, 183.

5. *See* Schafer, *Victim Compensation and Responsibility,* 43 Southern California Law Review (1970) p. 55; Schafer, *Restitution to Victims of Crime—An Old Correctional Aim Modernized,* 50 Minnesota Law Review (1965), p. 243.

6. Eglash, *Creative Restitution, Some Suggestions for Prison Rehabilitation Programs,* 20 American Journal of Corrections (Nov.-Dec. 1958).

7. S. Schafer, *The Victim and His Criminal,* p. 27.

8. Home Office, Compensation for Victims for Crimes and Violence, Cmnd. No. 1046, pp. 4, 5.

9. Home Office, Penal Practice in a Changing Society, Comnd. No. 645, p.17 (1959).

10. Cmnd. No. 645, above note 9, p. 17.

20 Composition, Restitution, Compensation: Making the Victim Whole

Donal E. J. MacNamara and John J. Sullivan

Criminology may be said to have addressed itself over the years first to the crime, then to the offender, and only relatively recently, at least in a scientific and structured approach, to the victim.

Attention to the victim, pioneered by Hans von Hentig,[1] first concerned itself with the contributory elements in the victim's personality and/or life-style, or his more specific conduct preliminary to and incident to the crime, which either increased his exposure to victimization or enhanced the seriousness (in terms of loss or injury) of the crime committed against him. It has been posited, for example, that prostitutes, homosexuals and those engaging in promiscuous extramarital sexual adventures, heavy drinkers and gamblers, and those who exhibitionistically make ostentatious display of money and gems are more likely to be victimized by criminals than those who are free of such vices and who live less conspicuously.

Secondary interest in the victim has been evinced by those, particularly but not exclusively in the United States of America, who set forth highly putative "rights" of the victim to be avenged or vindicated as a major rationalization for their denunciations of "defendant-oriented" judges and courts (e.g., the Warren Court[2]) and for their support of the death penalty and other extremely rigorous sanctions for offenders. This "lust for punishment" approach is sometimes extended to suggest a residual sadistic compulsion endemic in the population, which if not assuaged by frequent executions and long prison terms will find expression in mob violence (e.g., lynchings of alleged or convicted offenders).

Little attention has, however, been given to another victim-oriented approach, i.e., making the victim whole, restoring his losses of money or property, and/or providing compensation for loss of life, physical injury (with consequent loss of earning power and the costs of medical care), and the pain and suffering resulting from criminal assaults.[3]

In this brief article we will distinguish the contemporary victim compensation statutes from:

1. Early victim (or crime *composition*) procedures developed nonuniformly in early societies.

Reprinted from *The Urban Review* 6(3): 21-25, by permission of the publisher. Copyright © 1973 by APS Publications. Also, by permission of the authors.

2. The much more common though equally sporadic *offender-restitution-to-the-victim* schemes conceived partly as punishment and perhaps even more importantly as components of offender rehabilitation efforts and experimented with, at least in the United States in more recent years, largely by juvenile courts.[4]
3. The partial or full restitution sometimes voluntarily offered by adult criminal offenders, particularly in "white collar" crimes, to allay prosecution or to mitigate sentence.

Three Different Approaches

Although composition, restitution, and composition all allude to procedures for restoring the victim to his precrime condition, they differ basically in legal philosophy and very importantly in administration. Confusion of what was basically a civil tort approach (composition) with a punitive-corrective measure (offender restitution to the victim) and of both with the doctrine of the state's responsibility for protecting its citizens when such protection proved inadequate (compensation), has characterized much discussion of victim compensation legislative proposals in recent years. This confusion has created difficulties in the interpretation and administration of victim compensation laws.

Since Schafer et al.[5] have more than adequately surveyed the early history (and the legislative hearings leading to the enactment of the victim compensation statutes discussed herein) and since it is our principal purpose to discuss here the necessity for and the problems inherent in contemporary legislative approaches to the compensation of victims, we will not deal exhaustively with either composition or restitution. The former, albeit in many variant forms, can be identified in early tribal societies, in the formal codes of Moses and Hammurabi, in early Greek and Roman law, and indeed in the Europe, especially Germany, of the Middle Ages.

Composition was quite probably socio-economic in orientation and perhaps designed more to keep the peace between families and between tribes than as a deterrent, punitive, or rehabilitative response to crime.

It is apparent in the rather fragmentary materials that crimes by the rich and powerful against the lower social orders could be composed by relatively small payments in money, cattle, land, or other goods—while crimes committed by slaves, serfs, or the lower classes against their masters or against the persons or property of those of higher social strata (or violations of strongly held tribal tabus) could not be so composed, being instead punished by death, corporal penalties, enslavement, and confiscation of land or chattels.

A dual system in which the imposed composition, frequently a multiple of the amount stolen or the damage of injury inflicted, was divided between the victim (or his family or tribe) and the chief, noble, or king either as full retribution for the offense or as a part of a more severe penalty can be identified in a number of codes.

In such criminal incidents as involved victims and perpetrators of relatively equal social rank and military strength, composition was sometimes negotiable not only as to amount and kind but also as to period and conditions of payment. Such indeed was the custom among the Irish clans as late as the 12th and 13th centuries as is evidenced by many instances in bardic lore. Again the purpose seemed to be to avert unnecessary fighting among the all-too-warlike clans rather than to punish or rehabilitate the offenders.

The concept of *offender-restitution-to-his-victim* has proved more popular as a theory than feasible in practice. Without surveying at length all the abortive efforts to achieve so ethical and logical an equilibrium—and certainly without any intention of decrying the possible punitive, deterrent, and/or corrective values inherent in making the offender more literally "pay" for his criminal act—it must be noted that: a) only a minority of offenders are apprehended and convicted (who then would make restitution to victims whose attackers went unwhipped of justice?); b) offenders are largely of the lowest socio-economic stratum, judgment-proof to a man; c) the prison-earnings potential of offenders scarcely can be expected to meet a fraction of the costs of guarding, housing, clothing, and feeding them (to say nothing of the much greater costs of rehabilitating them); d) societal resistance to the re-employment of ex-convicts, and their lack of vocational skills insure that their lack of vocational skills insure that their post-prison employments will not prove sufficiently remunerative to permit any but token restitution payments; e) the costs to the state of administering a system of offender restitution to the victims of his crimes would exceed the sums actually collected for reimbursing the victims for their injuries and losses.

Certainly too, it is apparent that many crimes, particularly crimes against the person violative of the personal self-concept and dignity (e.g., forcible rape and forcible sodomy) and likely to result in psychological torment of long duration, would prove difficult to quantify in monetary terms (and impossible to be restituted within the limited financial resources of most perpetrators).

Civil Action Needed

In those few cases in which the convicted offender proved to have more than nominal assets, the victim might well gain more equitable restitution for pain, suffering, and emotional trauma through civil action (tort) for personal injury.

Instances of court-ordered restitution by juvenile court judges directed against either the offending juvenile or his parents have been more offender-oriented (i.e., attempting to teach him the lesson that he must pay for his misdeeds) rather than serious efforts to make the victims whole. In a number of vandalism cases against schools, churches, and cemeteries studied by the authors, the restitution ordered (usually in services rather than money) bore but an insignificant relationship to the actual extent of the damage done.

Restitution by adult offenders either as a condition of probation or voluntarily offered to fend off anticipated prosecution or to mitigate sentence has been largely limited, at least in our country, to cases of fraud, embezzlement, forgery, and other "white-collar" offenses. Indeed on more than one occasion such offers of restitution and their acceptance come perilously close to the compounding of felonies.

One notable current attempt at offender repayment to the victim of his crime is the Minnesota Community Corrections Center for Restitution, a small pilot program limited to male and female perpetrators of property crimes who opt voluntarily (as an alternative to imprisonment) to repay the identifiable and tangible losses suffered by their victims. Each inmate works out a "restitution plan" with his victim and remains an inmate of Restitution House (at which he must pay for his board and room and also contribute to the support of his family) until full restitution to his victim has been completed.

Let us now, however, proceed to a consideration in somewhat more specific detail of the victim compensation laws enacted over the past decade in a number of British Commonwealth countries and several of the American states: New Zealand in 1963; England in 1964; New York and California in 1965; Hawaii in 1967; Massachusetts and Maryland in 1968; Nevada in 1969; New Jersey in 1971; and the Federal Victim Compensation Act passed overwhelmingly by the United States Senate in September 1972. There are other victim compensation (and restitution) laws (notably in Cuba and Switzerland, in Canada and Australia, and, at least potentially, in several American states). To our knowledge, however, none of the Latin-American nations has adopted a system of *state compensation* to the victims of crime, although Argentina (and perhaps other nations of that continent) has provision for court-ordered restitution to the victim by the offender.

In 1971, England's victim compensation board (Criminal Injuries Compensation Board) processed nearly 10,000 claims, making grants which (while averaging $952.00) included one that totalled $119,000. Total claims paid April 1, 1971 through March 31, 1972, reached the record sum of $7,500,000 as compared to a 1970-71 total of $4,900,000, and a 1969-70 total of $4,500,000. The record total of $119,000 was awarded a young woman who was blinded and suffered other severe and continuing disabilities as the result of an assault with a concrete block by a former lover. Another grant went to a woman who suffered a heart attack two weeks after witnessing a robbery, but a man who was knocked from his motorcycle by a participant in a sidewalk brawl had his claim rejected since the English law requires that the injury be proximately incident to a crime and there was no showing that an actual criminal act was occurring. English law permits appeals from the decisions of the

Criminal Injuries Compensation Board first to a three-man review panel (only six percent of the 1971-2 decisions were reviewed) and then to the courts (only ten cases have been appealed to the courts since the law became effective; in eight of these the Board was upheld and in two cases the claim was returned to the Board for reconsideration).

Little purpose would be served by spreading on the record here the detailed legislative enactments and the even more voluminous procedural rules and regulations adopted in the several jurisdictions which are presently compensating the victims of crime. Instead let us confine ourselves to identifying some major similarities and a number of differences in the statutes, their interpretation, and their implementation—and, more importantly discuss briefly a number of the inadequacies and problems now all too apparent after several years of experience with ten compensation laws.

(*Victim compensation* laws should not be confused with so-called "good Samaritan" laws which provide compensation for citizens killed or injured while attempting to prevent a crime, apprehend a criminal, or in assisting a police officer in controlling a breach of the peace. A New York City ordinance of 1965 enacted following the killing of one Arthur Collins, fatally knifed after he ejected a disorderly drunk from a subway train, is an example of such "good Samaritan" legislation.)

Implicit in each of the victim compensation laws to be dealt with in this article is the legal responsibility of the state to protect its citizens from unprovoked criminal attack and the consequent liability of the state to compensate the victim when in fact such an attack occurs.

Major similarities in the various laws include:

1. Compensation for crimes against the person with demonstrable personal injury proximately resulting from the crime are compensable but crimes against property are not. This is largely a pragmatic distinction based on the anticipated difficulties of dealing with fraudulent or exaggerated claims (insurance companies have been plagued with such difficulties for decades); the astronomical costs of indemnifying even valid claimants with property losses (by far the highest incidence of crime is in this category— burglary, larceny, auto theft, etc.) have inhibited legislative support; and the availability of both governmental and private insurance coverage for most such property losses contributes to diminishing the urgency of support for such expanded coverage.

2. Generally no compensation can be claimed unless the injury results from an act specifically violative of the penal law (or, as in the case of the Hawaiian legislation, a violation specifically set forth as compensable in the victim compensation act).

3. Generally injuries resulting from violations of the motor vehicle and traffic codes (including driving violations which are misdemeanors and

felonies as, for example, drunken driving) are not compensable *except* for criminal assaults in which the vehicle itself was utilized as the assaulting weapon.

4. While some of the laws are somewhat unclear, or rather not sufficiently specific, the victims of intrafamilial crimes (wife-beating, incestuous rape or sodomy, sibling assaults, etc.) are not compensated.

5. Victims who initiate or provoke the criminal assault which results in their victimization are not compensable (but whether victims who ostentatiously display money or gems or who recklessly frequent areas of high crime incidence without good reason and are as a result assaulted and robbed should be compensated is left to the discretion of the board).

6. Offenders and their accomplices who may suffer injury consequent to their involvement in illegal acts are not compensable.

7. The administrative boards and commissions set up to administer the victim compensation laws may be said to have limited discretion (England), moderate discretion (California), or broad discretion (New York) in determining to what extent a victim himself provoked or enticed his own victimization and adjusting their awards accordingly.

8. Trivial injuries are usually not compensable. Thus England requires three weeks' loss of earnings; New York an out-of-pocket loss (e.g., for medical expenses) of not less than $100.00 or a two-week loss of earnings; Maryland and Massachusetts a two-weeks loss of earnings; California, Hawaii, and Nevada no minimum, with all three states discouraging trivial injury claims.

9. In England, Massachusetts, and Hawaii no showing of need is required in making a claim. But California, Maryland, Nevada, and New York direct that need be taken into account in determining both eligibility for an award and the extent of compensation awarded.

10. Maximum permissible compensation to a crime victim is difficult to determine in some jurisdictions, and in others it has already been increased by legislative action since the original compensation laws went into effect. The Federal Victims Compensation Act (approved by the United States Senate by an overwhelming vote on September 18, 1972, but not as yet passed by the U. S. House of Representatives) sets the upper limit of compensation at $50,000.00 per victim, a far more generous maximum than is permitted by any of the other compensation laws; Nevada and California, for example have $5,000.00 limits; New Jersey and Hawaii set the top payment at $10,000.00; New York allows up to $15,000.00 for loss of earnings but sets no limit for medical expenses (and has indeed made awards for medical expenses as high as $25,000.00 in at least one case); Maryland ties its allowances to the schedules in its state workmen's compensation law; England has no maximum in its law but in practice awards have been well below the more generous of the American maximum compensation payments.

11. Each of the laws sets forth criteria for determining the amount of compensation, usually limiting repayment to actual out-of-pocket losses (including
medical expenses, loss of earnings, loss of support for dependents of deceased victims). Hawaii permits consideration of "pain and suffering" but
Britain specifically excludes payment for "loss of happiness" and also for
"punitive damages."

Among the major problems encountered in the administration and implementation of the victim compensation statutes in effect over the past several years
have been:

1. Fraudulent claims and attempts at multiple recovery (e.g., seeking awards
   for injuries already compensated by insurance, hospital-medical plans, work-
   men's compensation, veterans benefits, and even by offender restitution).
2. Infinitesimal number of claims in proportion to the recorded or estimated
   numbers of compensable crimes; in New York for example the State Victims
   Compensation Law is little known. A survey of students at the authors'
   university, many of them professionals in the criminal justice field (police,
   corrections, probation, parole), disclosed that only a minority were familiar
   with the law and all were vague about its provisions; police do not inform
   victims of their right to an award, nor do hospitals, prosecutors, courts, and
   while the communications media, notably the *New York Times*,[6] have carried occasional articles describing the work of the Victims Compensation
   Board, the public on the whole, and compensable victims in particular, are
   uninformed.
3. Of those who do submit applications for compensation, fewer than half receive any award in New York State; and in all the jurisdictions the vast
   majority of the compensation awards do not even approach the already very
   low maxima.
4. In nearly all jurisdictions the bureaucratic red-tape and the long delays discourage applicants.
5. Apparently questionable awards have been made in some cases, violating
   either the statute itself or the criteria for eligibility.
6. Bills for medical expenses submitted by doctors, hospitals, and pharmacies
   seem in many cases to be highly inflated.
   Whether the somewhat less than spectacularly successful experience with the
currently operating victim compensation plans or, perhaps more likely, the financial stringencies plaguing many national and state governments have been responsible for a lessening of interest in the plight of the victim may be arguable but it
is now quite evident that the accelerated and widespread enactment of such legislation forecast after the New Zealand, England, California, and New York
schemes went into effect has been slow of realization. It is also apparent that
new and organized opposition to new plans and to expanded coverage in the

older laws has arisen both in legislative bodies and among tax-conscious members of the general public. Some resistance too has developed among criminologists and criminal justice specialists who see in victim compensation schemes the possibility of less aggressive cooperation by victims in the prosecution of their attackers. At any rate, it seems unlikely that new legislation will replicate the present laws. Creative and imaginative alternatives for the state's discharging of its obligations to its victimized citizens must be developed.

New York has paid out more than three million dollars to some 1,400 claimants, in large part for medical expenses. England's payments, on the other hand, are largely for loss of income, since its socialized medical scheme takes care of both doctors and hospital bills.

Perhaps a brief presentation of a few cases from the files of New York's Crime Victims Compensation Board will best illustrate a number of difficulties and problems inherent in such legislation and its efficient implementation.

Case Number One. Victim was shot to death while threatening to assault his killer with a claw-hammer. Victim and his assailant had engaged in a verbal dispute in a restaurant; victim left the restaurant, procured the hammer from his automobile, returned, attacked, and was fatally shot. In this case a compensation award was made to the victim's family covering burial expenses and other losses. In our opinion, this victim provoked the assaultive behavior and no award was justified.

Case Number Two. Victim visited a prostitute and while in her room was beaten to death; compensation was denied. Was this verdict based on *moral* or *legal* criteria?

Case Number Three. Victim was shot and paralyzed by a neighbor with whom he had initiated a verbal argument over the depredation of the neighbor's dog; victim's medical expenses exceeded $40,000.00 (largely paid for from a private insurance policy) and his out-of-pocket losses were fixed at $2,875.00 of which $1,615.00 was awarded as compensation by the Board. In addition to the question of how much provocation was involved in this case, there is also the question of the sufficiency of the award if indeed any award was justifiable.

Case Number Four. Victim jumped from a second-story window to escape two assailants; he was permanently disabled; an award of $152.00 per month for loss of earnings (up to a maximum of $15,000.00) and reimbursement for medical expenses was made. In this case, victim was 68-years of age (somewhat beyond the usual retirement age in American society); was the award for "loss of earnings" a charitable circumvention of the law?

Case Number Five. Victim, a young foreign student, was robbed, shot, and died sometime later as the result of his wounds; medical expenses amounted to $35,000.00, of which $10,000.00 was covered by an insurance policy; an award of $25,000.00 was made to the youth's parents to cover the balance. In addition to the question of inflated medical costs in this case, there is also a legal question: the youth was over his minority, was not resident with his parents, and they had no liability to pay his hospital and medical bills. Without the victim compensation, the hospital and medical costs would have been absorbed by the institution concerned.

Crimes of violence resulting in death, serious physical injury, loss of earnings, medical expenses, pain and suffering, and psychological aftermaths requiring long-term therapy show little evidence of abating. Deterrent and preventive measures can be only minimally effective in this category of crimes since the perpetrators are frequently emotionally disturbed (angry, fearful, drunk, under the influence of a narcotic, or engaging in compulsive behavior) or, perhaps a little less frequently, psychotic (manic-aggressive, paranoid, or sexually psychopathic). Police measures often prove minimally effective since these are "under-the-roof" crimes or attacks commited in dark, unfrequented places.

Despite the admitted difficulties of deterrence and prevention, there is little question in our opinion as to the liability of the state when such an unprovoked criminal attack is suffered by an innocent victim exercising due care.

Victim compensation laws and the boards or commissions which implement them are in most jurisdictions not even minimally discharging the state's liability to these victims of criminal assaults: Only a relative handful of victims, putatively eligible, make application for compensation; fewer than half of those who do file receive any compensation; the awards made are often parsimonious; large numbers of victims who have suffered injuries or losses are excluded from consideration; criteria set forth to guide the board's decisions have apparently been neither sufficiently clear nor effectively binding to prevent discretionary awards to ineligible claimants; awards for medical expenses have in some cases appeared to be excessive; and neither the laws nor their implementation have been subjected to rigorous evaluation.

We are of the opinion that crime victim compensation laws must be retained and expanded into those jurisdictions which have not as yet adopted such legislation. We feel, however, that the difficulties (enumerated *supra*) must be corrected. We suggest that there is great potential in a *mandatory crime victims insurance scheme*, modelled perhaps on a combined social security-workmen's compensation amalgam, which would discharge the state's obligation to the victims of crime much more generously and much more generally than can be expected under the systems evaluated herein.

Notes

1. Hans von Hentig. *The Criminal and His Victim*. Hamden, Conn., Archon Books, 1967.
2. Donal E. J. Mac Namara and Edward Sagarin. "The Warren Court and the Administration of Criminal Justice," *Crime and Delinquency*, January 1972, pp. 49-58.
3. Stephen Schafer has published an excellent monograph, *Compensation and Restitution to Victims of Crime* (Montclair, N.J., Patterson Smith, 2nd ed., 1970, 211 pp.) and there is a growing bibliography in the professional journals dealing with either the legal philosophy underlying victim compensation laws or the provisions of specific victim compensation statutes. See also Dr. Schafer's *The Victim and His Criminal*. New York, Random House, 1968.

4. Argentina has a provision for court-ordered restitution by adult offenders to their victims.
5. Three excellent symposia on victim compensation are especially to be recommended: *Minnesota Law Review*, December 1965; *Southern California Law Review*, 43, no. 1, 1970; and *Trial*, May-June 1972.
6. Wayne King, "If You are Maimed by a Criminal, You Can be Compensated (Maybe)," *New York Times Magazine*, March 24, 1972, pp. 40-41, 122-125. See also Michael Stern. "English Crime Compensation Board Sets Records in Grants to Victims." *New York Times*, November 29, 1972. p. 2.

21

Victim-Induced, Victim-Invited, and Victim-Precipitated Criminality: Some Problems in Evaluation of Proposals for Victim Compensation

Michael Fooner

Proposals to compensate victims of violent crime[1] are gaining widespread support in the United States, but studies analyzing victim behavior suggest legislators should be alert to possibilities that some compensation schemes may:

a) contribute to the growth of crime;
b) add unwarranted complications to the administration of criminal justice.

. . . .

In summary, these are the issues that need to be dealt with if a coherent system of victim compensation is to be created:

1. Is the victim's entitlement to compensation qualified by his behavior in connection with the crime?

If a Texas tycoon visits a clip-joint and flashes a fat roll of bills, gets hit on the head and rolled — would he be entitled to compensation? If a man enters a liaison with another's wife and gets shot by the husband, should his dependents be compensated? If a woman goes walking alone in a disreputable neighborhood, and is assaulted, would she be entitled to compensation?

Unless the answer to such questions is a flat "yes," the adjudication of victim compensation as a "right" would be embarking as upon a vast sea of confusion.

On the surface it may seem simpler to by-pass the issue of "right" and declare for victim compensation as a matter of social policy—a logical extension of the welfare state approach. The apparent simplicity may quickly prove illusory, for:

2. Is the victim's entitlement to compensation on an indigency basis to be qualified by apprehension of an offender and determination by a court of his guilt?

Reprinted from *Science*, 2 September 1966, 153 (3740): 1080-1083 by permission of the publisher. Copyright © 1966 by the American Association for the Advancement of Science. Also, by permission of the author.

There are two levels to this problem: First, if a severely injured man reports to police he's been mugged and robbed and the police cannot apprehend a suspect, how is the administrator of compensation to know he is in fact victim of a crime? The administrator of compensation must determine whether it was a criminal act or an argument—and who started it, and who precipitated the violence? What shall be the role of the witnesses, and of investigators? More important is the second level of problems: How will law enforcement officials and the courts evaluate victim testimony if victim compensation may be at stake?

In evaluation of proposals for victim compensation, criminologists may need to think very hard about such questions and about the probable effects on the administration of criminal justice.

These are pragmatic problems; there is another problem which may at this time seem speculative, but is nevertheless quite important:

3.   To what extent will a particular proposal for victim compensation contribute to a temptation/opportunity pattern in victim behavior?

In previous studies it has been pointed out that large numbers of our fellow Americans have tended to acquire money-handling habits—generically designated "carelessness"—which contributes to the national growth of criminality. How the victim helps the criminal was sketched in reports of those studies.[2]

It was made abundantly clear that human beings in our affluent society cannot be assumed to be prudent or self-protective against the hazards of crime. . . . Among the victims of burglary, statistically the most prevalent crime in the United States, are a substantial number of Americans who keep cash, jewelry and valuables carelessly at home or in hotel rooms with easy access for the burglar through door or window. Victims of automobile theft, one of the fastest growing classes of crime, include drivers who leave the vehicle or its contents invitingly accessible to thieves. And so on with other classes of crime.

As pointed out in previous studies, when victim behavior follows a temptation/opportunity patterns, it: (1) contributes to a "climate of criminal inducements," (2) adds to the economic resources available to criminal societies, and (3) detracts from the ability of law enforcement agencies to suppress the growth of crime.

It would seem to follow, therefore, that:

A. If "society should assume some responsibility for making the victim whole," it should also require victim-behavior that will diminish temptation/opportunity situations for offenders. This could be done through educational programs on citizen-defenses against criminality, plus legislative provisions which make victim compensation contingent upon actions not being contributory to the crime. Similar standards might be studied for adaptation to casualty insurance practices, voluntarily or through legislation.

B. Insurance company experience probably offers considerable material for study of the victim-compensation problem. Among other things, there is a seeming paradox: if the beneficiary of a life insurance policy causes death of the insured the claim will not be paid, but with burglary insurance an individual can be careless or imprudent to the point of "inviting" theft and still be compensated for a loss. "Insured" thefts seem to be a law enforcement problem of growing significance.[3] The relationships between compensation and carelessness, and carelessness and criminal incentives need to be studied for guidance in creating a workable victim compensation system.

   C. Provisions for compensation of the citizen injured while assisting a law officer or while on his own initiative restraining an offender can be administered effectively only if standards of citizen behavior are carefully defined. Payment of compensation must be on such basis as to discourage the vigilante and the busybody. A large-scale educational effort would have to be conducted so that citizens will know their obligations and rights.[4]

   Careful criminological research is needed to help resolve these issues, and to avoid opportunism, contradictions and serious stresses in public finance.

Notes

1. E.g., see *Interdisciplinary Problems in Criminology: Papers of the American Society of Criminology*, 1964, Edited by Walter C. Reckless and Charles L. Newman, Columbus, Ohio, 1965, pp. 159-190.
2. M. Fooner, "The Careless American: A Study in Adventitious Criminality," a paper presented at the American Society of Criminology joint annual meeting with the American Association for the Advancement of Science, Symposium on Psychiatry, Psychology and Criminology, Philadelphia, December 29, 1962.
3. C. H. Rolph, *Common Sense About Crime and Punishment,* New York, 1961, p. 78.
4. M. Fooner, *Crime in the Affluent Society,* A Summary Statement on Cause of Crime and a Program of Crime Prevention Education, prepared for the Third United Nations Congress on Crime Prevention and Treatment of Offenders, Stockholm, August 1965.

22

Sex Offenses against Children and Minors: Some Proposals for Legal Reform

Francine Watman

The Stereotype versus Sexual Behavior Patterns

The Offense Behavior

It is commonly believed that the sex offender imposes adult forms of sexual behavior on his victim. The offense behavior is believed to involve considerable coercion and, not infrequently, violence. The most prevalent stereotype of sex offenses against children and minors has crystallized around the frightening rape-murders that are so highly publicized. Public indignation caused by some sexual atrocities which have been committed has impelled many individuals to ignore the important differences between varying kinds of offensive sex behavior.

Most people think that forcible rape or sodomy is typical of sex offenses committed against children or minors. Public indignation based on the abhorrence of stereotypic sex offenses has been manifested in the "special legislation passed in many jurisdictions providing for the commitment and treatment of the so-called 'sexual psychopath', or 'abnormal sex offender' " (Schur, 1969:222). Although these laws were originally intended to isolate the really dangerous sex criminal, they are purposively ambiguous and vague so as to cover diverse types of deviate sexual behavior which differ in their degree of social danger. The very vagueness of these sex-psychopath statutes has caused them to be employed primarily when minor sex offenses have been committed (Ploscowe, 1962:214). These laws have evolved largely as a consequence of erroneous beliefs about the offense behavior in which the offender actually engages.

The actual sexual activity that takes place in a sex offense against a child or a minor may range from slight physical contact of any kind to vaginal coitus (Sudnow, 1969:251). Between these two extremes lies a wide area of possible behavior: touching, casual or more extensive petting (genital or non-genital), mouth-genital contacts, attempted coitus, anal coitus and vaginal coitus. The great majority of the sexual acts consist of the same kind of sex play that is found among prepubertal children and minors. "The nature of the act corre-

Paper presented at the Interamerican Congress of Criminology, Caracas, Venezuela, 1972. Printed by permission of the author. The original paper has been slightly revised.

sponds to the level of maturity expected at the age of the victim rather than at the age of the offender. It is not, as popularly imagined, that the adult imposes adult forms of sexual behavior on the victim" (Gigeroff et al., 1968:17). Penetration and intravaginal coitus is rare among sexual acts with children: not only is it not feasible with the majority of young children involved, but it is clearly not the offender's intention in many cases (Gigeroff et al., 1968:17).

The Offender

Sex offenders are treated as if they comprised a separate and homogeneous group of criminals. This is particularly true of the popular view of sex offenders who choose children and minors as their victims. The senile child molester who may be pathologically dangerous is a stereotype frequently associated with these sex offenders. These offenders are also believed to be members of the lower socio-economic classes and to commit progressively more heinous sex crimes, starting with a relatively innocuous offense such as exhibitionism and culminating ultimately in forced rape.

The research which has been surveyed in this paper demonstrates a striking lack of documentation for these stereotypes. The most definitive work on sex offenders has been done by Gebhard et al (1965) in their book *Sex Offenders*. Their findings indicate that a great variety of men commit sex offenses against children and minors. They are dispersed throughout society geographically, occupationally, and demographically (age-wise). Some offenders are repeaters, others display a low rate of recidivism (Gigeroff et al., 1968:21; Gebhard et al., 1965:195). Some offenders have a long history of prior offenses, sex-related as well as other offenses, for others this offense is their first reported criminal activity. Quite often it is a thinly veiled line which separates the sex offender from the socially sanctioned adult male.

The Victim

The entire question of victimology is particularly pertinent in analyzing sex offenses against children and minors.[1] Our idea is that innocent children, or at least children who would prefer to remain innocent, are seduced by cunning and wicked males. To what degree is an offense triggered by the advances, either overt or implied, of another person? The offense may be neither acceptable to the social mores, nor fit the offender-victim stereotype.

The "victims" of these sex offenses are very much like "every mother's child." They come from every type of home and family life, every intelligence level and every neighborhood. Some are very young, others approach the age of consent. The "victim" is often a willing sexual partner and even sometimes a seductive one, but if this person is under a certain age our social ethics definitely necessitate legal protection of this object-victim in such a situation (Gebhard et al., 1965:794; Gigeroff et al., 1968:19; Ploscowe, 1955:261; Trainer, 1966).

Doubtlessly, there are some victims who are forced to acquiesce to the desires of a sex offender. It is viewed as a heinous crime if these victims chance to be children or minors. In view of the fact that these offenders are not always deemed harmful psychologically or physically, we may question the value of punitive measures (Seward, 1946). It was noted that severe aggression is not common in sex offenses against children and minors; it was also noted that the sexual activity engaged in corresponded to the level of maturity expected at the age of the victim rather than at the age of the offender. Therefore, the victim is usually in little physical danger.

For victims in their late teens it is especially problematic to ascertain if there is truly a victim. The female has almost arrived at the age of consent. Should a male be penalized because the laws, in the geographical environment where he is situated, set a high limit to the age of consent?

When viewing a considerable number of sex offenses against children and minors, we meet victims who consent tacitly, cooperate, conspire or provoke. Should the right of a female minor to "consent" to sexual contact in all instances be limited by the law? Are her civil rights being violated?

The prevalent stereotype of children or minors as victims of a sex offense can seriously impede the determination of a "just" verdict. The offender may be unduly penalized for harming an innocent and unwilling victim, in fact, there may not really be a victim—in the common sense use of the term.[2]

Victim-Offender Relationships

There are always two partners in a sexual offense: the offender and the victim. As has been shown, on one hand, the prototype of the innocent victim brutalized by the sexual psychopath is not always a useful model of a sex offense against children or minors. This model must be revised to reflect more realistically the varieties of the relationship between perpetrator and victim (see Hentig, 1948:383-5).

On the other hand, a relationship between offender and victim may suggest more, rather than less culpability on the offender's part. For example, the intimacy of a family tie is expected to place a special obligation on a more mature member not to intrude sexuality into the relationship.

A multi-dimensional view of crime should emphasize the varieties of the relationships between victim and offenders rather than consider the criminal's behavior and the victim's behavior as two separate and distinct forms of conduct (Schafer, 1968).

Although children are frequently warned to be wary of male strangers, the available data indicates that most sex offenses against children and minors are committed by men the victims know.

The previous subsections have established that there is a discrepancy between the stereotypes of the sex offense behavior, sex offenders, victims, and victim-offender relationships and the evidence that is available.

In view of stereotypic images of sex offense behavior, and of the individuals involved in sex crimes involving children and minors, we might do well to consider revising our statutes. The major difficulty is that criminal legislation has gone beyond attempting to control socially harmful sexual acts and has attempted to legislate morality.

The general view of the functions of criminal law, expressed by the Wolfenden Committee in Britain, presents guidelines to prevent overlegislating. "Criminal sanctions, it urged, should be used to maintain public order and decency, to protect individuals from offensive and injurious behavior and from exploitation and corruption. Beyond what might be necessary to carry out these purposes, the criminal law should not interfere with the private lives of citizens" (Schur, 1969). Moral repugnance alone was not considered a sufficient reason for invoking criminal sanctions.

Effectiveness of Sex Crimes Laws

There are numerous reasons why sex crime laws may not be effective deterrents: 1) The extreme difficulty of detecting such conduct may encourage the offender to believe that his criminal activities will not be attended to by the authorities; 2) The existence of some of these prescriptions tends to create a deviant subculture (e.g., adolescent fellators (Reiss, 1964)); 3) Since the "victim" may actively invite the offense, the offender may not perceive his culpability; 4) The offender may believe that no secular harm can be shown to result from such conduct; he may view the behavior as relatively innocuous and, consequently, not perceive it as criminal; 5) Based on what is known about offenders-unconscious motivations, pathology (e.g., senile men), they may suffer from diminished capacity to obey the criminal laws; 6) Social class norms may indicate that the moral sense of the community will tolerate the conduct and not invoke the criminal sanctions; 7) Conflicts between norms may confuse the offender's interpretation of what is considered appropriate behavior; 8) The rarity of the enforcement of the sex crime laws may be known.

The rarity of enforcement and the lack of pressure to use criminal sanctions when a sex offense has been committed reflect, in part, the disproportion between the penalties and the demonstrable harm of the behavior. The courts may view existing penalties as too severe and may, therefore, be reluctant to convict offenders. The deterrent value of the laws is affected by this attitude to the extent that potential offenders are aware of this judicial viewpoint and even if the courts do not, in fact, maintain this view, potential offenders may not be deterred from committing an offense because they may expect the courts to show a reluctance to convict.

Following Beutel's (1957) suggestions, let us now ask how we can most appropriately and effectively deter males from sexually engaging children or minors, and, also, provide suitable punishment for those who do offend. Let us also question the objectives of these laws to determine if they should be altered or abandoned.

Existing sex crime laws reflect stereotypic beliefs, consequently, although the penalties they impose are disproportionate to the actual criminal conduct, they may be proportional to the stereotype of offense behavior.

One of the difficulties that reform will have to overcome are the popular beliefs concerning sex offenses committed against children and minors. To the public, the sex offender is typified by the senescent pedophile. He is conceived of as a stranger. It is believed that he inflicts adult forms of sexual activity on an unwilling and innocent child. The purity of the victim is usually considered unquestionable. This stereotypic belief complex is supported by the mass media in the sensationalistic coverage they give to sex crimes in which children or minors are involved. When such a crime is reported, it serves to "substantiate" stereotypes. Once again, parents will admonish their children "to be wary of strangers."

The retention of these stereotypes probably weakens any attempts at reform of our antiquated criminal code. However, there is an additional difficulty presented by the existing laws. When an accused individual is prosecuted under these laws, it appears as though there is a strong correlation between the criminal activity and the stereotypes. These laws assume that the crime is perpetrated by a male. Consensus between participants is not a legal defense. The virtue and morality (or a lack of it) of the female is legally irrelevant. There is assumed to be an unwilling and innocent victim. *The Penal Law of the State of New York* differentiates between various offense activities: rape, deviate sexual intercourse, sexual abuse and incest. These laws, however, make it seem that the offender alone determines the activity (e.g., inflicts adult forms of sexual behavior on the victim). The age of the victim is another consideration in the determination of charges which will be made against the accused.

Reforming Sex Crime Laws

The rigorous methodology of experimental jurisprudence requires more extensive research on sex crimes against children and minors before a firm commitment can be made to changes in the law which might better effectuate the policy for which it was created. First, there should be made available, to legislators and other concerned individuals, more and better information.

It is long overdue that our legislatures take cognizance of the fact that women can be as guilty of sex offenses as men. Hentig has remarked upon the extent to which younger girls and even children are victims more in a technical legal sense than in fact. He cites in support of this contention the observations of F. Leppmann, a noted medicolegal expert, who has pointed to the fact that "very small girls do not make any resistance, do not try to escape and show 'semi-compliance', a mixture of curiosity and fear, body intactness, and mental challenge" (Hentig, 1948:406). Since most sex offenses against children and minors are viewed as consensual or "semi-consensual" (not in the legal sense of the term — age of consent), although not legally valid, the inequity of sex crime laws indicate that the need for updating is well grounded.

Secondly, the perils of overlegislation should be examined and their significance integrated into the legislators' perspective. The third requirement, growing out of the research mentioned above, is that a wider range of dispositions be made available as penalties for sex crimes against children or minors.

The Need for Education

A concerned effort must be made to re-educate the public about sex offenses committed against children and minors, simultaneously with the attempts to revitalize our ailing sex crime laws. Public education is necessary because the public influences legislation and appropriations for suitable treatment. An uninformed, punitive public encourages simplistic solutions like long jail terms and inhibits realistic solutions. Unless this effort is part of the goal, any proposed changes seem doomed to failure. Stereotypic thinking about sex offenses involving children and minors and the present sex crime laws relevant to these offenses are mutually reinforcing.

Attention should also be directed to preventing sex offenses against children and minors. Probably the most constructive measures for combatting sex criminality are informal community-level educational programs aimed at informing parents and children and minors. More careful investigation of prospective foster parents and of adults whose vocations bring them into frequent associations with children and minors will also aid in the prevention of these offenses, since propinquity has been found to contribute to the commission of sex offenses.

Another measure to decrease the number of sex crimes committed against children and minors has been suggested by Berl Kutchinsky, a noted criminologist-psychologist. He found that the decrease in such sexual offenses as peeping and physical interference with children (short of rape) in Denmark could not be explained by a change in sexual mores or liberalized attitudes towards these crimes by the public or by the police. The explanation he viewed as most likely was the recent legalization of pornography.

A Final Word

During the past decade, various segments of American society have vociferously demanded the liberalization of laws that govern their lives. Numerous activities of the Civil Rights Movement of the 1960's, the Fem Lib Movement and Gay Liberation Front demonstrate the quest for a more humane legal system. Their importance for the present topic under consideration, sex offenses against children and minors, rests on the trend they indicate. This trend can be viewed as the extension of civil rights to formerly impotent political forces. An experimental program establishing an advocacy system for children may be one logical extension of this trend. Another logical extension of this trend may be the revision of some of our irrelevant sex crime laws.

Notes

1. The term *child,* as used in the context of this paper, refers to children up to the age of twelve. The term *minor*, as used in the context of this paper, includes all females and males below the age of consent.
2. Victim—"a person who suffers from a destructive or injurious action or agency; a person who is deceived or cheated" (*Random House Dictionary of the English Language*—College Edition, 1969).

References

Beutel, Frederick Keating   *Some Potentialities of Experimental Jurisprudence*
      1957   *as a New Branch of Social Science.* Nebraska: Lincoln University Press.

Gebhard, Paul H.,   *Sex Offenders.* New York: Harper & Row.
John H. Gagnon,
Warden B. Pomeroy,
and Cornelia U. Christenson
      1965

Gigeroff, Alex K.,   "Sex Offenders on Probation: Heterosexual Pedophiles."
J. W. Mohr, and   *Federal Probation* 32: 17–21.
R. E. Turner
      1968

Hentig, Hans von   *The Criminal and His Victim.* New Haven: Yale University
      1948   Press.

Ploscowe, Morris   "Sexual Patterns and the Law." In *Sexual Behavior in*
      1955   *American Society. An Appraisal of the First Two Kinsey Reports.* Jerome Himmelhoch and Sylvia Fleis Fava (eds.) New York: Norton.

1962   *Sex and the Law,* rev. ed. New York: Ace Books.

Reiss, Albert, Jr.   "The Social Integration of Queers and Peers." In *The Other*
1964   *Side.* Howard Becker (ed.) New York: Free Press.

Schafer, Stephen   *The Victim and His Criminal: A Study in Functional Respon-*
1968   *sibility.* New York: Random House.

Schur, Edwin M.   *Our Criminal Society: The Social and Legal Sources of*
1969   *Crime in America.* New Jersey: Prentice-Hall.

Seward, Georgene   *Sex and the Social Order.* New York: McGraw-Hill.
1946

Sudnow, David   "Normal Crimes: Sociological Features of the Penal Code in
1969   Public Defender Office." In *Crime and the Legal Process.*
                William J. Chambliss (ed.). New York: McGraw-Hill.

Trainer, Russell   *The Lolita Complex.* New York: Paperback Library.
1966

United States Code   1964 Edition — Title 18.
1964

23 Recommendations

*Prince George's County (Maryland) Task Force
to Study the Treatment of the Victims of
Sexual Assaults*

Task Force Recommendations

1. Every rape victim suffers trauma whatever her outward appearance or behavior. Therefore, police should take the victim to the hospital as soon as possible after initial contact. The hospital should provide a room for the police interview, especially if the victim is made to wait. An effort should be made to have someone present with the victim at all times.
2. In the hospital, rape victims should be given high priority, second only to life-threatening cases; they should be treated as rapidly and sympathetically as possible by personnel educated to the trauma the victim is undergoing.
3. There should be sufficient mental health workers, preferably female, on 24 hour duty in the County hospital for crisis intervention in rape cases.
4. The victim should be given information at the hospital on venereal disease, legal procedures, expected emotional reactions, the possibility of pregnancy and who to contact for help in these areas.
5. Follow-up counselling should be made available to the victim and family.
6. Payment to the hospital should not be responsibility of the victim. The County should provide payment for rape cases if the third party payments are exhausted. Appropriate County budgeting is a necessity.
7. Post-graduate and in-service medical training should include lectures on rape and treatment.
8. Trained Women Police Officers/Detectives should be available for the interview. Plainclothes Officer would be preferable to uniformed police officers.
9. There should be more training and retraining for police, men and women, in sensitivity and understanding of the rape victims. This would be general training for *all* police men and women and intensive training in interviewing for the Officers/Detectives who will be assigned to this task.

From the *Report* of the Task Force to Study the Treatment of Victims of Sexual Assaults, Prince George's County, Maryland, March 1973, pp. 5-8. Fred R. Joseph, Esq., Chairperson.

10. In the meantime, instruct the officer that he should not "interrogate," but question; that the questioning should be limited to a reasonable amount of time and should have direct bearing on the medical and legal aspect of the rape.
11. The threat of "false report" charge should not be used to intimidate the victim.
12. As far as possible, one officer should deal with each case and keep the victim informed on its progress.
13. There should be provisions for police and hospital complaint cases to be reviewed for appropriate action by the Human Relations Commission, the Commission for Women, the State's Attorney's Office, and/or the Grand Jury.
14. Hospital regulations should be amended to be consistent with Maryland Law. It should *not* be required that minors have their parents present during the examination or that parents must sign a consent form. Such practices discourage some minors who do not want their parents to know that they are seeking help when it is most needed.
15. The Task Force recommends the adoption of an enlightened and progressive Code relating to sex and abuse. Part 130: *Sex Offenses* of the proposed Criminal Code of the State of Maryland Commission on Criminal Law, represents an important step forward and deserves serious consideration and careful study by the Maryland State Legislature.
16. While the Task Force understands and supports the right of a defendant to a full and fair trial, it is imperative that the trial court limit the trial to the issues and prevent the trial from focusing on the chastity of the victim as opposed to the commission of a criminal act by the defendant.
17. The Task Force recommends that the Criminal Injuries Compensation Board Brochure be made available to all rape victims so that they will be informed of the possibility of receiving compensation. The Criminal Injuries Compensation Board is too little known, and victims of crimes should be made to realize that compensation is available in certain cases.
18. The Task Force recommends that its Report be circulated to the Judges of all courts to improve judicial understanding of problems involving sexual abuse in Prince George's County.
19. The Task Force recommends a community education program, designed to heighten awareness of the crime, the personal, legal, and medical aspects. This would include the addition to school Family Life Programs of such topics as defense against rape, police and court procedures, implications of submitting a false report, etc.
20. The Task Force recommends that it be designated to review within one year the results of the County legislative, executive and administrative actions taken as a result of the Task Force's findings and recommendations.
21. While the focus of the Task Force's investigation has been on women and girls, it is equally important that emphasis be placed on sexual abuse and

assaults on males–particularly the young males. Additionally, from a preventive and rehabilitative standpoint, an investigation is necessary into the area of sexual abuse with focus upon the sexual abuser.

22. The Task Force recommends that its report be circulated to all Prince George's County Police forces and to police forces in all other municipalities, counties, and the state, as well as to police departments in Washington, D.C. and Virginia, with the hope that its report will improve law enforcement understanding of problems involving sexual abuse throughout the Washington Metropolitan area.

Part V Bibliography

In general, three symposia on victim compensation are especially to be recommended:

Minnesota Law Review 1965, 50: December; *Southern California Law Review* 1970, 43: 1; *Trial: The National Legal Newsmagazine* 1972, 8: May-June.

Atiyah, P.S. *Accidents, Compensation, and the Law.* London: Weidenfeld and Nicolson, 1970.

Bentel, D.J. "Selected Problems of Public Compensation to Victims of Crime," *Issues in Criminology* 1968, 3 (2): 217-231.

Bloemertz, C.B. *Die Schmerzensgeldbegutachtung* (Punitive Damages Expert Opinion). 3. neubearbeitete Auflage. Berlin: Walter de Gruyter, 1971.

Brainard, C.H. "The Threshold Impact on Injury Victims' Recoveries," *Trial* 1972, 8 (4): 32-33.

Cameron, B. "Compensation for Victims of Crime: The New Zealand Experiment," *Journal of Public Law* 1963, 12.

Cahen, R. "La Psychanalyse face au Génocide. Prophylaxie du Génocide dans la Perspective de la Psychologie Analytique," *Etudes Internationales de Psycho-Sociologie Criminelle* 1968, 14 (15): 56-77.

Chappell, D. "The Emergence of Australian Schemes to Compensate Victims of Crime," *Southern California Law Review* 1970, 43 (1): 69-83.

Childres, R.D. "Compensation for Criminally Inflicted Personal Injury," *New York University Law Review* 1964, 39: 444-471.

————. "Compensation for Criminally Inflicted Personal Injury," *Minnesota Law Review* 1965, 50: 271-283.

Clark, G. de N.   "Compensation for Personal Injuries. Damages and Social
                     Insurance," *Law Society Gazette* 1967, 64 (7): 339-343, (8):
                     408-412, (9): 476-481.

―――――.   *Compensation to Victims of Crime and Restitution by Offen-
                     ders.* Canadian Corrections Assocation (Ottawa) 1968.

Coon, T.F.   "Public Defender and Victims Compensation Legislation.
                     Their Part in the Criminal Justice System," *Bulletin of the
                     Society of Professional Investigators* 1971 (June): 25-31.

―――――.   "Crime Costs Insurers 9m pounds in First half of 1968,"
                     Security Gazette (London) 1968, 10 (11): 484.

―――――.   "Crime May Cost the Criminal," *FBI Law Enforcement Bulle-
                     tin* 1971, 40 (3): 28.

―――――.   "Current Legal Developments. Faults Liability (Tort)," *Inter-
                     national Comparative Law Quarterly* 1970, 19 (4): 715-717.

De Francis, V.   "Protecting the Child Victim of Sex Crimes Committed by
                     Adults," *Federal Probation* 1971, 35 (3): 15-20.

Downes, D., and   "Social Reaction to Deviance and Its Effect on Crime and
P. Rock   Criminal Careers," *British Journal of Sociology* 1971, 22 (4):
                     351-364.

Duplissie, A.J.   "Compensating Victims of Crimes of Violence," *International
                     Criminal Police Review* 1969, 24, (224): 8-10.

Feeney, D.T.G.   "Compensation for the Victims of Crime," *Canadian Journal
                     of Corrections* 1968, 10 (2): 261-271.

Floyd, G.E.   "Compensation: A Comparative Study," *Trial* 1972, 8 (May-
                     June): 14-27.

Fooner, M.   "Some Problems in Evaluations of Proposals for Victims Com-
                     pensation," *International Criminal Police Review* 1967, 22
                     (206): 66-71.

Fox, S.S., and   "Crisis Intervention with Victims of Rape," *Social Work* 1972,
D.J. Scherl   17 (1): 37-42.

Fry, M.   "Justice for Victims," *The Observer* (London), July 7, 1957.

Furstenberg, F.F., Jr.   "Public Reaction to Crime in the Streets," *American
                     Scholar* 1971, 40 (4): 601-610.

Gaylord, C.L.   "Fault, No Fault, or Strict Liability," *American Bar Association
                     Journal* 1972, 58: 589-593.

Geis, G.   "Compensation for Crime Victims and the Police," *Police*
                     1969, 13 (5): 55-59.

Geis, G. et alii   "Public Compensation of Victims of Crime: A Survey of the
                    New York Experience," *Criminal Law Bulletin* 1973, 9 (1):
                    pt. I; 1973, 9 (2): pt. II.

Hamilton, P.   "The Police and the Security Industry. I and II," *Police Journal*
                    1968, 41: 261–267, 297–303.

Hardy Ivamy, E.R.   " 'Hit and Run' Victims," *New Law Journal* 1968, 118
                    (5361): 1000.

Hayman, C.R. et al. "A Public Health Program for Sexually Assaulted Females,"
                    in H. Gochros and L. Schultz, *Human Sexuality and Social
                    Work.* New York: Association Press, 1972, 321–333.

Hellner, J.   "Damages for Personal Injury and the Victim's Private Insur-
                    ance," *American Journal of Comparative Law* 1970, 18 (1):
                    126.

Honderich, T.   *Punishment: The Supposed Justifications.* London: Hutchin-
                    son, 1969.

Hook, S.   "The Rights of Victims of Crime," *Congressional Record,*
                    February 17, 1972, and March 4, 1972.

King, W.   "If You are Maimed by a Criminal, You Can be Compensated
                    (Maybe)," *New York Times Magazine,* March 26, 1972:
                    40–41, 122–125.

Klein, H.   "Holocaust Survivors in Kibbutzim: Readaptation and Re-
                    integration," *Israel Annals of Psychiatry* 1972, 10 (1): 78–91.

Kutner, L.   "Due Process for Crime Victims," *Trial* 1972, 8 (May-June):
                    28–30.

Lamborn, Le R.   "Remedies for the Victims of Crime," *Southern California
                    Law Review* 1970, 43 (1): 22–53.

Légal, A.   "Les Garanties d'Indemnisation de la Victime d'une Infrac-
                    tion," *Prisons et Prisonniers* 1963 (59–60): 834–836.

Legislation and Reports.

                    *Annual Report of the Crime Victims Compensation Board,
                    State of New York.* Albany, N.Y., 1971.

                    "Indemnification of Private Citizens: Victims of Crime," Ch.
                    5, Government Code of California.

                    "Criminal Injuries Compensation," Ch. 351, Laws of Hawaii.

                    "Criminal Injuries Compensation Act," Article 26 A, Anno-
                    tated Code, State of Maryland.

"Compensation for the Victims of Violent Crime," Ch. 258 A, General Laws of Massachusetts.

Untitled, New Jersey Statutes 52: 4 B-1-21, 1971.

"Crime Victims Compensation Board," Sections 620–635, Article 22, Executive Laws of the State of New York.

Analysis of S. 2994, Victims of Crime Act of 1972. U.S. Law Enforcement Assistance Administration. Washington, D.C.: U.S. Government Printing Office, 1972.

S. 1191, A Bill to Establish a National Center on Child Abuse and Neglect. Congressional Record 1973, 119 (39): Tuesday, March 13.

Linden, A.M.   "International Conference on Compensation to Innocent Victims of Violent Crime," *Criminal Law Quarterly* 1969, 11 (2): 145–149.

————.   "Victims of Crime and Tort Law," *Canadian Bar Journal* 1969, 12 (1): 17–33.

————.   "Rescuers and Good Samaritans," *The Modern Law Review* 1971, 34 (3): 241–259.

Marshall, D.   "Compensation: New Atonement for Old Guilt?" *Canadian Bar Journal* (Ottawa) 1971, 2 (4): 24–26.

McClellan, J.   "Victims of Crime Act of 1972: Society's Moral Obligation," *Trial* 1972, 8 (May-June): 22–24.

McGrath, W.T.   "Compensation to Victims of Crime in Canada," *Canadian Journal of Corrections* 1970, 12 (1): 11–24.

Miers, D.   "Compensation for Victims of Crimes of Violence: The Northern Ireland Model," *Criminal Law Review* 1969, (November): 576–587.

Morris, T.   "Compensation for Victims of Crimes of Violence," *The Modern Law Review* 1961, 24 (6): 744–747.

Mueller, G.O.W.   "Compensation for Victims of Crime: Thought Before Action," *Minnesota Law Review* 1965, 50: 213–221.

O'Connell, W.E., and   "The Negative Nonsense of the Passive Patient," *Rational* P.G. Hanson   *Living* 1972, 6 (1): 28–31.

Pečar, J.   "Vpleteni 'opazovalci' -viktimološka razclemba" (Involved Bystanders–Victimological Aspects), *Revija za Kriminalistiko in Kriminologijo* (Ljubljana) 1971, 22 (3): 172–184.

Prince George's County Government, Maryland   *Report of the Task Force to Study the Treatment of Victims of Sexual Assaults.* Upper Marlboro, Maryland, 1973.

Prince, M.   "Versicherung gegen Verbrechen? Weshalb nicht?" (Insurance
                 against crime. Why not?), in A. Mergen, *Kriminologie-Morgen.*
                 Hamburg: Kriminalistik Verlag, 1964 (vol. 14), 151–157.

Reckless, W.C. and   *Interdisciplinary Problems in Criminology:* Papers of the
C.L. Newman (eds.)   American Society of Criminology. Columbus, Ohio: Ohio
                 State University Press, 1965 (esp. pp. 159–190).

Ross, I.   "The Victims of Crime Deserve a Break," *Readers' Digest*
                 1967 (July): 173–176.

Rubin, S., and   "Developments in Correctional Law," *Crime and Delinquency.*
J.E. Glen   1968, 14 (2): 155–170.

Schafer, S.   "Restitution to Victims of Crime: An Old Correctional Aim
                 Modernized," *Minnesota Law Review* 1965, 50: 243–254.

————.   *Compensation and Restitution to Victims of Crime.* Mont-
                 clair, N.J.: Patterson Smith, 1970.

————.   "Victim Compensation and Responsibility," *Southern Cali-
                 fornia Law Review* 1970, 43 (1): 55–67.

————.   "Corrective Compensation," *Trial* 1972, 8 (May–June): 25–27.

Shank, W.A.   "Aid to Victims of Violent Crimes in California," *Southern
                 California Law Review* 1970, 43 (1): 85–92.

Schomburg, E.   "Nachgehende Betreuung der Kindlichen Opfer von Sittlich-
                 keits-verbrechen" (Care of Child Victims after Indecent
                 Assaults), *Polizei* 1968, 59 (2): 53–55.

Schomerus, D.H.   "Der Paedophile und sein Opfer in Teologischer Sicht" (The
                 Pedophiliac and his Victim in a Theological View), *Beiträge
                 zur Sexualforschung* 1965, 33: 80–87.

Smigel, E.O.   "Public Attitudes toward Stealing as Related to the Size of
                 the Victim Organization," *American Sociological Review*
                 21: 320–327.

Starrs, J.E.   "A Modest Proposal to Insure Justice for Victims of Crime,"
                 Minnesota Law Review 1965, 50: 285–309.

Stoll, H.   "Penal Purposes in the Law of Tort," *American Journal of
                 Comparative Law* 1970, 18: 3–21. Other relevant articles on
                 the contemporary roles of the law of tort are published in
                 the same volume (1–168).

Tapper, C.   "Criminal Injuries Compensation Board Releases," *The Modern
                 Law Review* 1965, 28 (4): 460–463.

————.   "The Second Report of the Criminal Injuries Compensation
                 Board," *The Modern Law Review* 1967, 30 (3): 319–321.

Tedeschi, G.   "Recovery of Compensation for Personal Injuries Caused by
                    the Victim's Negligence" (In Hebrew), *Hapraklii* 1965, 21 (3):
                    371–376.

Tiley, J.   "The Rescue Principle," *The Modern Law Review* 1967, 30
                    (1): 25–45.

U.S. Congress,   *Crime in America: In the Nation's Capital.* Washington, D.C.:
House of   U.S. Government Printing Office, 1970.
Representatives

U. S. Congress,   *The Impact of Crime, Crime Insurance, and Surety Bonds on
Select Committee   Small Business in Urban Areas.* Washington D.C.: U. S.
on Small Business   Government Printing Office, 1970.

U.S. Congress,   *Crimes Against Banking Institutions.* Washington D.C.: U.S.
Government   Government Printing Office, 1964.
Operations Committee

University of Kansas, *First Annual Burglary and Larceny Seminar: A Report.*
Governmental   Special Report no. 108. Lawrence, Kansas: University
Research Center   of Kansas, 1961.

Van Beek, M.M.   "The Change in the Role of the Victim of Crime," *T. Strafr.*
                    1970, 79 (4): 193–204.

Van Rensslaer, S.L. "A Compensation Board at Work," *Trial* (Cambridge,
                    Mass.) 1972, 8 (3): 20–21.

Weeks, K.M.   "The New Zealand Criminal Injuries Compensation Scheme,"
                    Southern California Law Review, 1970, 43 (1): 107–121.

Wilson, P.R.   "Crime and the Public," *Australian and New Zealand Journal
                    of Criminology* (Melbourne) 1971, 4 (4): 223–232.

Wolfgang, M.E.   "Victim Compensation in Crimes of Personal Violence,"
                    Minnesota Law Review 1965, 50: 223–241. Also in Italian, in
                    La Scuola Positiva (Milano) 1964 (3): 1–11.

————.   "Social Responsibility for Violent Behavior," *Southern Cali-
                    fornia Law Review* 1970, 43 (1): 5–21.

Yarborough, R.W.   "The Battle for a Federal Violent Crimes Compensation
                    Act: The Genesis of S.9," *Southern California Law Review*
                    1970, 43 (1): 93–106.

Index

List of Contributors

Michael Agopian, California State University at Los Angeles.

Elliot Aronson, University of Texas.

Duncan Chappell, Center for Law and Justice, Human Affairs Research Center, Battelle Research Institute, Seattle.

Robert Crosby, Resource Management Corporation, Bethesda, Maryland.

Vahakn Dadrian, State University of New York at Geneseo.

Russell Dynes, The Ohio State University.

Michael Fooner, Consultant, New York City.

Gilbert Geis, University of California at Irvine.

Daniel Glaser, University of Southern California.

Maurice Goldsmith, Columnist, *Science and Public Affairs.*

Seymour Halleck, University of Wisconsin Medical School.

Hans von Hentig, University of Colorado (1941).

Roger Hood, Institute of Criminology, University of Cambridge, England.

Bruce Jacob, Emory University.

David Landy, The University of Rochester.

Donal MacNamara, John Jay College of Criminal Justice, The City University of New York.

Beniamin Mendelsohn, Lawyer, Jerusalem, Israel.

Willem H. Nagel, Institute of Criminology, University of Leiden, The Netherlands.

E. L. Quarantelli, The Ohio State University.

Richard Quinney, New York University.

261

William Ryan, Psychologist, New Haven, Connecticut.

Stephen Schafer, Northeastern University.

Leslie Sebba, Institute of Criminology, The Hebrew University, Jerusalem, Israel.

Robert Silverman, The University of Western Ontario, Canada.

David Snyder, Resource Management Corporation, Bethesda, Maryland.

Richard Sparks, Institute of Criminology, University of Cambridge, Cambridge, England.

John Sullivan, John Jay College of Criminal Justice, The City University of New York.

Francine Watman, Foy, Falcier Associates, Inc., New York City.

Marvin Wolfgang, University of Pennsylvania.

About the Editors

Israel Drapkin, M.D., has been professor of Criminology and director of the Institute of Criminology at the Hebrew University of Jerusalem since 1959. Formerly, he was director of the Institute of Criminology of Chile (1936-59) and professor at the University of Chile (1950-59). He has served as correspondent to the United Nations Social Defence Section since 1950; United Nations Expert in Israel (1957) and at the Asia and Far East Institute for the Prevention of Crime and Treatment of Offenders, UNAFEI (1965-68). He has been visiting professor at Haile Selassie I University (Addis Ababa), Central University of Venezuela, University of Pennsylvania (Philadelphia) and The American University (Washington, D.C.).

Emilio Viano, Ph.D., is assistant professor of Sociology and the Administration of Justice and director of the Institute for Comparative Justice Studies at The American University in Washington, D.C. He was formerly on the research staff of the National Council on Crime and Delinquency in New York City. He has published widely in the field of criminal justice. Among works he co-authored are: *Management of Probation Services: A Bibliography*, vol. I (220 pp.), and vol. II (237 pp.); and *Decision-Making in Administration of Probation Services* (253 pp.), published by the National Council on Crime and Delinquency, New York, N.Y. Dr. Viano is also the co-author of a volume on major social problems for law enforcement personnel to be published shortly by Nelson-Hall. Several articles by Professor Viano have appeared in the *Canadian Journal of Criminology and Corrections, Sociology and Social Research, Quality and Quantity: European Journal of Methodology.*